Saint Tikhon of Moscow

INSTRUCTIONS & TEACHINGS

for the American Orthodox Faithful (1898–1907)

Saint Tikhon of Moscow

INSTRUCTIONS & TEACHINGS

for the American Orthodox Faithful (1898–1907)

Translated and Edited by Alex Maximov and David C. Ford

St. Tikhon's Monastery Press

MMXVI

Saint Tikhon of Moscow: Instructions & Teachings for the American Orthodox Faithful (1898–1907)

Published by:
St. Tikhon's Monastery Press
175 St. Tikhon's Road
Waymart, Pennsylvania 18472
Printed in the United States of America

ISBN: 978-0-9974718-1-6

DEDICATION

With heartfelt gratitude,
we dedicate this book to
All the Monks of St. Tikhon's Monastery,
both past and present,
who have been a great blessing for many,
and who continue to strive faithfully to fulfill
the vision of St. Tikhon,
when he and Fr. Arseny founded the Monastery
in 1905.

CONTENTS

Preface   i

A Note from the Translator   iii

Foreword *by Scott M. Kenworthy*   v

Introduction *by the Translators/Editors*   ix

In Place of an Introduction *to the Original Book in Russian*   xvii

From the Editor   xix

An Introductory Vignette   xxi

Year 1898

A sermon preached on ascending the archpastoral cathedra in San Francisco   2

A sermon preached at the Feast of the Nativity of Christ   6

Year 1899

From the homily preached on the Sunday of Orthodoxy at the San Francisco Cathedral   12

A sermon addressed to the parishioners of St. Mary's Church in Minneapolis, Minnesota   19

A sermon preached upon entering Sitka Cathedral   23

A sermon preached on the day of the Equal-to-the-Apostles
St. Prince Vladimir, the Enlightener of the Russian Land,
in the chapel in Ninilchik, of the Kenai parish   26

A sermon addressed to Serbs at the Church in
Jackson, California, on the 17th week after Pentecost   31

A response to the General Agent for education in Alaska,
Mr. Sheldon Jackson   35

Suggestion 1: To the Alaskan Spiritual Board, in connection
with the 100th anniversary of the appointment of the
Russian Orthodox bishop to America   37

Year 1900

Homily addressed to the newly ordained priest, Fr. Vladimir
Alexandrov, in the San Francisco Cathedral   40

A sermon preached at the cathedral in San Francisco on
the first Sunday after returning from a visit to Alaska   45

A sermon preached before the thanksgiving prayer
on the day of the 50th anniversary of the State
of California celebrations   48

Homily addressed to the newly ordained priest, Fr. Peter
Popov, at Holy Trinity Cathedral, San Francisco   51

The speech given in response to the speech of Bishop Grafton
at the consecration of his Bishop-Coadjutor, Reginald H.
Weller, at Fond du Lac, Wisconsin   54

Suggestion 2: To the North-American Spiritual Board
regarding the establishment of a girls' school-orphanage
in Alaska   57

Suggestion 3: To the North-American Spiritual Board as of
December 1, 1900 regarding accurate tabulation of the
actual number of parishioners in the parish   59

Reflection on the Feast of the Nativity   60

Year 1901

Reflection on the occasion of the arrival of the New Year
  (1901) and the new century (20th); in San Francisco   66

A sermon preached on Cheesefare Sunday   70

A sermon preached on the fourth Sunday of Great Lent
  in San Francisco   74

A sermon preached in the week of Antipascha
  (St. Thomas Sunday) in Galveston, Texas   79

A sermon on the Sunday of the Blind Man
  in Wilkes-Barre, Pennsylvania   82

Suggestion 4: Regarding the opening of a "Repository
  of Innocent" in the city of Sitka   85

Suggestion 5: Regarding the establishment of a "Society
  of Soberness" at parishes, and organizing modest
  entertainment on Sundays   86

A sermon preached on the 14th week after Pentecost
  at the consecration of a temple in the village of Vostok
  in Canada   88

Sermon preached on the Feast of the Elevation of the
  Cross at the Sitka Cathedral   93

Sermon in honor of the 60th anniversary of the arrival
  of the Most Reverend Innocent in Sitka, at St. Michael's
  Cathedral in Sitka, Alaska   96

Suggestion 6: To the clergy of the Aleutian Diocese   100

A sermon preached on the Feast of the Nativity of Christ   102

Year 1902

A sermon preached at the blessing of newlyweds
in San Francisco   108

A sermon preached at the consecration of the chapel
on the newly built battleship "Retvizan"
in Philadelphia, Pennsylvania   112

A homily addressed to the newly ordained priest, the editor
of *Svet,* Fr. Benedict Turkevich, in Allegheny, Pennsylvania   114

A homily preached at the ordination of the teacher Michael
Skibinsky, a Canadian missionary, into the priesthood   117

An open letter to the editor of the newspaper Svet
regarding the strike in the coal mines, in San Francisco   120

Suggestion 7: To the North American Spiritual Board
regarding the distribution of icons from Athos among
the Orthodox temples in America   122

A sermon preached at the consecration of the
New York church   124

A sermon preached at the consecration
of the Syro-Arabian temple in Brooklyn, New York   127

The Orthodox Mission in Alaska (North America): From
the report to the Council of the All Russia Missionary
Society in Moscow   129

A sermon on visiting the local missionary school,
at St. Mary's Church in Minneapolis, Minnesota   137

Year 1903

A sermon preached on the Sunday of Orthodoxy
in San Francisco, California   140

A sermon preached at the blessing of the Orthodox temple
in Chicago   147

A salutory sermon preached upon visiting
the Mayfield Parish 151

Suggestion 8: To the attention of the North American
Diocese regarding the establishment of a seminary 154

A sermon preached at the funeral service of the Right
Reverend Bishop Markell (Popel), in St. Petersburg, Russia 156

Year 1904

A sermon preached at the presentation of the hierarchical
staff to the Most Reverend Bishop Innocent of Alaska 162

A sermon preached at the New York Cathedral on
his first Sunday upon returning from Russia 165

A sermon preached for the week of the Prodigal Son
at the Yonkers church 169

A homily addressed to the newly ordained priest, Fr. Mikhail
Potochny, in the Russian Cathedral in New York City 173

A sermon preached after the liturgy at the presentation
of the episcopal staff to the Most Reverend Raphael,
Bishop of Brooklyn 176

A sermon preached on the day of His Majesty Emperor's
birth, in the San Francisco Cathedral 179

A response to His Holiness Meletius, Patriarch of Antioch 183

A letter of the most humble servant to
Tsar Nikolai Aleksandrovich 186

Resolutions 188

A sermon preached at the Vespers service on the eve
of the blessing of the side chapel in honor
of the Nativity of the Mother of God 191

Year 1905

Homily addressed to the newly ordained priest,
Fr. Michael Andreades   196

A sermon preached at the New York Cathedral on
the anniversary of the holy crowning; on May 14, 1905   200

A sermon preached at the farewell liturgy in San Francisco   206

A sermon preached at the presentation of the staff
to Archimandrite Sebastian (Dabovich) in Chicago   210

A sermon preached at the first service in the New York
cathedral on September 25, 1905   212

Opinions on the issues proposed for discussion at
the Pomestni Council of the All-Russia Church   214

A sermon preached on the Feast of the Nativity
at the New York Cathedral   230

Added notes concerning the development
of Orthodoxy in America   236

Year 1906

Address given at the consecration of St. Tikhon's Monastery
and Church in South Canaan, Pennsylvania   240

Sermons preached at tonsurings at St. Tikhon's Monastery   244

Year 1907

A sermon preached at St. Andrew's Church in Philadelphia   250

A sermon preached at the Liturgy at the Mayfield Church
on the opening day of the convention   253

Farewell sermon preached on the Sunday of Orthodoxy
in the New York City Cathedral   257

Afterword, *by the original editors*   263

PREFACE

THIS BOOK IS THE FRUIT of many concerted efforts on the part of people lovingly devoted to the beautiful memory of St. Tikhon, Patriarch of Moscow and All-Russia, who served as Bishop and then Archbishop of the Russian Missionary Diocese in North America from 1898 to 1907. The first of these people was Fr. Alexander Hotovitzky, who as editor of the *Amerikansky Pravoslavny Vestnik* (*Russian-American Messenger*), the national bi-weekly newspaper of the Diocese, made sure that many of Vladika[1] Tikhon's sermons and other messages to his flock appeared in print in that journal. Fr. Alexander would later be martyred back in Russia, in the gulag under Stalin in the late 1930s, earning his saintly crown.

Then, in the early 1920s, some 15 years after Vladika Tikhon had left America, and as he, as Patriarch of Russia, was suffering severe persecution under the Bolsheviks, a committee of church people in New York compiled many of his sermons and other messages into a book dedicated to the celebration of the 25th anniversary of his consecration to the episcopacy back in 1897. Entitled *Zaveti i Nastavleniya Amerikanskoi Pravoslavnoi Rusi Ego Svyateishestva Patriarkha Moskovskogo i Vseya Rusi Tikhona* [*Instructions and Teachings of His Holiness Patriarch of Moscow and All Russia Tikhon for the American Orthodox Russia*], it was published as installments in 1923 and 1926 in New York City.

---

[1] "Vladika" (also spelled Vladyko) is a term of address for any hierarch (bishop, archbishop, or metropolitan) in the Russian Orthodox Church. It carries a note of endearment as compared to the "official" terms of address, such as "Your Grace" or "Your Eminence" or "Your Beatitude."

But it was all in the Russian language! While a few of his sermons have been translated into English in the years since, this collection as a whole has not been published in English until now. The present volume appears mainly through the efforts of Mr. Alexander Maximov, a native Russian speaker, and Dr. David C. Ford, a native English speaker who provided editorial assistance.

The translators/editors wish to thank their ever-patient wives, Theresa Maximov and Dr. Mary Ford, for allowing their husbands the many hours required for this work, over a period of many years. We also wish to thank Archimandrite Sergius (Bowyer), the Abbot of St. Tikhon's Monastery and head of St. Tikhon's Monastery Press, who has given us great encouragement in producing this work. We also thank him for his patience. And we thank Fr. Matthew Markewich for doing an excellent job in formatting the manuscript for publication.

We humbly offer these many words of wisdom, pastoral care and love, and missionary vision by our greatly beloved Vladika St. Tikhon, in the prayerful hope that many will come to know this great Saint better through reading his words—and that we all will be inspired by him to continue the work of strengthening our beloved Orthodox Church in this land. May our Holy Orthodox Church in North America indeed thrive more and more through his wisdom, and his ongoing care and love for us, his beloved American flock.

Alex Maximov, translator
Dr. David C. Ford, editor
November 23, 2015
St. Alexander Nevsky

A NOTE FROM THE TRANSLATOR

I WOULD LIKE EXPRESS my deepest gratitude to all the wonderful people who helped us with prayer, advice, or an encouraging word regarding our translation. I want to thank Dr. David Ford for his patience and tireless efforts to bring our work to fruition.

I also would like to thank some special people. First of all, I want to thank my parents, Maxim and Galina. I would like to thank Fr. Abbot Sergius (Bowyer), Fr. Gabriel (Nicholas), Fr. Juvenaly (Repass), Fr. Gregory (Zaiens), Fr. Athanasy (Mastalski), Fr. Michael (Juk), Fr. Nicodemus (Kentop), Fr. Innokenty, Fr. Alexander, and all the fathers, brothers, and parishioners of St. Tikhon's Monastery and Church for their prayers. I would especially like to thank Robert Roth for his help, prayers, and patience.

I would like to thank Fr. Andrei (Rumyantsev) for his prayers and good wishes as well. I also would like to thank my teacher of English, Lyudmila Sharuda, along with Konstantin Kostirkin and Evgeni Komarov. Memory eternal to Dmitri Vishnyakov; may God's peace and love be with his family. I also would like to thank my daughters, Katherine and Anastasia, for valuable suggestions for this translation.

Above all, I want to give thanks to God the Father, the Son, and the Holy Spirit for allowing my unworthiness to touch the precious words of our beloved Saint. To Him belong glory and honor, now and forever!

–Alex Maximov

FOREWORD

by Scott M. Kenworthy

THIS VOLUME of St. Tikhon's sermons and other writings, newly translated and edited by Alex Maximov and David C. Ford, provides English-speaking readers access to the words of a figure of towering importance for the Orthodox Church both in America and in Russia. Born Vasilii Ivanovich Bellavin (1865–1925), St. Tikhon was bishop of the Orthodox Church in North America from the end of 1898 until the spring of 1907, longer than any bishop between the establishment of the diocese in 1870 and the Russian Revolution.

A decade after returning to Russia, in November 1917, Tikhon was elected Patriarch of the Russian Orthodox Church. The first patriarch since Tsar Peter the Great abolished the office two centuries earlier, he was elected by the great Russian Church Council at the very time when the Bolsheviks seized power. It was St. Tikhon's burden to lead the Russian Church at a time when a new, militantly atheist regime sought to eradicate religion by any means necessary. Patriarch Tikhon is therefore one of the most important Orthodox churchmen of modern times, and the opportunity for readers to acquaint themselves with his words through these translations is very welcome.

During his time in America, St. Tikhon made profound contributions to the fledgling American Church. In his very first sermon in San Francisco he promised his American flock: "From now on, I devote all of my strength and gifts to serve you." Since his diocese was no less than the entirety of North America, the challenges of keeping such a promise were enormous. He spent nearly half of every year traversing the continent, traveling tens of thousands of kilometers across the "Lower 48," Canada, and Alaska.

The America that St. Tikhon so tirelessly explored was in the process of being transformed by a new wave of immigration that brought an unprecedented level of ethnic diversity into the fold of the Orthodox Church in the New World. Until the 1880s, the Orthodox Church in North America was concentrated primarily in Alaska, but in the 1890s large-scale immigration to Canada and the "Lower 48" transformed the nature of the mission. In response, St. Tikhon made a whole array of profoundly important contributions to the American Church, as discussed below in the Introduction. He envisioned a unified Orthodox Church for North America that respected the diverse ethnicities and their traditions.

St. Tikhon's sermons and writings included in this collection also reflect the great impact that his experience in America had upon him. Just as he served longer than bishops before and after him, so also it was the longest appointment of his career. The sermons he gave while in America, which are unique in that he did not continue to publish his sermons after his return to Russia, are important in revealing his spiritual focus. Those things that were of enduring importance to him find expression here, such as the indispensability of education for the faithful. At the same time, he came to understand the distinct challenges for the Orthodox in the New World that were radically different from the Old World: in North America, not only were the Orthodox a small minority by comparison with Protestants and Catholics, but American culture—with its emphases on individualism and pragmatism—were often at odds with the traditional Orthodox ethos. St. Tikhon frequently admonished his American flock to persevere in their faith; even more, as in his parting sermon, he encouraged them—missionary clergy and laity alike—to share it with others.

St. Tikhon was greatly beloved by his flock in North America, as elsewhere. He was unusual among Russian bishops of the age in that he was accessible and approachable, distinguished by his humility, simplicity, and lack of ostentation. At the same time, he was incredibly hard-working and took his pastoral responsibilities with utmost seriousness—and expected his clergy to do the same. The great care he had for his flock—both clergy and laity—is reflected in these sermons and writings.

Father Petr Bulgakov, a classmate of St. Tikhon's at the St. Petersburg Theological Academy, settled in the United States in the 1920s. After St. Tikhon's death, Fr. Bulgakov urged Orthodox Christians in America to erect a monument to the Patriarch and to collect and preserve everything connected to St. Tikhon's American service, because "Tikhon's legacy is of the most vitally important interest and significance."[1] The collection and publication of St. Tikhon's Russian-language sermons and writings, newly translated in this volume, was accomplished in the mid-1920s.

Beyond that, however, it appears that few have heeded Fr. Bulgakov's words in America, despite recent interest in Russia and beyond.[2] But his project is no less relevant for Orthodoxy in America today than it was in Fr. Bulgakov's day. This translation of St. Tikhon's sermons and writings, therefore, is a worthy monument and a major contribution toward making his words and legacy available to new generations of Americans.

---

[1] "Patriarshii kurs," *Vestnik PSTGU II: Istoriia. Istoriia Russkoi Pravoslavnoi Tserkvi* 2/19 (2006): 34–109, p. 43.

[2] See especially the important works and collections of A. V. Popov: *Amerikanskii period zhizni i deiatel'nosti sviatitelia Tikhona Moskovskogo, 1898–1907 gg.* (St. Petersburg: Satis, 2013); *Amerikanskii period zhizni i deiatel'nosti sviatitelia Tikhona Moskovskogo: Pis'ma sviatitelia Tikhona* (St. Petersburg: Satis, 2010); *Amerikanskii period zhizni i deiatel'nosti sviatitelia Tikhona Moskovskogo: propovedi i stat'i* (St. Petersburg: Satis, 2011); and *Amerikanskii period zhizni i deiatel'nosti sviatitelia Tikhona Moskovskogo: Dokumenti* (St. Petersburg: Satis, 2014). See also A. B. Efimov and O. V. Lasaeva, *Aleutskaia i Severo-Amerikanskaia eparkhiia pri sviatitele Tikhone* (Moscow: Pravoslavnyi Sviato-Tikhonovskii gumanitarnyi universitet, 2012). The first English-language dissertation on St. Tikhon's service in America was written by an Italian: Monica Cognolato, "The Orthodox Church Does Not Build on Other People's Foundations: The Orthodox Church in America During Bishop Tikhon's Years (1898–1907)," Ph.D. dissertation (University of Padova, 2014).

INTRODUCTION

by the Translators/Editors

St. Tikhon's Life

VASILI IVANOVICH BELLAVIN, the future St. Tikhon of Moscow, was born in the village of Klin in the Toropets district, in northwestern Russia, on January 19, 1865. The son of a priest, he attended seminary in Pskov. After that, he attended the Theological Academy at St. Petersburg, where he flourished in his studies. Upon his graduation from there, in 1888, at the age of 23, he began teaching at the seminary back in Pskov. In 1891, he was tonsured a monk, being given the name Tikhon after St. Tikhon of Zadonsk, a beloved and very famous bishop in southern Russia in the 18th century.

Soon after that he was ordained a priest. Then, for several years, he taught in the seminary in Kholm, and briefly in the seminary in Kazan.

In 1897, at the young age of 32, Fr. Tikhon was made an auxiliary bishop in the Diocese of Kholm for the city of Liublin, in eastern Poland, where he had much contact with former Byzantine Rite Catholics, commonly called Uniates, who had been brought back to the Orthodox Church in 1875. These people's ancestors had been Orthodox for centuries, but had become subject to the Roman Catholic Church in 1596 through the Union of Brest-Litovsk, whereby seven of the nine Orthodox bishops in western Ukraine, under political pressure, accepted the authority of the Roman papacy. While serving in eastern Poland, the newly consecrated Bishop Tikhon had success in further assisting the transition of these people back to Holy Orthodoxy, the Faith of their fathers.

This experience would prove to be excellent preparation for his work in America, where many Byzantine Rite Catholics began immigrating in the 1880s. We find frequent references to the Unia in his sermons preached in America, including the fact that many of the members of his flock had recently returned to Orthodoxy from the Unia.

After about a year serving in Poland, Bishop Tikhon was sent to be the presiding bishop of the Russian Missionary Diocese in America, which dated back to the coming of the ten missionary monks from Valaam Monastery, near Finland, to Kodiak, Alaska, in 1794. As Bishop Tikhon ministered in Alaska and learned about the history of the Church there, he quickly came to greatly appreciate that heritage.

In 1870, three years after the sale of Alaska by Russia to the United States, the Holy Synod of the Russian Church established the Diocese of the Aleutian Islands and Alaska, centered in Sitka, Alaska. Two years later, the episcopal see was moved by Bishop John (Mitropolsky) from Sitka to San Francisco, in accord with the growing vision to bring Holy Orthodoxy to all the people living on the North American continent.

Arriving in New York City in December of 1898, the newly appointed Bp. Tikhon soon discovered that there were already some highly successful and saintly workers in this American vineyard, including several future Saints. First, there was Fr. Alexis Toth, who had brought St. Mary's Byzantine Rite Catholic Church in Minneapolis into Holy Orthodoxy in 1891, and who was now in Wilkes-Barre, Pennsylvania, in the midst of his ongoing outreach to Uniate immigrants from Eastern Europe, some 29,000 of whom, in 17 parishes, he would help to return to Holy Orthodoxy before his death in 1909. Then there was Fr. Raphael Hawaweeny, a highly energetic and deeply inspired missionary priest ministering to all the Arab-speaking Orthodox Christians in North America from his home church in Brooklyn, New York. Next, there was Fr. Sebastian Dabovich, a tireless Serbian-America missionary, and the first Orthodox priest to be born in the "lower 48."

There also was Fr. John Kochurov, priest of the flourishing Holy Trinity Cathedral in Chicago, who became the first priest martyred by the Bolsheviks in Russia in 1917. And in addition, there was Fr. Alexander Hotovitzky, priest of St. Nicholas Cathedral in New York City and editor of the national newspaper for the Russian Orthodox in America, the *Amerikansky Pravoslavny Vestnik* (*Russian-American Messenger*); he also died back in Russia, in a concentration camp, in 1937. As mentioned in the Preface, the bi-weekly *Vestnik* journal would become the main source for the sermons, "suggestions," and other material by St. Tikhon that are presented in this book.

There were also many active laymen in the Church in North America. Very often it was the laity, recent immigrants from Eastern Europe, who would purchase land and build a church in communities scattered across the continent. At the same time, there were many church members who evidently seemed to be more interested in the Church as an ethnically-oriented social club rather than as the embassy of the Kingdom of Heaven. Hence, in his sermons, we find St. Tikhon very often urging his flock to pay more attention to their spiritual life than to their material and social well-being in this world.

Bishop and then Archbishop Tikhon would lead the American Orthodox flock for over eight years. He was a truly visionary leader, recognizing the unique needs of the multi-national situation here. He greatly respected the liturgical practices, customs, and languages of all ethnic groups, yet he urged the use of English, and promoted missionary outreach. Well-known as a wise and gentle caretaker of souls, he was also very strong when the occasion demanded decisive leadership, so his preaching very often is marked by a loving yet firm tone.

In 1903 Bp. Innocent was consecrated as Bp. Tikhon's first auxiliary bishop, with oversight of the Orthodox in Alaska. In the next year, Bp. Tikhon consecrated Fr. Raphael Hawaweeny as another auxiliary bishop, with responsibility for the Arab-speaking Orthodox in North America; altogether St. Raphael would establish 30 Syrian Orthodox parishes before his repose in 1915. Also in 1904, Bp. Tikhon moved the episcopal see from San Francisco to New York City, which further indicated the Church's vision for evangelizing all of America. In 1905, he appointed Archimandrite Sebastian Dabovich administrator of the various Serbian Orthodox parishes in North America.

Two other highlights during his North American ministry also occurred in 1905—the founding of a theological seminary in Minneapolis, Minnesota; and the establishment of the first Orthodox monastery in the New World—St. Tikhon's Monastery, in South Canaan, Pennsylvania, which he loved, even spending a large part of the summer of 1906 there.

In 1906, the first Orthodox service book ever to be published in English was printed with Archbishop Tikhon's ongoing support and encouragement. Compiled and translated by Miss Isabel Hapgood, this book is still in use today.

In February of 1907, the First All-American *Sobor* (Council) was held in Mayfield, Pennsylvania, with clergy and lay representation from every parish. The theme of the *Sobor* was "How to Expand the Mission." But by then, very poignantly, the greatly beloved Vladika Tikhon had already been summoned to return to Russia to a new assignment there. So it was at that *Sobor* that St. Tikhon gave a very touching farewell speech to his greatly beloved American flock. He preached his very last sermon before leaving America in his beloved cathedral church in New York City; this sermon is also very touching, as he pours out his heart to his beloved flock there.

In the Spring of 1907, Vladika Tikhon returned to his Russian homeland where he was assigned as the bishop of the ancient city of Iaroslavl. In the summer of 1917 he was made Metropolitan of Moscow. Later that year, at the Great Council of the Church of Russia, held in Moscow in 1917 and 1918, he became Patriarch of All

Russia. After suffering much under the fanatical, anti-Christian rule of the Bolsheviks, he died in a private hospital in Moscow as a Confessor for the Faith, on March 25, 1925. It is possible that he died by poisoning, either intentionally or accidentally.

His Instructions and Teachings

Various characteristic dimensions of St. Tikhon's heart and mind and soul are revealed and expressed in the sermons and other directives printed in this book. First of all, we see very vividly demonstrated, over and over again, St. Tikhon's deep love and profound knowledge of the Holy Scriptures. His sermons are suffused with Scriptural quotations and references—along with quotations from hymns and prayers, and from various Church Fathers, although to a much lesser degree. In two sermons preached at ordinations to the priesthood, he refers to the Prophet Jeremiah calling the written Word of God a *fire* and *hammer* (Jer. 23:29) burning the dross and breaking up the rockiness in our souls. He urges the newly ordained priests, as well as all his people, to immerse themselves in the Scriptures.

Another characteristic of his that comes through in these sermons is intense love for his homeland, the motherland, holy Russia. He speaks often of the beauty of churches/temples in the Russian land, and how dear they are to the Russian people—and how he hopes the members of his American flock will continue to love their places of worship, humble and simple though they usually were in comparison to grand cathedrals in the Russian lands!

He also reveals a strong love and respect for the reigning Tsar Nicholas II, as especially expressed in his homilies on the Tsar's birthday (May 6, 1904) and the anniversary of his crowning (March 14, 1905), as well as the letter he writes directly to the sovereign (April 29, 1904). St. Tikhon's defense of benevolent autocracy as the best and most appropriate type of government for the Russian people, along with encouraging of his flock to explain this view to their

fellow Americans misunderstanding the Russian system of government, is particularly interesting.

His great concern for the material welfare of his American
flock—especially the impoverished Orthodox Native Americans in
Alaska—is vividly expressed in these writings. However, his dominant concern is, of course, for their spiritual well-being. Very often
we find him urging others to resist the lure of pursuing wealth and
entertainments at the expense of concentrating on the health of their
souls. And he repeatedly exhorts them to be Orthodox Christians
not just in name, but most importantly in deeds, truly living the
Christian life not only for their own spiritual welfare, but also so
that the light in their lives might attract outsiders to the Orthodox
Church.

He also many times urges his people to be strong in Holy Orthodoxy, and therefore to steadfastly resist the attempts of Protestants
and Roman Catholics to lure them away from the True Faith. His
profound and deep conviction that Orthodoxy is indeed the true and
complete Faith of Christ comes through very powerfully in these
texts.

As part of this dominant concern for protecting his flock from
foreign intrusions, St. Tikhon several times talks about the pressing
need for education—not just for the children, but also for the adults.
His Suggestion in 1901 for a "Society of Soberness" is especially
interesting along this line, as he directs that supplemental teaching
through various appropriate readings be brought to the people after
the celebration of the Divine Liturgy every Sunday—to help also in
minimizing drunkenness!

We see, in addition, a keen interest in the history of Orthodoxy
in America, as demonstrated especially in his directive for a museum
to be established in Sitka, Alaska, to be dedicated to the memory
of the remarkable and outstanding missionary bishop, St. Innocent,
who served in Alaska as priest and then bishop from 1824 to 1867.
Archbishop Tikhon's specific instructions were to collect and house

every kind of artifact associated with St. Innocent during his time in Alaska.

One particular gem in this collection of writings is his sermon of January 31, 1902, addressed to newlyweds for whom he has just celebrated the Sacrament of Marriage. This is one of the most profoundly beautiful and wise presentations on marriage, and its sanctity before God, that we know of. And of course, what makes this homily even more remarkable is the fact that it was delivered by someone who had no personal experience of the married way of life.

Finally, what we think is most striking in these writings—what impacted us repeatedly as we did our translation work—is St. Tikhon's tremendously strong—we might even say *adamantine*—faith in Christ. Everything he says and writes is penetrated with rocklike faith—which undergirds his profound love for and devotion to the Lord Jesus Christ, and to His Holy Church.

With all of this, it's no wonder St. Tikhon was the man selected by the Lord—by Whose direction and allowance all people and nations live and act, as St. Tikhon well knew—to be the leading churchman to have to face and deal with the atheistic and rabidly anti-Christian Bolsheviks. His eight years of experience in America, with his Church being misunderstood, if not outright under attack, in various ways, and existing without any support from the government, was also part of his preparation for defending the Church in Russia in the face of much more hostility and attack. Remarkably, the Bolshevik revolutionaries were in the midst of seizing the reins of government in Moscow, in October of 1917, at the very moment when St. Tikhon was being selected, first by ballot and then by lot, to be the new patriarch of the Russian Church.

TROPARION

Tone 1

Let us praise Tikhon, the patriarch of all Russia, and enlightener of North America, an ardent follower of the apostolic traditions, and good pastor of the Church of Christ, who was elected by divine providence, and laid down his life for his sheep. Let us sing to him with faith and hope, and ask for his hierarchical intercessions: Keep the church in Russia in tranquility, and the church in North America in peace. Gather her scattered children into one flock; bring to repentance those who have renounced the True Faith. Preserve our lands from civil strife, and entreat God's peace for all people.

IN PLACE OF AN INTRODUCTION
TO THE ORIGINAL BOOK IN RUSSIAN

Report of the Publishing Committee to His Beatitude,
Metropolitan Platon, and the resolution of His Beatitude
on the report, written by the editors of the 1923/1926
Collection of Instructions and Teachings *by St. Tikhon*

December 14, 1923. Godspeed! Metropolitan Platon.[1]

PUBLISHED IN THE YEAR 1922 by the Publishing Committee at the St. Nicolas Cathedral, the booklet "Patriarch Tikhon" was distributed by the diocese in the number of 1000 copies. The results of the publication of this booklet are such that hope is present that a new edition will be circulated just as successfully.

The name of His Holiness, our Patriarch Tikhon, is so much alive among the Orthodox in America that it is desirable to give the Orthodox people more precise and clear information about the views and spiritual make-up of His Holiness during the time of his archpastoral service in America. Making use of the fact that Vladika Patriarch blessed publishing extracts from his *Instructions and Teachings for the American Russian Orthodox* in the publications of the time during the years between 1898 and 1907, the publishing committee

---

[1] This was Metropolitan Platon's affirmative response to the request by the Publishing Committee for his blessing upon their work. Metropolitan Platon served as head of the Russian Missionary Diocese in America from 1907 (succeeding Archbishop Tikhon) until 1913, and then as head of the Metropolia (which embraced most of the Russian-American Orthodox after the Missionary Diocese dissolved in the throes of the Russian Revolution) from 1922 until his death in 1934.

has chosen to publish sermons of His Holiness Patriarch Tikhon during his time as the Bishop of the Aleutians and North America.

Presenting this thought for the archpastoral consideration of Your Beatitude, the Publishing Committee most respectfully asks Your blessing for this publication of the sermons of Vladika Patriarch Tikhon.

Your Beatitude's most humble servants:

Cathedral Priest Leonid Turkevitch[2]
Priest Petr Popov
Priest Vasili Lisenkovitch

November 21, 1923
New York City

---

[2] This was the future Metropolitan Leonty, who headed the Metropolia from 1950 until his death in 1965.

FROM THE EDITOR[1]

IN THIS PRESENT collection of the homiletic works of His Holiness Vladika, our Patriarch Tikhon, an historical order in the arrangement of the sermons of His Holiness is used. Aside from the natural flow, this order was considered the best, since with it the reader unknowingly is introduced to the spectrum of the subjects that interested Vladika during the time of his preaching in America. These words and sermons represent in a way the archpastoral diary of Vladika, in which the main aspects in the life of the American Orthodox Church that the Archpastor paid attention to are indicated. Rereading these "Instructions and Teachings" of His Holiness to the American flock, the pastors and those in their care, the reader involuntarily is present amidst the flow of life of the American Church, enters the many-sidedness of its parts, recalls its distant past, contemplates what was contemporary for the Hierarch, and detects similarities or differences between what took place then and what exists in its present life.

As it is clear on its own, the words and sermons of His Holiness preached during visits to churches and parishes which were passed on not entirely accurately and completely by the chroniclers of the time could not be included in the collection. No matter how significant and how interesting they are, yet their place is in the historical reproduction of the life and work of His Holiness in his years of administering the American Orthodox Church. This task should be

---

[1] The (unnamed) editor of the original collection of these sermons, which were published in Russian in New York City in 1923 and 1926.

fulfilled in another publication. The present one accomplishes only what was offered to the reader's attention already in the year of 1918.

The content is broken down into parts for the purpose of simplifying the publishing side of the undertaking, as well as highlighting the historical order in the arrangement of the homiletic works. Nevertheless, with the whole-heartedness of His Holiness's personality, the image of Vladika in every part is present as invariably full and deep in his Christian character that is purely Russian Orthodox, and at the same time entirely universal, catholic.

AN INTRODUCTORY VIGNETTE

The Stay of His Eminence, the Most Reverend Tikhon, at St. Tikhon's Monastery, and His Visits to the Neighboring Parishes;[1] *by Igumen Arseny, Co-Founder of the Monastery and Orphanage*

O N   T H E   7th [/20th, Friday] of July [1906] the Most Reverend Archbishop Tikhon left stifling New York, the place of his cathedra, and came for a summer vacation to St. Tikhon's Monastery. In truth even this summer vacation itself represents a whole number of archpastoral activities in the cloister and the neighboring parishes.

At the cloister the Most Reverend Vladika, with the archpastoral simplicity that is distinctively his, shared and sometimes led the labors of the brethren in feats of prayer and in household affairs; he tried to understand, thoroughly, the particulars of the newly organized life of the first inhabitants [of the monastery]; he gave instructions whenever necessary, and in everything he clearly demonstrated how precious to him the habitation he had organized is, and how the fire of the monastic calling is aflame within himself.

This sojourn of Vladika will comprise a memorable part of the brief history of our first young cloister, and we suppose that it will put into the hearts of the worthy Archpastor's successors the desire to imitate and to continue to patronize and guide the holy habitation.

At the cloister, the Most Reverend Vladika is only a dear and honorable guest, but we will see how close to him are its needs and its

---

[1] Translated by Alex Maximov and Fr. Juvenaly (Repass); taken from a *History of St. Tikhon's Monastery*, to be published by St. Tikhon's Monastery Press.

ways, in general. Here his Archpastoral eye noticed that the amvon in the temple is too big and not very useful; instead of giving orders to the subordinates and yelling, typical of many in these situations, Vladika takes an ax, a hammer; and together with a novice, he starts to remake the amvon, and almost [by] himself he sweeps up the shavings after the work is done, and, completely calm, goes on to his office work.

In the field, in the woods, in the meadow, at the apiary one can often see Vladika working with the brethren. Right here a monk is working on constructing the holy gates, and Vladika himself is guiding him and hands him the necessary boards. There the brothers are cutting the wheat in the field, and the Archpastor, in spite of high midday heat, is with them; and here, outside, the fruits of the first labors—beautiful green cucumbers—are collected with joy, and Vladika counts them and with his own hands brings them to the pile. And there the orphan-children, spread through the orchard, are picking apples, and their father-benefactor is amidst them. A stroke of the bell calls the laborers to the modest lenten meal; and the Archpastor, without fail, goes to the common meal, blesses it, and shares it with everyone, not giving himself any exceptions. It is not for nothing that the holy habitation is called "Tikhonovskaya," since in everything and everywhere we can see St. Tikhon!

And truly the Archpastor's cell is not meant for rest. There, from 5 and sometimes even 4 o'clock in the morning, the desk becomes covered with papers; late at night his pen is at work and brings to life the complex structure of the dispersed American mission; next to him, not sitting untouched, are the *Otechnik*,[2] the Works of St. Tikhon,[3]

---

[2] This was a certain kind of prayer book.

[3] These would have been the works of St. Tikhon of Zadonsk (1724–1782), a beloved bishop of southern Russia, for whom St. Tikhon of Moscow was named at his monastic tonsuring. One of St. Tikhon of Zadonsk's most popular works was called *Counsels on the Particular Duties of Every Christian*. It has been published in English with the title *Journey to Heaven: Counsels on the Particular Duties of Every Christian* (Jordanville, NY: Holy Trinity Monastery, 1991).

Unseen Warfare,[4] and many other fruits from the gardens of ascetics. And in front of a holy icon, with a lamp lit up at the beginning and the end of the day, there arises a cell-prayer for the flock, those in his care, for everyone and everything...

This anchoretic-monastery life of Vladika is interrupted and diversified by trips to the neighboring parishes for archpastoral services on Sundays. None of the neighbors are forgotten. All parishes—poor and well-to-do, populous and not—had the pleasure of receiving the exalted guest.

On August 13/26, 1906, the monastery community observed the feast day of its patron saint, Tikhon of Zadonsk. The Divine Liturgy was celebrated by Archbishop Tikhon, assisted by the monastery and visiting clergy, who had traveled to South Canaan for the occasion. During this service Brother Andrew (Repella) was tonsured and received the mantia of a monk, being given the name of Anthony. On the following day another novice, Brother Seraphim, was also tonsured a monk in the monastery church by the Archbishop.

When we had entered the temple, a *molieben* to St. Tikhon[5] was served, at the conclusion of which the monastery Igumen, Arseny, presented the Most Reverend guest of honor the icon of the Savior from the brethren and the building committee, with the following word of salutation:

> Your Eminence, most Merciful Archpastor and Dear Guest of Honor!
>
> The brethren of St. Tikhon's Monastery, who have delighted in your long stay with us, truly rejoice now.

---

[4] This popular work on spiritual warfare was first written in Latin in 1589 by a Roman Catholic priest named Fr. Lorenzo Scupoli. It was edited and translated into Greek in 1796 by St. Nicodemus of the Holy Mountain (Athos), one of the two compilers of the famous *Philokalia*, the greatest collection of texts from the Eastern Fathers on the spiritual life. The book was further edited, and translated into Russian, in the late nineteenth century by St. Theophan the Recluse (1815–1894); a fourth printing of this edition was published in Moscow in 1904.

[5] This was a prayer service dedicated to St. Tikhon of Zadonsk, asking for his intercessions.

Today is our first patronal feast and your name day. On this joyful and solemn day you are with us. Many times we have felt your kindness and good will, which you offered to us humble monks, and today we are receiving it in abundance.

It is not a magnificent cathedral temple, not a rich temple of some famous and renowned city of our mission that is receiving you on the most joyful day of your Name; but it is the humble temple of our youthful, infant cloister, which has sprung up in the midst of thick forests, that is honored by your choice. Thanks be to the Most Merciful God; and to you, our most kind Archpastor and Father, go with our filial greetings for your Name Day, and from pure hearts, 'Many Years'!

It may be that this joy and honor is the first and the last for us, since premonition foretells this, and there is also the will of Providence which cannot be changed, and so let it be! And so that you will have a visible pledge of our love and admiration, and remember us everywhere in the places of your service, we have decided to present you on this day of our common joy this holy image of the Savior. Accept this gift from us: it is not so valuable in material terms, but it is infinitely precious on account of Him Who is depicted here. Let the Savior who is portrayed hereon, bless your paths until the hour when He will say to you, 'O good and faithful servant, enter into the joy of your Lord!' [Matt. 25:21, 23].

The Most Reverend Vladika accepted the holy icon with reverence, kissed it, and said in response that he would always keep this holy gift as a memory of the days spent at the habitation, offering prayers before it for the brethren and for the monastery's well-being. After this, a little girl from the orphanage stepped out and greeted the Most Reverend guest of honor with best wishes on his angelic day.

The orphan's well-thought out and heartfelt speech moved everybody so much that those around the dear guest of honor, together with him, shed a tear.

YEAR 1898

1. A sermon preached on ascending the archpastoral cathedra in San Francisco.

2. A sermon preached at the Nativity of Christ.

A SERMON[1]

*Preached on ascending the archpastoral cathedra
in San Francisco on 11/23 December, 1898*

AT THIS FIRST VISIT of mine to you, beloved brethren, the words come to my mind said by the Lord at one time through the Prophet Hosea, "and I will say to them who were not my people, Thou art my people; I will have mercy on her who had not obtained mercy" (Hos. 2:23).[2] These words referred to the heathen and meant that when many in Israel, the chosen people of God, did not come to know Christ, then the Lord revealed Himself to those who did not seek Him (cf. Rom. 10:20; Is. 65:1), and called the heathen to His Church.

According to the unspeakable mercy of God, the heathen who lived within the boundaries of Alaska and the Aleutian Islands were called to the Church of Christ. They were catechized and enlightened with the light of the Christian Faith by the Valaam monks, who were the first here to sow the seeds of the Evangelical preaching. After them, their holy undertaking was continued by pastors and Archpastors who succeeded them, and especially among them—Archpriest Ioann Veniaminov (later on, Innocent, Metropolitan of Moscow),[3]

---

[1] Printed in *Amerikansky Pravoslavny Vestnik*, 1899, #2, pp. 50–51.

[2] Scriptural quotations may not match those in any English translation since St. Tikhon was using a Russian translation of the Bible.

[3] Fr. Ioann Veniaminov served as a married missionary priest in Alaska from 1824 to 1840. After his wife's death, he served as the first bishop of Alaska, from 1840 to 1867. Then he was made Metropolitan of Moscow. He died in that office in 1879. In 1977 he was glorified as a Saint by the Russian Orthodox Church as "St.

2

and my predecessor, the Most Reverend Nikolai,[4] a man mighty in word and deed.

And my unworthiness, through the will of God, was called to the apostolic service here, and here now I will "say to them who were not my people, 'Thou art my people'; I will have mercy on her who had not obtained mercy" (Hosea 2:23). Before, we were strangers to each other and did not know each other; but from now on, through the Lord Himself we will become closely connected in the mutual relationship of a bishop with his flock and a flock with their bishop.

In the writings of the Fathers of old, this relationship is compared to a marriage, with the bishop considered to be the groom, and the flock—his bride. And just as the husband loves his wife to such an extent that he leaves his father and mother and cleaves to his wife, and becomes intimately close to her, a bishop in the same manner must come to love his flock. And just as a wife obeys her husband, so the flock should obey their bishop.

Having this kind of understanding of the relationship of a bishop with those in his care, being betrothed to the Aleutian flock,[5] I left the beloved motherland, my elderly mother, people familiar and close to me, those who are dear to my heart, and departed to a far-away land—to you, people not familiar to me, so that from now on you become my people and my beloved ones. From now on, all of my thoughts and care I direct to you and to your benefit. From now on, I devote all of my strength and gifts to serve you.

I come to you with love, brethren—and I ask you to accept me with love as well. My love will be expressed in concern and care for

---

Innocent, Apostle to America."

[4] Bishop Nikolai (Ziorov) served as the bishop of the Russian Missionary Diocese in America from 1891 to 1898. As St. Tikhon's immediate predecessor, he did much to lay the groundwork for St. Tikhon's ministerial success.

[5] He refers to "the Aleutian flock" because in 1898 the Russian Missionary Diocese in America was still called the Diocese of the Aleutian Islands and Alaska. The name was changed to the Diocese of the Aleutian Islands and North America in 1900.

you in serving you; and your love should be expressed in being obedient to me, in your trust in me, and in assisting me.

I direct the words regarding assistance above all to my closest coworkers—the pastors of the Aleutian Church. I enter this country for the first time; I know it little. But you have labored here for a long time, long before me; many of you have become intimately linked with it, and some were even born here. I hope in my forthcoming service that you will do a great service to me with your knowledge of this land and its people, and that with your experience you will become for me true coworkers, men of advice and reason.

I ask for assistance and cooperation with me not only from the pastors, but also from all of my beloved flock. The Holy Apostle Paul wisely compares the Church of Christ with a body, and a body has not one member, but many (1 Cor. 12:14). And they do not have the same office (Rom. 12:4), but each one has its own: the eye—its own, the hand—its own; and each member is necessary and cannot do without the other. They all care for one another, and there is no discord in the body (1 Cor. 12:25–26). In the same manner you, brethren, "are the body of Christ, and members in particular" (1 Cor. 12:27). "Unto every one of us is given a field according to the measure of the gift of Christ" (Eph. 4:7), "for the perfecting of the saints, for the work of the ministry, for the edifying of the body of Christ" (Eph. 4:12).

Therefore, "with true love grow into Him, from Whom the whole body fitly joined together and compacted by that which every joint supplieth, according to the effectual working in the measure of every part, maketh increase of the body unto the edifying of itself in love" (Eph. 4:15–16). As St. Chrysostom long ago said, "Do not shift everything off on the clergy; you can do much yourselves, you know each other better than we do."[6]

---

[6] St. John Chrysostom (347–407), a priest in Antioch and later Archbishop of Constantinople, was one of the greatest Church Fathers. Chrysostom's words that St. Tikhon is quoting here can be found in his Homily 30 on Hebrews.

Therefore, brethren, edify each other, "warn those who are unruly, comfort the feeble-minded, support the weak, be patient toward all. See that no one renders evil for evil unto any man; but ever follow that which is good—both among yourselves and to all men" (1 Thess. 5:14–15). "May the God of all grace, Who hath called us unto His eternal glory by Christ Jesus, make you perfect, and establish, strengthen, and settle you. To Him be glory and dominion for ever and ever. Amen" (1 Peter 5:10–11).

A SERMON[7]

Preached at the Feast of the Nativity
of Christ in December of 1898

THOSE OF YOU, brethren, who paid close attention to this service, could not but notice how often the Holy Church repeats today in its hymns the angelic glorification at the birth of Christ, "Glory to God in the highest, and on earth peace, good will toward men" (Luke 2:14). In this manner, the Church points out that this feast of the Nativity of Christ is most of all the feast of peace, goodwill, and joy.

And indeed, from the very fall of our forefathers up until the coming of Christ, there had not been true peace on earth. Man was at peace neither with God, nor with people, nor with himself.

Through his sin man disrupted his peace with God, since how can there be communion between the truth of God and the lie of man, between light and darkness? People who had fallen in the eyes of God were "the children of wrath," "sons of disobedience" (Eph. 2:2–3); their sacrifices and offerings did not please the Lord; and He would not accept the holocaust for sins, because "it is impossible for the blood of bulls and goats to take sins away" (Heb. 10:4).

Not having peace with God, people did not have peace among themselves. They were not brethren, children of one father; they were adversaries, directing all of their thoughts towards dominating one another. One kingdom would conquer another, and one nation would oppress another; everywhere there were "wars and rumors of

[7] Printed in Russian in the *Amerikansky Pravoslavny Vestnik*, 1899, #3, pp. 82–85.

wars" (Matt. 24:6) under the burden of which the earth wailed, being soaked in blood.

And if people had peace neither with God nor among themselves, then there could be no peace in their souls, for his conscience convicted the fallen man unceasingly for breaking the law: "There is no wholeness in my bones because of my sin, for my inequities have overwhelmed me; they are like a heavy burden, beyond my strength"; "I am stooped and bowed down utterly; all day I go in mourning"; "I am numbed and severely crushed; I roar with anguish of heart" (Ps. 37:4, 5, 7, 9; LXX)—this is how the Psalmist lamented. The best of heathens also felt the lack of peace in their souls, and being unable to instill it there, they fell into deep anguish and despair.

But then there comes into the world the long expected and desired King of peace, and there are no bounds to His peace (cf. Is. 9:6–7). Christ brings peace in every manner: He reconciles people with God, and He teaches them that they all are brethren, children of one heavenly Father, and therefore they must love one another. He also brings peace and joy into the soul of man. Therefore the angels at His very birth already sing "on earth peace, good will toward men."

But perhaps you might ask—where is peace on earth, since from the coming of Christ until this day we see conflicts and wars; when at the present time one nation rises against another and one kingdom against another; when even now discord, hostility, and animosity are seen so often among people? Where are we to look for peace, which was brought and left by Christ (cf. John 14:27)?

"It shall come to pass in the last days that the mountain of the Lord's house shall be established in the top of the mountains"; "all nations will stream toward it" "and beat their swords into plowshares and their spears into pruning hooks," "and they will not train for war again" (Is. 2:2, 4); "every man shall sit under his own vine undisturbed" (Mic. 4:4). This kingdom of peace on earth, which was foretold by the Prophets of the Old Testament, is indeed the Church of Christ; and it is in it [the Church] that peace should be sought. Here man is given peace with God, since in the mysteries he is purified from sin and becomes a child of the Lord, pleasant to Him.

Here also in the services offered to God, in the mysteries, in the order and life of the Church, a Christian draws peace and delight and calmness for his heart. The nature of man is transformed and renewed, and into his meek, gentle, truly humble, merciful, and loving soul comes the God of peace and love.

And a Christian then experiences the heavenly bliss of which there is nothing higher on earth. No troubles or sufferings of any kind can overshadow this blissful peace in a Christian. On the contrary, we know from the history of the Church of Christ that holy men even rejoiced in suffering and boasted in sorrows, captivity and prisons, deserts and dens of the wicked. Amidst all deprivations they were placid and calm, perhaps more so than people who live with all the comforts and prosperity ever feel. They are not afraid of death itself; they calmly expect its approach and depart to the Lord in peace.

Peace is dispersed everywhere in the Church of Christ. Here people pray for peace in the whole world, for the unity of all; here all call one another brethren, and help one another; here everybody is loved, and even enemies are forgiven and cared for. And when Christians listen to the voice of the Church and live according to its commands, then they truly have peace and love. Recall the first Christians who were united in heart and soul, who even shared their possessions (cf. Acts 2:44 and 4:32). But when, on the contrary, people distance themselves from the Holy Church and live according to their own will, then egoism, division, discord, and wars reign in their midst.

In our days, brethren, days that are not particularly distinguished by peace—when the sword, so to say, hangs in the air, and when nations compete with one another in arms—in our time there has resounded a powerful call for peace. To our great joy, compatriots, this call resounded from the height of the Russian throne from our Most Pious Emperor Nicholas II.[8] And to our comfort his call finds

---

[8] This Tsar Nicholas II ruled Russia from 1894 to 1917. For the Christ-like, humble way he and his entire family met their death at the hands of the Bolsheviks

approval and sympathy with various nations, including the people we live amidst.

May it be during these saving days, when the Holy Church sings the angelic song of peace on earth, that the voice of our Emperor, that calls nations to peace and invites them to "beat their swords into plowshares," will resound from land to land and grow from strength to strength. Let also all the friends of peace be convinced that the Orthodox Church, whose first-born son calls everyone today to peace, is indeed the kingdom of peace on earth.

"Become wise, ye nations, for the God" of peace and love "is with us!"[9] And therefore, all those who thirst for peace, those who labor and are burdened [cf. Matt. 11:28], come to the Church of Christ, and here you will find peace for your souls [cf. Matt. 11:29]. Amen.

---

on July 17, 1918, they have been glorified as Passion-Bearing Saints by the Russian Church.

[9] These words are sung repeatedly in the Orthodox vigil service for the Nativity of Christ.

YEAR 1899

3. From the homily preached on the Sunday of Orthodoxy.

4. A sermon preached to the parishioners of the Minneapolis Church.

5. A sermon preached upon entering the Sitka Cathedral.

6. A sermon preached in the chapel of Ninilchik in Alaska.

7. A word preached to the Serbs on the 17th Sunday after Pentecost in the city of Jackson, California.

8. A response to the General Agent for public education in Alaska.

9. Suggestion (1st) regarding the 100th anniversary of the tonsure of the Russian bishop in America.

FROM THE HOMILY[1]

*Preached on the Sunday of Orthodoxy at the San
Francisco Cathedral in the Spring of 1899*

THE FIRST SUNDAY of the Great Fast is called the Sunday of
Orthodoxy. It is called this because it is the day of "the Triumph
of Orthodoxy," and on this day an "Office of Orthodoxy" is served
at the cathedrals. This service was established in the middle of the
ninth century in memory of the victory of the Orthodox Church
over heresies—and especially over the heresy of iconoclasm, which
had taken hold of many in the Church of God at that time.

But, brethren, the Orthodox Church has reasons not only to com-
memorate the Triumph of Orthodoxy that once took place, but also
even now to live the victory of Orthodoxy and to celebrate it. Indeed,
should we not rejoice and thank the Lord that He, the Merciful One,
watches His Church—that He has preserved Her from Her enemies
unharmed and undefeated even to this day?

After all, the Church of Christ suffered various afflictions and
persecution not only during the first centuries. And not only during
the time of the Ecumenical Councils did false teachers, mistaking
their own wisdom for the wisdom of God, attack Her. No. From the
first days, and until the end of time, the Church has been, and still
is, at war on this earth. Until the end of time She will be likened to
a ship with sailors that sails in the midst of a furious, roaring sea,

[1] Printed in *Amerikansky Pravoslavny Vestnik*, 1899, #7, pp. 186–192.

which is ready to shake the sailors off the ship at any moment, and to sink the ship itself in the waves.

And it seems that the further this ship sails along, the harder the waves whip against it and the fiercer they attack it. First, during the early centuries, there were external persecutions against Christians by pagans. Then, after the Church had triumphed over them, there appeared a danger even more severe, but now from a different direction. The misfortunes from heathens had ended, but now perils started coming from the Church's own countrymen, "perils among false brethren" (2 Cor. 11:26). Attacks started coming from within—heresies and schisms arose one after another from within the depths of Christianity itself.

Of course, the Truth of God prevailed over the lies of man. But the members of the Church may not lay down their victorious weapons. Now they will have to struggle, not with ancient heretics, but with new adversaries—with unbelievers, with all kinds of deniers and false representatives of powerful science. And one can never say that through the course of time this struggle will dissipate—for hardly has the Church prevailed over one enemy before a new adversary arrives. Evil is like some sort of hydra, on which in the place of a decapitated head a new one grows.

And at the end of time the evil one will pull all his strength together, and in the person of the Antichrist will enter into a bitter battle with the Church of God. And for the Church in those days, there will be great sorrow (cf. Matt. 24:30), which has not been seen from the beginning of time (cf. Matt. 24:21). And while in the past some blooming, glorious local churches became poor and deserted, at the end there will be even more desertions. But there has never been—and we believe, according to the word of Christ, there never will be—a time when all of the universal Church of Christ will disappear from the face of the Earth. No, "the foundation of God stands firm" (2 Tim. 2:19); the Church of Christ is built on an immovable rock "and the gates of hell shall not prevail against it" (Matt. 16:18).

The fiercer the waves hit this immovable rock, the further they fly away from it.

Sometimes the enemies of the Church of Christ are ready to celebrate a complete victory over the Church, for it seems to them that they have done away with Her. But what happens next? Like risen waves, having hit the ship, disappear back into the sea and are no longer seen, and cannot be distinguished from other waves, so do the enemies of Christ, having arisen against the Church of God, return back into the oblivion from which they came, and the ship of the Church once again continues its triumphant journey forward. Every new year we live through confirms more and more the certitude of the fact that "the truth of God will endure forever" (Ps. 116:2, LXX), and the gates of hell will not prevail over the Church of Christ.

How can we not rejoice at that—we, the members of the Orthodox Church—and how can we not thank God for victory over the enemies! How can we not celebrate, in light of the fact that the Church of Christ is a kingdom not of this world, and does not possess any worldly means and earthly attractions! This kingdom, which is oppressed, persecuted, and powerless, not only did not ever perish in the world, but grew and defeated the world. How can we not celebrate at the thought that despite all sorts of violence, attacks, and opposition, the Orthodox Church has preserved the Faith of Christ, as a priceless treasure, in all its original purity, wholeness, and flawlessness, so that our Faith is "the Faith of the Apostles, the Faith of the Fathers, the Orthodox Faith."[2]

The fact that the Orthodox Church has preserved the original teaching in purity and flawlessness is acknowledged by many—even among those who do not belong to the Church. However, they add at the same time that (supposedly) the Orthodox Church does not reveal its righteousness and truthfulness in any way, that it does not attract anybody to itself, that it does not grow and succeed on earth; that having set a goal of preserving the original teaching, the

---

[2] These words are part of the proclamation at the end of the Sunday of Orthodoxy service.

Orthodox Church has become introverted, secluding itself from everything else, coming to a standstill at the freezing-point; that life has come to a halt in it; that indeed it has become a lifeless church. At the least, some say, it does not possess the most important sign of vitality—namely, the spirit of missionary activity.

Perhaps it is true that the life of the Orthodox Church does not catch the eye as much and does not shine with so many bright colors as the life of other church communities, where there is more noise and luster, but where in return there are fewer innermost fruits of the Spirit of God. In particular, it is true that we do not have such widely organized missionary establishments—such "congregations" for the "propagation of faith"[3]—as the communities of other confessions have; and we do not spend as much money on this pursuit as they do. But nevertheless, the Orthodox Church remembers Christ's commandment to spread the evangelistic message, and the spirit of missionary activity is not at all foreign to Her—only, Her missionary work has a different character.

When spreading Christianity, the Orthodox Church does not have the habit of building on the foundations put up by others—establishing Christianity in places where it has already been preached. Yet other Christian communities often gather the crop where others sowed first, and they do not hesitate to seize "the sheep from the neighbor's yard" with money and force. The Orthodox Church stays away from those methods which are sometimes permitted by missionaries of other confessions. She does not use unlawful means to convert people to Christianity, She does not strike bargains with the prejudices and passions of man, and She does not distort the purity of the evangelical Truth in order to acquire for Herself more members, since She is concerned not only about the number of the faithful, but also about the quality of their faith.

---

[3] St. Tikhon must have had in mind specifically the Sacred Congregation for the Propagation of the Faith (the Propaganda) of the Roman Catholic Church, a missionary organization established in 1622.

But the most important fact is that the Orthodox Church conducts Her missionary work quietly, with humility and reverence, being conscious of the powerlessness of man and the strength of God. Missionaries of other confessions often do not mind to make noise, to make a din about their work. They meticulously record their heroic deeds so that the whole world might know of their actions and glorify them, and it is for this reason that they are much spoken about.

But the Orthodox messengers of the Good News act differently. They undertake their holy endeavor not to gain glory for themselves from people, but to receive the mercy of God for themselves and salvation for others. They do not trumpet their own successes before the world, and they attribute them not to themselves but to the might of God.

For example, this is what our great missionary Metropolitan Innocent says about himself: "Could I, speaking in all fairness, count it as my own merit or consider it some sort of heroic deed that I went to America? Could I possibly take credit for myself for anything good and useful that was done in my presence or through me in those places where I served? Of course not—at least, I should not. God sees how hard it is for me to read or hear when I am praised for something, and in particular when something that was done by others, or at least not by myself alone, is ascribed solely to myself. I must admit, I would like, if only it would be possible, that my name would not be mentioned anywhere aside from regular lists and records."[4]

And other Orthodox missionaries are distinguished by the same humility; there is nothing showy or artificial in their activity. That is why, perhaps, people know little about our missionaries. But the greatness of their deeds, which could serve as a worthy spectacle for angels and men, is by no means reduced because of that.

Let us look, for example, at the history of our North American mission. Its history indeed can tell of deeds that can amaze us by

---

[4] From *The Writings of Innocent, Metropolitan of Moscow*, Volume 1 (Russian Synodal Publishing House, 1886). See footnote 3 on page 2.

the heroism reflected in them—and that even more so, because the heroes, the messengers of the Good News, themselves did not attribute any importance to their feats, seeing in them just a modest fulfillment of their own holy duty. Without the slightest hesitation they started off to the most far-off, inhospitable lands—which even now, with the improvements in the means of communication, scare most people.

In these lands they suffered all sorts of deprivation and adversities just to bring to Christ people who were unaware of the [Divine] Law. Nothing could stop them from this—neither sorrow, nor cramped conditions, nor persecution, nor a sword, nor hunger, nor danger, nor depth, nor height, just as it is written: "for Thy sake we are killed all the day long" (Rom. 8:36).

And killed they were indeed—let us recall even Hieromonk Juvenaly,[5] one of the enlighteners of the Aleuts. And not by men alone were our missionaries killed, but by the elements too; let us recall the valiant leaders of our mission, Reverend Joasaph[6] and Reverend Nestor,[7] who perished in the bottomless pit of the ocean.

Can a Church that produces such selfless messengers of the Good News, who passed through the unreachable wilderness preaching Christ, and there gave their lives for the Faith of Christ—can a Church like this be accused of being lifeless, inactive, without a missionary spirit, and not concerned about spreading the Gospel?

As recently as last year the Orthodox Church had a new success in its missionary work when it was joined by several thousands of

---

[5] St. Juvenaly, Protomartyr of North America, was one of the original ten missionary monks who left western Russia and arrived in Kodiak, Alaska, in 1794. He was martyred three years later by natives as he was spreading the Gospel in mainland Alaska far to the north of Kodiak.

[6] Archimandrite Joasaph (Bolotov) was head of the Mission in Alaska when he was consecrated as Bishop of Kodiak on April 10, 1798, while on a visit in Irkutsk, Siberia. However, he died at sea in May of 1799 as he was returning to Alaska.

[7] Bishop Nestor (Zakkis) led the Russian Missionary Diocese in North America from 1879 until his death at sea on June 30, 1882.

Nestorians with Urmian Bishop Mar Jonah.[8] Is this not a new victory, and is this not a new "Triumph of Orthodoxy"?

Let us, brethren, thank the Lord, Who is beneficent to us. And for our part, let us care for the preservation of the Holy Orthodox Faith, and its spread amidst those who are unaware of the Law of the Lord. Amen.

---

[8] Bishop Mar Jonah of the Assyrian Church in Sunurgan and Urmia in northwestern Persia converted to Russian Orthodoxy together with his diocesan flock in 1898.

A SERMON[9]

*Addressed to the parishioners of St. Mary's Church
in Minneapolis, Minnesota, on April 25, 1899*

IN VISITING THE PARISHES of our God-preserved diocese, I chose to come to your parish first, not because it was the first one on the way from our cathedral city [San Francisco]. I am visiting you first, brethren, because you were the first from among the local (American) Uniates to rejoin the Orthodox Church. You are the first-born for Her, the first-fruits from former Uniates.[10]

Being the first-born in the ranks of God, as well as in family life, has an important meaning. Many rights and advantages are conferred upon the first-born compared with the others. The Lord's blessings pour abundantly upon them: "May God bless you, may God give thee the dew of heaven and the fatness of the earth, and plenty of corn and wine. May people serve thee and nations bow down to thee. Be lord over your brethren, and let thy father's sons bow down to

---

[9] Printed in *Amerikansky Pravoslavny Vestnik*, 1899, #10, pp. 272–273. This was the first sermon that St. Tikhon preached on his first journey of pastoral visitation since his arrival at his cathedral in San Francisco the previous December. He emphasizes how he made sure that the first church he visited on this trip would be St. Mary's, the first of the former Uniate parishes to come back home to Holy Orthodoxy.

[10] St. Alexis Toth was the priest at St. Mary's Byzantine Rite Catholic (Uniate) Church in Minneapolis, Minnesota, who in 1891 brought his entire flock into Orthodoxy in the Russian Missionary Diocese. Bishop Vladimir came personally from San Francisco to Minneapolis to receive them.

thee"—this is how the patriarchs of the Old Testament blessed their first-born (Gen. 27:28–29).

And here the whole of Israel, the God-chosen Jewish people, the first-born beloved by God—how many blessings were poured on these people, to whom some time ago belonged "the adoption, and the glory, and the covenants, and the giving of the law, and the service of God, and the promises" (Rom. 9:4); "unto them were committed the oracles of God" (Rom. 3:2); "and of whom as concerning the flesh Christ came" (Rom. 9:5). Many rights of the first-born came into the everyday order of human life from the divine order of the universe—the first-born receives known rights over his brothers, he receives a much greater part of the inheritance, and in the royal family he inherits the throne of his father.

Upon you, brethren, as the first-born to Orthodoxy from the Uniates, great and abundant favors, generously and in full measure, were poured out here by the hierarchs of the Orthodox Church. I consider it unnecessary to name them, since I believe that your grateful heart itself will tell you what and how much was done for your benefit.

But, my brethren, being the first-born not only gives known rights, but also bestows upon the bearers special obligations of primary importance. Thus, the Jews devoted their first-born to God. And to the Jewish people themselves, these first-born and the chosen ones of God, the Lord gives a commandment: "Ye shall be holy, for I am holy" (Lev. 11:44).

And so you, brethren, are the first-born, the "peculiar people," "a generation chosen" by the foreknowledge of God to announce to those who do not know the miraculous light of Orthodoxy its truth and might (cf. 1 Peter 2:9). As the older ones in the family should be an example for the younger ones, so you should be an example and serve as "an example ... in conduct, in spirit, in faith, in purity" (1 Tim. 4:12) for those newer ones who have reunited with the Orthodox Church later than you did. "Let your light so shine before men" around you "that they may see your good works and glorify" (Matt.

5:16) our Holy Orthodox Church, whose members, through the mercy of God, you became eight years ago.

Among the many virtues that your life should be adorned with, I will point out only those that are required from Christians by the Gospel and the Apostle[11] which were read today. Right now is the "Week of Thomas." The Apostle Thomas for some time was not a witness of the glory of the risen Lord, and he doubted the resurrection of Christ itself. But with all his heart he wanted to see the risen Lord and believe in Him, and he saw and believed (cf. John 20:24–29).

Through the will of God, you, brethren, for some time having been in the darkness of the Unia, did not witness the glory of the Orthodox Church. But through the Providence of God some of you learned in San Francisco about the existence of the Orthodox Church, you became interested in it yourselves, and you let the others know about it. And like the Apostle Thomas, you proclaimed with joy, "Here in the Orthodox Church is 'my Lord and my God'" (John 20:28). So to you, like Christ said to Thomas, one might say, "Be not faithless, but believing" (v. 27).

Having joined the Orthodox Church, you tasted and saw "that the Lord is good" (Ps. 33:9, LXX). "Therefore, brothers, stand fast, and hold the traditions which ye have been taught" (2 Thess. 2:15) in the Orthodox Church. "Let us hold fast the profession of our faith" (Heb. 10:23), remembering the first days when you had become enlightened by the light of the Orthodox Faith, for which you suffered quite a lot of grief and insults (cf. Heb. 10:32–33). And "not forsaking the assembling of ourselves together, as the manner of some is" (Heb. 10:25), but on the contrary, "exhort and encourage one another to love and to good deeds" (Heb. 10:24).

And you, taking as an example the first Christians, whom we read about today in the Acts of the Apostles, be of the same mind in the Church of God (cf. Acts 2:46 and 5:12). The first Christians were strong through this very unanimity in the Church; they had one

---

[11] This is to say, the Gospel and Epistle readings; in this case, for St. Thomas Sunday, the Epistle reading was Acts 5:12–20.

heart and one soul; quite often their possessions were held in common as well (cf. Acts 2:44 and 4:32). Peace, love, compassion, and mutual aid reigned among them. Any Christian community should strive for these virtues—and yours above all, since it is the oldest among the local ones.[12]

"May the God of Peace, Who brought again from the dead our Lord Jesus, that great Shepherd of the sheep, ... make you perfect in every good work" (Heb. 13:20–21). And may He affirm you in Orthodoxy and like-mindedness. Amen.

---

[12] He is thinking of the Church in America as a local church, with St. Mary's parish being the first of the former Uniate parishes to have become Orthodox.

A SERMON [13]

Preached upon entering the Sitka Cathedral on June 29, 1899

IT IS NOT without feeling emotional that I am entering this holy temple for the first time, and I think this emotion is understood by you, brethren, also.

This temple was once a cathedral. Here in Sitka the Aleutian hierarchs once lived—the first among whom was the ever-memorable Metropolitan Innocent. [14] Here was the center of Church life and of the administration of the local church; here also was the center of the civil administration of this land.

But, according to the word of the Most Wise, "to every thing there is a season, and a time to every purpose under the heaven" (Eccl. 3:1); and you in Sitka have it different now from the way things were some thirty years ago. Though until this day the center of the civil administration of the land is still here, the ruling authority itself is no longer Russian, as it used to be, but American. [15]

And what about the Orthodox Church?—will it remain, and will it stand here with the changes and different trends? Some forecasters turn up who say that in twenty-five years there will not be even a trace of Orthodoxy left in Alaska.

---

[13] Printed in *Amerikansky Pravoslavny Vestnik*, 1899, #15, pp. 394–395.

[14] See footnote 3 on page 2.

[15] St. Tikhon is referring to the sale of Alaska by Russia to the United States in 1867, and to the fact that the civil administration of the U.S. Territory of Alaska was centered in Sitka.

The fortunes of the world, of kingdoms and people, are in the hands of God. He, the All-Mighty One, "bringeth down and bringeth up, maketh rich and maketh poor, maketh alive and killeth" (1 Sam. 2:6–7; 1 Kingdoms 2:6–7, LXX). The fortunes of the Orthodox Church in Alaska are in His hands as well, and we only have left to humble ourselves therefore "under the mighty hand of God," "casting" all our "care upon Him; for He careth for us" (1 Peter 5:6–7).

But while placing our hopes on God, let us not, brethren, have our spirit lazy and relaxed. You have heard in the Gospel read today that the Church of Christ is built and founded on the immovable rock of confessing faith in Christ, the Son of God (Matt. 16:18). And in whoever's heart the Faith in Christ lives steadfast, there, although unfavorable circumstances and various misfortunes might occur, the Church of Christ stands firmly. Whether we transfer ourselves in thought to the first centuries of Christianity, or recall the time that is closer to us, how a hundred years ago the Christian Faith was being established within wild Alaska, we will see everywhere that among those people who were poor materially but were rich in faith, love, and patience, the Church of Christ grew, and became firm, and well-to-do also.

And you, brethren, while keeping this in mind, build up within your hearts a firm foundation for the Faith in Christ; be the stones that are firm and living (cf. 1 Peter 2:5). Having partaken of the beneficent word of God in the Orthodox Church and having displayed in it the labor of love, show, according to the word of the Apostle, the same zeal until the end (cf. Heb. 6:5 and 6:10–11).

Therefore, brethren, watch ye, be vigilant towards visible and covert attacks on your faith, be strong against your enemies, and stand fast in the Orthodox Faith, which you received from your fathers as a sacred and priceless heritage. Preserve it ardently and protect it like the apple of the eye, and become strong in it from strength to strength. Then, though an enemy should encamp against you, do not fear (cf. Ps. 27:3), nor be disturbed. For the foundation of God—the holy Orthodox Church—will stand firm with you, and "the gates of hell," according to the word of the Savior, "shall not prevail against it!" (Matt. 16:18).

A SERMON [16]

Preached on the day of the Equal-to-the-Apostles St. Prince Vladimir, the Enlightener of the Russian Land, in the chapel in Ninilchik, of the Kenai parish, on July 15, 1899

THROUGH THE PROVIDENCE OF GOD, my visit to you, brethren, coincides with the day when our Russian Orthodox Church joyfully celebrates the memory of the Equal-to-the-Apostles Prince Vladimir, Enlightener of Russia. And I, for your edification, according to the commandment of the Apostle to "remember your leaders" (Heb. 13:7), will offer you, brethren, a word about who Prince Vladimir was, and what he is glorified for by the Holy Church.

Holy Prince Vladimir was a great prince of Russia more than 900 years ago, when Russia was not holy, or Orthodox, as yet—when our forefathers did not know the true God; they were heathens, and worshiped idols. And Prince Vladimir worshiped idols, too. But being gifted from God with a bright mind and a heart sensitive to truth, he could not but see that the idols were not God, that vain was the service to them, and that the heathen faith was a lie and a delusion. And the Prince started to think hard concerning how to learn about the true God and to find the right faith.

When different nations heard that the Russian prince wanted to change his faith, they each started sending their ambassadors to him, praising their own faith. The Jews came, and the Muslims, and the Germans from the Pope. But Vladimir did not like their faith, and

---

[16] Printed in *Amerikansky Pravoslavny Vestnik*, 1899, #17, pp. 458–460.

the Prince told the ambassadors from the Pope, who also had tried to convert Russia into the Latin faith previously, "Go away; our fathers did not accept you."

Imprint, my brethren, this wise answer of Prince Vladimir in your minds and in your hearts. Although you have the right Faith and do not have any need to change it, and you are not thinking of changing it, nevertheless we live in a country where there are many different faiths, some of which promote themselves widely. I know that even around this place representatives of different sects do not mind spreading their false teachings even amidst the Orthodox, especially the young children, whom they take to their orphanages while traveling "over sea and land" (cf. Matt. 23:15).

Of course, not all of you are able to refute their false teachings and prove the superiority and true nature of the Orthodox Faith when meeting them. So in this case, answer them with the words of St. Prince Vladimir: "Go away; our fathers did not accept you." Let the sectarians, if they wish to discuss faith, go to your spiritual father. Listen to his voice, and not that of the false teachers.

Among those who came to visit Prince Vladimir was also a Greek monk, who announced the right Faith to him, and Vladimir's soul inclined towards his words. But following the advice of his boyars[17] he also decided to send select people to different nations, for them to see how different people pray to God, how they live, and whose faith would seem to them to be the best. Many different countries did the ambassadors visit, but their souls were not inclined toward any of their faiths. And when they came to Tsargrad[18] and saw the Orthodox service to God there, it fascinated and delighted them so much that they thought that they were in heaven and not on earth, and right away they decided that the Orthodox Faith is the only right faith.

Here you can see, brethren, how much the temple of God and the service in it mean in matters of faith. The temple is the house of God,

---

[17] Boyars were members of the highest rank of aristocracy in Kievan Rus.

[18] The Russian name for Constantinople (literally, Caesar's city).

the preferred habitation of God on earth. Here a Christian learns the law of the Lord, is enlightened by the light of the Faith in Christ; here he is sanctified by the mysteries and the grace of the Holy Spirit, which heals his spiritual and bodily infirmities, and which is poured abundantly on him; here his prayers are enhanced by the prayers of the multitude of faithful pastors and the heavenly forces themselves, who serve invisibly with us.

After this, it is hardly necessary to incline you with many words to come to your temple as much as possible. Imitate the righteous man of the Old Testament in this, who rejoiced when he would be called to the temple (cf. Ps. 122:1), whose soul sought to be there like a deer seeking a spring (cf. Ps. 42:1), and who asked of the Lord only one thing—to dwell in the house of the Lord, and see the beauty of the Lord, and visit His holy temple (cf. Ps. 27:4).

When visiting your temple, brethren, take care of its splendor. It is sinful before God, shameful before other people, and harmful for our soul, if our temples of God are squalid. King David did not want to live in a rich cedar palace while the Ark of the Covenant stayed in a tent—the tabernacle (2 Sam. 7:2). Every good landlord takes care of the splendor of his home. Is it possible, then, that a whole Christian community is incapable of taking care of the splendor of their temple?

The Lord loves those who love the splendor of His house and will not leave them without His great mercies and rich generosity. Perhaps you have heard it from your parents and experienced it yourselves, also, that when you care for your temple and donate to beautify it, then the Lord sends you "earnings" and "jobs" through which you can easily satisfy all your daily needs. And by devoting some of your generosity to the temple of God, you also "prepare for yourselves a treasure in heaven, where moth does not corrupt nor thieves break through" (Matt. 6:20).

When the ambassadors told Prince Vladimir about the Orthodox Faith and services, then he decided to accept the Orthodox Faith; he was baptized, and he baptized his people. But the Prince did not become a Christian only in name; in his life also he became a different person, not the one he used to be while he was a heathen. He restrained his sensual passions, abandoned former sinful habits, became restrained, meek, and merciful, and thought only of how to please the Lord with his new life, which with the help of God he did attain.

And so, brethren, we, having been baptized in Christ, must "put off the old man, which is corrupt according to the deceitful lusts," leave sinful thoughts and deeds, and "put on the new man which after God is created in righteousness and true holiness" (Eph. 4:22, 24), and live in holiness according to Christ's commandments. But do we always act in this manner? Do we always fulfill our Christian obligations? What are our cares, labors, and thoughts directed to? Are they directed to glorifying God with our good deeds and to serving Him only, or are they directed entirely to earthly needs and cares, to food, clothes, shelter?

We are Christians, but what kind of lives do we have? Do we occasionally do things that cause our Faith and our Christian name to be reviled? Let us not, in this case, for our own justification, refer to the weakness of human nature, to the fact that a man is not an angel, and cannot be without sin. The example of St. Vladimir shows us that a man, even in old age (from the *kontakion*[19] to St. Vladimir), with ingrained old habits, can, with the help of the grace of God, leave his deeds of vanity and become adorned with the splendor of good deeds.

St. Prince Vladimir, having become a Christian, started to ardently care for the enlightenment of the Russian people. For this purpose he established schools at churches, where he ordered his subordinates to send their children, to have them learn the law of Christ.

My brethren! There is a wise saying displayed in your school: "Learning is light, ignorance is darkness"; and an illiterate person is often called "benighted." This is particularly true when applied

---

[19] A *kontakion* is a certain type of hymn.

to the knowledge of the truths of faith. Could a person who knows almost nothing about God, about the salvation of the world, about the future life, about his soul, be called a true Christian? To believe, it is necessary to first know what to believe in; and in order to know, one must learn. That is why we have schools established at churches where children are taught the law of the Lord. There is such a school at your chapel. And if you want for your children true benefit and goodness, then send them to the church school to be taught. Here they will learn the fear of God, which is the beginning of any wisdom (cf. Ps. 111:10, Prov. 9:10, Sirach 1:18), and from here they will come out as good Christians and right believers.

St. Vladimir peacefully departed to the Lord on the 15th of July, 1015. The Church canonized him for his God-pleasing life, and for the great and holy undertaking of baptizing Russia, from which a hundred years ago the light of the Faith of Christ penetrated these lands as well. "Thy people celebrate thy repose" (from the *troparion*[20] to St. Vladimir); and we pray to the Lord, who chose Vladimir "like another Paul" (from the *troparion*). And we pray with the words of St. Vladimir himself at the baptism of Russia: "O Lord, Who is great and wonderful! Look upon Your new people. Grant them, Lord, to see You, the true God, and implant in them a steadfast faith."

---

[20] A *troparion* is another kind of hymn.

A SERMON

Addressed to Serbs at the Church in Jackson, California, on the 17th week after Pentecost, on October 3, 1899

"BE YE NOT unequally yoked together with unbelievers" (2 Cor. 6:14). With these words begins today's reading from the Apostle, and to them in particular, beloved brethren, I wish to draw your attention.

St. Apostle Paul wrote once to the Christians of Corinth that they should not associate with non-believers and idol-worshipers. He meant, obviously, not day to day contacts in routine matters, since otherwise the Christians would have to completely withdraw from the world (1 Cor. 5:10), but association in matters of faith, in service to God. In this respect there ought not to be anything in common between the Corinthians and heathens, since what kind of concord can there be between Christ and Belial, and what kind of agreement between the temple of God and idols? (2 Cor. 6:15–16).

But are these instructions of the Apostle applicable to you, brethren? You do not live among heathens, but among Christians. And if it is acceptable to associate even with heathens in daily matters, then why would it be forbidden for you to have religious, prayerful contacts with other Christians, who believe in the very same Christ, the Son of God, Who came in the flesh? Well, brethren, but even though they serve the same Lord along with you, nevertheless do not forget that you are *Orthodox*. In other words, you glorify God the right way and serve Him rightly, but they are non-Orthodox. In other words, they glorify God differently from how you do, and therefore not in a completely right and true way. May they not be offended if we apply to them the expression of the Apostle that they "hold the truth in unrighteousness" (Rom. 1:18).

And if we possess the fullness of truth, then what need is there in this case for us to turn to other church communities for prayerful consolation, and even more—for the Holy Mysteries? Would it not be similar to when someone thirsty rejects a pure spring and starts drinking from turbid streams? Or when someone who can tell the difference exchanges a precious native gem for its imitation, although a skillful one? Or when some reasonable man, when crossing a wide and rapid river, rejects a sound and reliable boat and prefers to it a fragile vessel with which he could drown at any moment? If we are wise in everyday matters, then why would we be in matters of faith like children forever changing our minds about what we believe because someone has cleverly lied to us and made the lie sound like the truth? (cf. Eph. 4:14).

May this not take place among you, brethren! "Be ye not unequally yoked together" (2 Cor. 6:14). Stand fast in the Orthodox Faith and be strong (cf. 1 Cor. 16:13). If the merchant in the Gospels who acquired the pearl sold all his estate to buy it (Matt. 13:45–46), then would you not care to preserve the precious treasure of the holy Orthodox Faith inherited from your fathers, who endured suffering and deprivation for it?

In our time, brethren, quite an effort is made to preserve one's national character, to preserve in a foreign land one's communal peculiarities, one's own native language, one's dear customs, so that a Slav, for example, would remain everywhere a Slav, a German, a German, and so on. If this kind of care exists among you, then it is quite praiseworthy. The Lord Himself appoints a motherland for a person and a place of habitation. Every person who is sensible and has an unspoiled heart loves his motherland, his people, his home-land. Being far away from them, he remembers them night and day, like the ancient Jews, who cried out to Jerusalem in the Babylonian captivity, "If I forget thee, O Jerusalem, let my right hand forget her cunning; if I do not remember thee let my tongue cleave to the roof of my mouth" (Ps. 136:5–6, LXX). And whoever renounces his nation and his homeland, this kind of person is like one who renounces his parents; he does not have any worth and significance, just like a coin without an image and inscription.

And if it is necessary to support, preserve, and protect one's national character, then how much more is it necessary to preserve the holy Orthodox Faith? Although the national character is beneficial for the successful development of a person, nevertheless it only has a temporary significance in this earthly life, and not in the future, eternal life, since "there is neither Greek nor Jew, circumcision nor uncircumcision, barbarian, Scythian, but Christ is all, and in all" (Col. 3:11). It is not the preservation of one's national character that will be required to receive the future kingdom of heaven, but the right faith in Christ. This should be on your mind, brethren, even more so, because your preservation of the Orthodox Faith is also the best and the most reliable way to preserve and support your national character.

"Godliness," the true right Faith, "is profitable unto all things, having promise of the life that now is, and of that which is to come" (1 Tim. 4:8). The history of different peoples eloquently testifies that faith, virtues, and truth elevate a nation, and sins debase nations. Only that nation is great, powerful, and glorious in which a firm faith in God lives, and an unyielding hope in Him—so that "through faith it subdues kingdoms, … is made strong out of weakness, waxes valiant in battle" (Heb. 11:33–34). If it sins before God, it repents before Him also, and in its tribulations turns not to foreign gods, but only to the One True God, and receives help and salvation from Him. Recall, for example, the Jewish people: were they strong and terrifying to their enemies when they bowed to the foreign yoke and served Baal and Astarte, or when they remained faithful to the beneficent Jehovah?

Recall the history of your own people. Was the Serbian nation not tough and grew in strength and glory when it was faithful to the Orthodox Faith of its fathers, and when it remained in unity of thought and brotherly love? Those were the golden days for Serbia, when men of faith and national character labored in it—St. Sava, the patron of your temple and of the Serbian people, his father Stefan Nemanja, his brother crowned by him, and Stefan VI Dusan. On the contrary, hasn't the Serbian nation become weak, and hasn't it been growing weaker even unto this day, from division into various parties, from their internecine animosity, and most importantly from their spiritual swaying, from bowing to the foreign yoke, from servility to a foreign and alien civilization, from coldness towards the Orthodox Faith, and betraying the traditions of the Fathers? True it is!

"We beseech you also, brethren: be ye not unequally yoked together with unbelievers" (2 Cor 6:14); "be not carried about with divers and strange doctrines" (Heb 13:9); "Stand fast and hold the traditions which ye have been taught" (2 Thess. 2:15); "Remember them which have the rule over you, who have spoken unto you the word of God" (Heb 13:7); and do not turn away from them that called you into the grace of Christ "unto another gospel, which is not another; but there be some that trouble you, and would pervert the gospel of Christ" (Gal. 1:6–7)—"Jesus Christ the same, yesterday, and today, and forever" (Heb. 13:8). Amen.

A RESPONSE[21]

*To the General Agent for education in Alaska, Mr.
Sheldon Jackson, on December 11, 1899*

Merciful Sir!

I am enclosing the geographical map, sent by you to me, in which
I marked places where the churches and chapels of the Orthodox
mission are located. Along with it, I enclose a list of our churches,
schools, priests, and teachers. One may see from this list that in spite
of a scarceness of funds, our mission, according to our strength and
ability, does quite a bit to spread Christianity in Alaska and enlighten
and ennoble the native population.

The goal of Russifying the local land is completely falsely
attributed by some to our mission, as well as to our schools. The
fact that we care to support, and as much as possible to spread, the
Orthodox Faith in Alaska, to guard its members from the influence
of other missions we do not hide at all, and we do not make con-
cessions in this respect; and I think you will not deny the legality of
these actions of ours.

The fact that we pray for the Russian tsar is only because he is the
patron of the Orthodox Church, and the local Orthodox clergy and
schools are supported through his generosity; but we do not force
anyone at all to pray for him as our ruler in the local land. On the
contrary, along with prayers for him, supplications are offered for the
President of the United States.

---

[21] Printed in *Amerikansky Pravoslavny Vestnik*, 1900, #4, pp. 82–84.

The fact that Slavonic-Russian is taught in our schools is because our church service language is Slavonic (only certain prayers are translated into the local language and into English), and to understand it, of course, its study is required.

And these are all reasons for us to be accused of a Russification effort. Yet is it not strange to talk about this after the voluntary transfer by the Russian government of its possessions in America to the government of the United States! I have brought this subject up because you, as the person standing at the helm of power, can easily dispel the prejudice of the ill-wishers towards our mission.

As the general agent for public education in Alaska, you may also draw the benevolent attention of your government to our schools. You, of course, will not deny the fact that our schools exist in places where there are often no government or public schools, and the state language (English) is taught in them; therefore they, in my opinion, would be fully entitled to the government subsidy. Their confession here is irrelevant—the state would not be paying for the Orthodox Faith being taught there, but for the English language being taught there, for the future citizens being brought up there, and for the uneducated native population being ennobled. And for the state itself, it would be much more profitable in places where the entire population is Orthodox to provide a subsidy to the Orthodox schools that already exist, rather than to establish its own special public schools, and create with this a completely unnecessary duplication.

This is what my view on this matter is, and I have allowed myself to express it before you in the hope that you, as an educated laborer in public education, would sympathize with the efforts of others directed towards the same noble goals. I will be very glad if, when visiting San Francisco, you will honor me with a visit also.

SUGGESTION I [22]

*To the Alaskan Spiritual Board, in connection
with the 100th anniversary of the appointment
of the Russian Orthodox bishop to America*

ONE HUNDRED YEARS AGO, in 1799, on April 10th, during the week of Palm Sunday, the tonsure of Archimandrite Joseph (Bolotov) to the rank of a bishop took place in Irkutsk.

Archimandrite Joseph came to Kodiak Island in September of 1794 at the head of a troop of Valaam monks to enlighten the heathen, who resided in the Aleutian Islands and Alaska, with the light of faith in Christ. The Lord blessed the labor of the missionaries with success: in two to three years they turned to Christ up to ten thousand heathen. The cause of Orthodoxy advanced here with such success that the Holy Synod saw the necessity to establish an archpastoral cathedra in the Aleutian Islands. Archimandrite Joseph was appointed and tonsured a bishop for this cathedra. But according to the unknown Providence of God, it was not destined for the Reverend Joseph to enter Kodiak Island, which had been enlightened by him, in the rank of a bishop, for the ship the new bishop was traveling on from Asia was destroyed by a storm, and the ocean swallowed Reverend Joseph and his companions in its waves.

Our holy obligation is to remember our teachers, who preached the word of God to us (Heb. 13:7). In fulfillment of this obligation, I suggest for the clergy of the Aleutian Diocese to remember its

---

[22] Printed in *Amerikansky Pravoslavny Vestnik*, 1899, #5, pp. 138–139.

first hierarch, Reverend Joseph, on the hundredth anniversary of his tonsure,[23] on the 10th of April of this year, on Lazarus Sunday, in the Divine Liturgy; and after its conclusion to serve a *panikhida*,[24] preceded by a speech about the hierarch who perished.

In order to immortalize the memory of Reverend Joseph, name the existing church-parish school in Kodiak "The Joseph School."

---

[23] Meaning the day of his consecration as a bishop. Normally a *panikhida* service is performed on the anniversary of a person's death, but in Bp. Joseph's case, this date was (and still is) unknown.

[24] This is a prayer service specifically asking the Lord to have mercy on the soul(s) of certain persons.

YEAR 1900

10. Homily addressed to the newly ordained priest, Fr. Vladimir Alexandrov.

11. A sermon preached at the cathedral in San Francisco on the first Sunday after returning from a visit to Alaska.

13. A sermon preached before the thanksgiving prayer on the day of the 50th anniversary of the State of California celebrations.

13. Homily addressed to the newly ordained priest, Fr. Peter Popov.

14. The speech given in response to the speech of Bishop Grafton in Fond du Lac.

15. Suggestion (2nd) regarding the establishment of a girls' school-orphanage in Alaska.

16. Suggestion (3rd) regarding accurate tabulation of the actual number of parishioners in the parish.

17. Reflection on the Feast of the Nativity.

HOMILY[1]

Addressed to the newly ordained priest, Fr. Vladimir Alexandrov in the San Francisco Cathedral on March 6/19, 1900

ICONGRATULATE YOU, beloved, upon receiving the grace of the priesthood. When our soul comes into contact with Divine grace, it is softened from its usual bitterness—like wax is made soft from the action of fire. I think your soul is in a similar state in these holy and exceptional moments of your life, and I am taking this opportunity to give you instruction for your new service. For your part, imprint it in your mind, and incline to my words not only with the ear, but also with the heart [cf. James 1:22]. Among the many things [that could be said], I consider it timely to give you[2] guidance concerning what is required of you as a priest.

With your new priestly authority you enter a place that is familiar to you, so you know in part what is required there. Your flock consists of Greeks, Arabs, and Slavs. For many years they have gone without a priest. Having come to this land to seek subsistence for themselves—their daily bread—they perhaps have thought little about the heavenly bread, "the one thing needful" [cf. Luke 10:42]. Because of this, their hearts could not help but become hardened, and when they were given the gift of spiritual consolation in the person of a priest, perhaps their hearts were not sufficiently set alight with the holy fire and were not consumed with love for things Divine. They

---

[1] Printed in *Amerikansky Pravoslavny Vestnik,* 1900, #8, pp. 154–156.
[2] Literally, "announce in your hearing" (*oglasit slukh tvoi*).

do know that it is *in their midst* that "Wisdom has built for herself a house," and that it is *for them* that "She has killed a beast and spread her table" (Prov. 9:1–2). Nevertheless, it is still necessary to call them in the streets and from the gates and upon the mountaintop (cf. Prov. 8:2–3), urging them to forsake their foolishness and to prefer Divine knowledge over pure gold (cf. Prov. 8:19 and 9:6).

Well, what about it? Should we burden ourselves with this? But indeed, we are slaves of Wisdom, whom She sends for this very purpose. And for this purpose, today you are being sent by Her. Therefore, preach the Good News not only to those who thirst for this; do not feel it is a burden to search for those who are not seeking you, to open yourself up to those who are not inquiring, to stretch out your hands to those who are disobedient and unruly (cf. Is. 65:1–2). Others quite often travel over sea and land to win a single convert (cf. Matt. 23:15). Be quick to help, and work hard to persuade, all those who are cold towards their mother, the Holy Orthodox Church.

The other part of your flock consists of those reunited from the Unia.[3] They have shown their love for the Orthodox Faith, as you yourself know, through good deeds. Try then to make sure that they do not cool in their first love, but abound in it.

Take care that this church community, which is still small, may grow like the mustard seed in the Gospel into a tree with many leaves (cf. Matt. 13:31–32), under which those who are not yet in our "yard" may find refuge. And it will attract others most of all if the services in it are conducted fervently, with splendor; and if its church life is distinguished for its piety; and if the members of the community live in peace, love, and agreement—like brothers.

The foundations in some respects have already been laid there; it is only necessary to strengthen and develop them. But in other areas nothing has been started. For instance, there is no church school there; you must see that one gets organized. I say to you—and I do not keep silent about this in front of anyone—that the future of

---

[3] These were former Byzantine-rite Catholics, probably from Galicia and/or Bukovina, on the eastern edge of the Austro-Hungarian Empire.

Orthodoxy in this land depends on church schools, and that these schools are especially crucial here, since in the public schools of this country, as you yourself know, the Law of God is not taught.

What I have said up to this point pertains to the external works that you will be involved with in the future. But don't think that you can limit yourself to these things only. Perhaps just the external activities would be enough for some other position, but this is by no means enough for a pastor, even though some of the pastors do devote almost all of their service to external activities.

Have you directed your attention, beloved, to the words of the Savior, "Many will say to Me, 'Lord, Lord! Have we not prophesied in Thy Name? Have we not exorcised demons with Thy Name, and done many miracles?' Then I will solemnly declare to them, 'I never knew you. Go away from Me, you evildoers!'" (Matt. 7:22–23)? And so? Does this mean that it is possible to be a pastor, to preach Christ, to do miracles by His Name, and yet not be recognized by the Lord? Yes. And fear this, so that you do not suffer the same fate!

Remember that the success of pastoral labors does not depend so much on external activities; rather it is the result of spiritual *podvigs* [i.e., struggles and labors] and the virtuous life of the pastor himself. A priest can only ever be a true builder of souls, and their guide to Christ, when he builds himself up spiritually, and in his heart[4] follows the path of Christian self-perfection. Indeed, it cannot be any other way, since this is the law of the spiritual life! "It is necessary," says St. Gregory the Theologian, "first to purify yourself, and then to purify others; to become wise, and then to make others wise; to become light, and then to enlighten others; to become holy, and then to make others holy."[5] One elder, experienced in the spiritual life, used to say, "You will not inspire more good in someone else than you have in yourself."

---

[4] Literally, "in his own conscience" (*v svoei sovesti*).

[5] Oration 2, "In Defense of His Flight from Pontus," part 71 (*Nicene and Post-Nicene Fathers*, second series, vol. VII, p. 219). St. Gregory the Theologian was a great Church Father of the 4th century.

Therefore, in order for your pastoral labors to be successful, before everything else you must attend to your own enlightenment and purification. The Most Holy Master of all pastors, Christ Himself, before setting forth upon His great labor[6] of service for the human race, spent forty days in the wilderness in fasting and prayer. And following the example of the Master of all pastors, all true pastors of Christ have begun their pastoral service with feats of inner self-perfection. So you too should start with this, *especially* since due to circumstances, after having been ordained you will not immediately enter into external pastoral activities. They will remain for some time in the hands of your elder fellow-servant of Christ.[7] Therefore, use this transitional time to prepare yourself for the great work of pastoral service.

Today, through the laying on of hands from me (one who is unworthy), God's grace has descended upon you. Let it not be fruitless in you (cf. 1 Cor. 15:10). To accomplish this, "do not quench the Spirit" (1 Thess. 5:19) which you have received, but kindle it in every way possible. I will briefly point out to you some of the ways to kindle the Spirit.

The first is prayer. As our body cannot live without air, so our soul cannot survive without the breath of the All-Powerful One—without the grace of God; and grace is attracted to a person most of all through zealous and ardent prayer to God. St. John of the Ladder, who is remembered by the Holy Church today, calls prayer a "solicitor of the blessed gifts."[8] And our contemporary, the great man of prayer, Pastor John of Kronstadt, considers it food, strength, firmness of soul, air, light, life-giving warmth, heavenly rain—that refreshes, fills, and impregnates our soul.[9]

---

[6] *Podvig* in the original.

[7] Presumably he is referring to Fr. Dimitri Kamnev, the priest in Seattle who was still overseeing the mission parish he started in Wilkeson.

[8] See Step 28.1 of *The Ladder of Divine Ascent*, by St. John Climacus, a great monastic saint of the 7th century.

[9] See *The Spiritual Counsels of Father John of Kronstadt*, edited by W. Jardine Grisbrooke (Crestwood, NY: St. Vladimir's Seminary Press, 1981), pp. 9–11 and 22–23.

In short, without prayer there cannot be true spiritual life. Therefore, if prayer is crucial for every believer, it is all the more necessary for a priest, whose very purpose is to offer prayers to God for himself and for the people (cf. Heb. 5:3). Therefore unceasingly exercise yourself in prayer. Do not limit yourself to the prayers in the services of the Church; but within the walls of your house, in silence and in solitude, kindle and cleanse your soul with prayer to God.

To kindle the grace of God in yourself, exercise yourself also in reading the Word of God. The Word of God is a *hammer* that crushes and softens our stony hearts; it is a *fire* that burns away the uncleanness of our sins and warms our cold hearts (cf. Jer. 23:29). It is "useful for teaching, for reproof, for correction, and for training, so that the man of God may be perfected, equipped for every good work" (2 Tim. 3:16–17).

Therefore be instructed in the Law of the Lord day and night (cf. Ps. 1:2). Make a rule for yourself to read the Word of God every day, and read it with reverent attention. Then, what seemed long familiar to you in it—what formerly did not make a strong impression on you—will suddenly have new meaning and significance for you, as if you are hearing it for the first time. This will make your soul tremble; and peace, joy, and tender feelings will descend into your heart.

I still have much to say to you, but perhaps now, due to your tiredness, you would not be able to grasp it all. Instead, accept the booklet entitled "Hierarchical Instruction for Newly-Ordained Priests," and through reading it edify and strengthen yourself unto salvation. And I will pray to God that He will make you a good pastor, "rightly dividing the word of truth" (2 Tim. 2:15).

St. John of Kronstadt was a beloved parish priest famous throughout Russia for his wonder-working prayers and great outreach to the poor; he died in 1908.

A SERMON [10]

Preached at the cathedral in San Francisco on the first Sunday after returning from a visit to Alaska, on June 10/23, 1900

THE GOSPEL READ TODAY contains a narration of how the Savior Christ miraculously, with five loaves of bread and two fish, fed more than five thousand people who followed Him. What is remarkable in this narration is not only the miraculous feeding of so many people with such little food, but the most touching attitude of the Lord to the needs of the people. For the compassionate Christ took pity on the people who had not provisioned any food for themselves, and who felt hunger in the meantime. At the suggestion of the Apostles to let the people go to the villages to buy food for themselves, He replied, "Give them something to eat" yourselves (Matt. 14:16).

This story by the Evangelist came to my mind not just one time, brethren, during my visit to the parishes in Alaska—and particularly to the Kwikpak and Kuskokwim missions. And now during my first service after returning from there, the Gospel selected in the rubrics is read of how Christ took pity on the hungry people and miraculously fed them. The inhabitants of the far north, where Christ destined me to have just visited, often find themselves in this helpless state, which causes one to feel pity for them. No longer ago than last winter and spring, they experienced a great shortage of food and suffered severe starvation. And this summer, sicknesses and "social

---

[10] Printed in *Amerikansky Pravoslavny Vestnik*, 1900, #16, pp. 318–319.

diseases," which were brought there by white people and from which the natives die quickly, have joined the hunger.

Is someone helping them in their pitiful state? Yes, they are being helped—but unfortunately, by others, not by us. Jesuits, for example, are helping; they were so foreseeing that they reserved food not only for themselves and those of their own faith, but they give to our Orthodox, just as they take our Orthodox into their orphanages. They give and take in confidence that those whom they help will turn to their faith. And their hopes are not fruitless, for out of gratitude, some of those who used to be with us left us. Like Esau, who sold his first-born birthright for food, some of our people sell the truth of Orthodoxy for food and shelter and go into the spiritual slavery of Papism, understanding neither Orthodoxy nor Latinism, and simply thinking that Christ is the same both here and there.

What about us? Why don't we help? We have only a few people, and our means are scarce. And what can one or two persons do for thousands of natives? We do not have real schools there, and we are only dreaming about an orphanage. And one can only be amazed and thank God that with the current unfavorable conditions we have churches and faithful there, and sometimes we even hear a specific request from the natives for our missionaries to come to them.

The compassionate Christ told His disciples, "Give them something to eat yourselves." We must help our brothers in the Faith. It does not matter that they belong to a different, less civilized race. It is not civilization at all—which shamefully is preached by some—wherein the sole idea is that the white race must not only be prevailing in the world, but must wipe out the other "colored" races; and if the natives die, it's for the better, so it's not worth taking care of them. True civilization consists in giving as many people as possible access to the benefits of life, to elevate the lower races to the level of the higher ones. Since all people originate from one man, all are children of one Heavenly Father; all were redeemed by the most pure blood of Christ, in Whom "there is neither Jew nor Greek, slave nor free" (Gal. 3:28). All are brothers and must love one another—love one another not only in words, but in deeds as well. And so in the name of this love of Christ, we must help our brothers of the far north.

How to help? An example of this was already given in the earliest Church of Christ at the time of the Apostles. At that time, a great need was threatening the Church communities in Palestine due to hunger, so Christians from other countries decided that each one of them would send help, according to their means, to their brothers living in Judea (cf. Acts 11:28–30). The Apostles themselves were often engaged in the collections, and the Apostle Paul collected especially generous gifts from the Greek churches. This method finds followers up to this day in different church communities, which often support their entire missions this way. And we, brethren, should adopt it.

With God's help we hope with time to establish a missionary society, which would provide help and assistance for the Orthodox to satisfy their spiritual, and in part their bodily, needs. Each one of you must give according to what he has inwardly decided for this holy undertaking; and the all-powerful God will multiply His favors among you so that you may always have enough of everything and even a surplus for good works (cf. 2 Cor. 9:7–8).

The Lord Who kindly accepted two mites from a widow, and Who promises a reward even for a cup of cold water offered to one's neighbor, will not leave your zeal and diligence for the benefit of your brothers in the Faith without His heavenly blessing, which attracts earthly blessings as well!

A SERMON[11]

*Preached before the thanksgiving prayer on the day
of the 50th anniversary of the State of California
celebrations, on August 14/27, 1900*

AT THE PRESENT TIME we are celebrating the 50th anniversary of our State of California joining the common union of the United States. I consider it unnecessary to prove that this unification has been favorable, bringing benefit to this land; if all of us did not acknowledge its usefulness, today's celebrations would not be taking place. And I will not examine at length the issue of how and what the present celebration should be marked with—this is a matter for the civil society and is the subject of its care and discussions. As a representative of the Orthodox Church, as a bearer of spiritual views, I only consider it my solemn duty to draw your attention to the fact that you should not forget God at the present festivities.

The 50th anniversary celebration itself is a custom from the Bible, for speaking through Moses, God Himself ordered that the 50th year be celebrated as a holy one (cf. Lev. 25:8–17). And of course, the first and foremost thought of any of the faithful during this kind of celebration should be of God, and of gratitude to the One from Whom we receive everything, "in Whom we live, and move, and have our being" (Acts 17:28). "Every good gift and every perfect gift is from above, coming down from the Father of lights" (James 1:17).

---

[11] Printed in *Amerikansky Pravoslavny Vestnik*, 1900, #18, pp. 358–359.

48

All blessings are given to us from God, and they are so numerous and so common that we have become accustomed to them, and out of habit we do not notice, we do not feel them—just as we do not notice, for example, that air surrounds us everywhere. We appreciate the blessings only when we become deprived of them. But when we have them, then we forget the Lord and all His giving.

The Hebrew people represent a striking example of this kind of disregard. The Lord led them to the fertile land where milk and honey flowed, and gave them bread, wine, and anointing oil. They had a multitude of cattle, and much silver and gold. But their hearts became proud, and they forgot their Savior Who had delivered them from the Egyptian toil (cf. Deut. 8:14). "'The ox knows his owner, but Israel,' says the Lord, 'did not come to know Me.' It has forsaken and spurned its Holy One and started serving strange gods." For that, the Lord became angry with them and gave His Kingdom to others (cf. Is. 1:3–4; cf. Deut. 31:16 and 20).

My brethren! We, through the mercy of God, like Israel, live in a good land—a land of wheat and barley, grapes and honey, a land where silver and gold are not scarce, where everything is abundant (cf. Deut. 8:7–10). And so? Do we always thank the Lord who gives us blessings? Or on the contrary, have our hearts become proud? (cf. Deut. 8:14). And in our blindness do we think that all of this abundance is the fruit of our labor and the work of our hands? (cf. Deut. 8:17). Do we audaciously ask, "What has God given to us?" Yet "He filled our houses with good things" (Job 22:17–18).

May we not, like Israel, fall by following their example of disobedience (cf. Heb. 4:11). May the Kingdom of God and all of our blessings not "be taken away from us and given to a nation bringing forth the fruits of it," as was read in today's Gospel (Matt. 21:43).

Let us hasten to give thanks to God for His beneficence to us. And let us pray that He "extend His mercy to those who know Him" (Ps. 35:11, LXX; Ps. 36:10, KJV), and that from now on He, the Merciful One, may deliver "His holy church, and this city and country, from every evil, thus giving peace and tranquility" (from the Liturgy of St. John Chrysostom).

HOMILY[12]

Addressed to the newly ordained priest, Fr. Peter Popov, at Holy Trinity Cathedral, San Francisco, on September 17, 1900

I CONGRATULATE YOU, beloved Fr. Peter, with the grace of the priesthood. The merciful Lord, Who has foreseen the best in you, today through my unworthiness elevates you from a lower service to a higher, from protodeacon to priest. In you today the word of Christ, which has been read by you yourself in the Holy Gospel, has come true: "Well done, thou good and faithful servant: thou hast been faithful over a few things, I will make thee ruler over many things: enter thou into the joy of thy Lord" (Matt. 25:21).

For your Christian life, meek temper, obedience, exemplary performance, diligence in service, and loyalty in small matters, you are being entrusted with things of greater importance. You are being appointed as priest of a sizable parish (in Bridgeport, Connecticut), where many things still need to be arranged, completed—brought to fruition—for the benefit of the Holy Orthodox Church. In addition to that, I am appointing you to provide some guidance to the neighboring parishes in your deanery.

Try hard to "make yourself worthy of God's approval, a workman who has no cause to be ashamed, following the straight course in preaching the truth" (2 Tim. 2:15). In order to do this, "Do not neglect the gift" that already lives within you, which you have received today through the laying on of my hands (1 Tim. 4:14). Work hard

---

[12] Printed in *Amerikansky Pravoslavny Vestnik*, 1900, #19, pp. 378–379.

with this "talent" given to you; do not conceal it, but multiply it (cf. Matt. 25:14–30).

"Stir up the gift of God" (2 Tim. 1:6) which has descended upon your soul, for it burns our lies; it cleanses the heart of impure, vile, idle, and harmful thoughts; it extinguishes the flame of passions in our flesh; and it expels the seeds of pride, which are often mixed within us with the good seed, with praiseworthy intentions and deeds.

Therefore, taking care to warm up this gift within you—to purify, to perfect yourself—should be your first and highest priority, since the success of your pastoral service will depend most of all on this. Purification and self-perfection are achieved through sorrows and suffering, through self-denial and a cross (Mark 8:34)—which are commanded by Christ in a different part of the Gospel read today. As gold is purified in the hearth, where the impurities are separated from the metal, so our soul is purified from sinfulness through sorrows and suffering—in the midst of which the outer man smolders, but the inner man, created in God's image, is renewed (cf. 2 Cor. 4:16).

Through the way of suffering and the Cross went the Most Holy Master of all pastors, Christ Himself; this is proclaimed by the Cross of the Lord displayed today.[13] Anyone who wants to serve Him must follow the same path. If the God-man Himself rejected His human will, put it in complete submission to God's will, and called out, "Let it be as Thou wouldst have it, not as I, Father" (Matt. 26:39), then even more so we, powerless and sinful, must reject ourselves, submit our sin-loving will to the will of God, and carry out not our will, but the will of the One Who has sent us. If He, while being the Son, "learned obedience through suffering" (Heb. 5:8), then even more so we cannot attain moral perfection without saving sorrows. If He endured offenses, and abuses, and terrible sufferings, and the life-giving Cross, while being innocent, then even more so we must

---

[13] This homily was delivered on the Sunday after the Feast of the Elevation of the Life-Giving Cross, on September 14, so a flower-bedecked cross would have been prominently displayed in the church.

endure suffering, which we rightly deserve through our sin, without complaint. In one word, each one of us must crucify himself with Christ.

Perhaps you are disconcerted, that on a day of true celebration, joy, and praise for you, I give you words about the Cross—words about sorrows and suffering. But recall that even on Tabor, during the glorious Transfiguration of the Lord, Moses and Elijah spoke of His passage[14] which He was about to fulfill in Jerusalem (Luke 9:30–31). The cross, sorrows, and suffering, if understood correctly and endured in a Christian manner, lead to glorification: "Now is the Son of Man glorified," spoke Christ of Himself at the beginning of His suffering (John 13:31). And true is the word of the Apostle: "if we suffer with Christ, we will be glorified with Him" (Rom. 8:17). Therefore we should rejoice, not only when we are given to believe in Christ, but also when we suffer for Him (cf. Phil. 1:29).

Let, therefore, this holy Cross, which is given to you today, always remind you of the path of the cross ahead. Yet at the same time, it will also make this path easier for you, since the life-giving Cross is our strength, might, power, deliverance, shield and protector, victory and firm foundation.[15]

---

[14] "Exodus" in the original Greek.

[15] These words and phrases are taken from various hymns for the Feast of the Elevation of the Life-Giving Cross (September 14).

THE SPEECH[16]

*Given in response to the speech of Bishop Grafton at the
consecration of his Bishop-Coadjutor, Reginald H. Weller,
at Fond du Lac, Wisconsin, on November 8, 1900*

Most honorable fathers and brothers in Christ!

Having received the courteous invitation of Most Honorable
Bishop Grafton to come to the consecration of his coadjutor, I considered it my pleasant duty to accept this invitation in the hope that
the True Head of the Church of Christ perhaps would make my trip
here fruitful. I will not try to predict whether it will be followed by
any results and consequences for your church. But I would only mention some useful observations which I personally have made while
staying in your midst, which could have certain meaning in the eyes
of our Church in the important matter of Church unification.

It would be unnecessary to say to this honorable gathering how
the division of Christians is unpleasant to Christ, yet pleasant to
non-Christians—and how much it weakens our strength and our
achievements. It is unnecessary to say this, since the importance and
holiness of unification in Christ is deeply felt by all of you. And
we, brethren, must not only pray for the desired hour when all of
us would be one flock with One Pastor, Christ, to come as soon as
possible, but we must ourselves make every effort and labor for this
holy undertaking. Perhaps it will happen when we are gone, but we
must sow for it, since the Lord will remember in His Kingdom not

---

[16] Printed in *Amerikansky Pravoslavny Vestnik*, 1901, #21, pp. 452–453.

only the one who reaps but also the one who sows. Let him "rejoice" who, according to the word of the Savior, both "sows and reaps" (cf. Gal. 6:7; John 4:35–38).

I do not doubt that you, enlightened fathers, realize all the seriousness of this great matter of unification.

Sometimes we are reproached of being unnecessarily slow. To counter that, I will quote two of our folk proverbs: "Measure seven times, cut once"; and, "Do things in haste and you will make people laugh." Every important matter should be very well thought out and have a firm solid foundation, for it is unlikely that someone wants to build on sand. I think that this kind of sober attitude is quite applicable to the great matter of unification of the Churches.

In order to achieve this highly desirable goal, conscious study and acquaintance with each other are necessary, as the late hierarch of the Russian Church, Metropolitan Isidor of St. Petersburg, wrote in his message to the Episcopal Church. We, until recently, have rarely come in contact with you, and therefore we know little about you, and you perhaps have looked at us through the eyes of Rome.

Thanks be to God! The All-Merciful Providence lately has been raising up men of counsel and reason, friends of veracity and truth, and the fog has been clearing up. A good step towards this was made by your Episcopal Church in America, and for this the credit and thanks go to you!

Going back to the beginning, with great magnanimity towards the Episcopal Church, I cannot but express gratitude to His Grace Bishop Grafton for giving me this great opportunity to acquaint myself better with your beliefs. I will not hide from you that within the Orthodox Church we are confused by the fact that in your 39 consecrated Articles only two sacraments are considered mysteries. Today's solemnity of the bishop-coadjutor's consecration and the statements you made yesterday clearly testify that the priesthood, just like Baptism and Eucharist, are considered by those who are present here to be mysteries. And I am pleased to witness this for my Church today, and to report about your opinion concerning the Filioque and other matters. This is the tangible benefit I have received from my present visit, of which I have spoken earlier.

If I would be allowed to express a wish, it would be that the Episcopal Church and its worthy representatives would go further in defining their beliefs according to the ancient, Orthodox-Catholic Tradition. In my opinion, a great and convenient opportunity for this would be the general convention of Episcopalians, coming up in October of next year in San Francisco.

And now, according to a Russian tradition, allow me to offer a toast and wish many years to their Graces—Bishop Grafton and the newly ordained Bishop—and all who are present here, fathers and brothers in Christ.

SUGGESTION 2

*To the North-American Spiritual Board regarding
the establishment of a girls' school-orphanage
in Alaska; on November 17, 1900*[17]

THERE HAS BEEN a need felt since a long time ago to establish a girls' school-orphanage in Alaska.

During my inspection of the parishes in Alaska, I had the comfort of seeing how the local women are devoted to the Orthodox Church, how they love to come to the temple of God, and how they try as well to bring up their children (sometimes born in mixed marriages) in the Orthodox Faith. I can say without exaggerating that in some places the Orthodox Faith is upheld by women only. This is apparent to the missionaries of other faiths, who often direct all of their efforts to taking Orthodox girls (mostly orphans) to their own orphanages, to bring them up in the spirit of their teaching, and through that to undermine the strength of Orthodoxy in Alaska.

Unfortunately, up until now we have not had our own school-orphanage, so we unwillingly have had to allow the most undesirable of circumstances to take place—Orthodox girls being brought up in the orphanages of other faiths. Although even there they were not left without any care by the Orthodox pastors, this care was not always accompanied with the desired success, due to the fanaticism, resourcefulness, and shamelessness of the missionaries of

---

[17] Printed in *Amerikansky Pravoslavny Vestnik*, 1900, #23, p. 479.

other faiths (such cases many times have been announced in our *Vestnik*).[18]

Now, through the mercy of God and thanks to the All Russia Missionary Society,[19] there is an opportunity to establish our own special school in Alaska with an orphanage for at least twelve orphans. In light of that, I recommend that the Fathers—the deans of Sitka and Unalashka—discuss *without any delay* the particular matters regarding the establishment of a girls' school-orphanage, and present their suggestions to me.

---

[18] That is, the national periodical of the Russian Missionary Diocese in America, call the *Russian-American Messenger* (*Amerikansky Pravoslavny Vestnik*).

[19] This was a society of clergy and laity established in Russia by Metropolitan Innocent in 1870 for the purpose of promoting international missionary work by the Orthodox Church.

SUGGESTION 3

To the North-American Spiritual Board as of December 1, 1900 regarding accurate tabulation of the actual number of parishioners in the parish

ONE OF THE PRIESTS of our diocese, to my question of "how many parishioners he had," reported to me in writing that "there would be no more than 400 parishioners, although on paper there are more than 600." In another place, men who were almost a hundred years old, who have already passed into eternity, were counted among parishioners until recently.

I suggest to the Spiritual Board to explain to those who need it, that only those persons should be reflected "on paper" who actually belong to the Church, and all sorts of "paper" acquisitions will not be praised, but will be held against the priests.

REFLECTION[20]

On the Feast of the Nativity on December 25, 1900

T HE FEAST OF THE NATIVITY breathes with a spirit of peace, benevolence, quiet joy, heavenly simplicity. A quiet night blankets the fields of Palestine; above them is the starry sky with the "star of the King of Judea" shining brightly. The bustle of the day dies out in Bethlehem, overflowing with visitors. In a simple manger lies an Infant wrapped in a cloth; the loving Mother leans over Him with a joyful smile. The righteous Joseph is here as well, immersed in reverential contemplation of the great mystery. And the shepherds, simple and pure of heart, have come to pay their respect to Christ Who has been born. And in heaven the choirs of angels sing, "Glory to God in the highest, and on earth peace, good will toward men" (Luke 2:14).

Peace and good will! Does that mean the end of hostility and discord? At last, the long awaited and much welcomed King of Peace is born, and "of His peace there is no end" (Is. 9:7), since He brings peace to all, reconciling man with God, with his neighbor, and with his restless conscience. The kingdom of Christ, the kingdom of peace, arrives!

Nevertheless, even now "one nation rises against another, one kingdom against another." On the one hand there is an angelic song of peace, and on the other there are "wars and rumors of wars" (Matt. 24:6–7)! This antimony has continued until our days, and now is confirmed by the events that are happening in front of our eyes.

---

[20] Printed in *Amerikansky Pravoslavny Vestnik*, 1900, #24, pp. 484–487.

Two years ago a powerful call of the Tsar was heard from the height of the Russian throne, calling the nations to peace, inviting them to beat their spears into sickles and their swords into plowshares (cf. Is. 2:4). What happened next? Hardly had the conference at The Hague, that had convened at the initiative of the Russian Tsar, finished its sessions, when a war flared up in the south of Africa between Christian nations, one of which even had its representatives at the conference. And later, all of the main Christian states of the world were forced to send troops to heathen China.

Where does this duplicity come from? Why is there talk of peace, and preaching about it, that is met with sympathy and approval everywhere, but in reality there is war, waged with brutality, that causes joy and delight in the victors?

The explanation of this contradiction within man has already been given by the holy Apostle Paul long ago: "For I know that in me (that is, in my flesh), dwelleth no good thing: for to will is present with me; but how to perform that which is good I find not. For the good that I would I do not: but the evil which I would not, that I do" (Rom. 7:18–19). As long as sin abides in our inner man, and until the Kingdom of God—truth, peace, and joy and the Holy Spirit (cf. Rom. 14:17)—becomes established *within* us, until that time it cannot reign *outside* of man in the society and in the state. And until that time there will be discord and wars among people.

But the closer the nations come to Christian ideals, and the more they become imbued with Christ's commandments, the less hostility, division, and warlike vehemence is in them. We no longer compare the ancient world, where "a man was like an animal unto another man," to the Christian world, where all are considered brothers and children of one heavenly Father. Within that Christian world itself, the most peace-loving and meek are the nations that in spite of their external strength and might, realize their sinfulness and poverty in front of the King of kings, and are strangers to an arrogant attitude towards other nations.

This is the way our "Holy Russia" is, the way the "God-bearing" Russian people are. And this is not some sort of self-deception and self-praise, but the truth—which is vividly supported by the latest events.

During the present war in China, who had to suffer and endure more than Russia? Was not the daring assault of the enemy directed only against the Russian lands? Was it not the Russian roads that were destroyed? It would seem that the Russian state had more reasons and grounds than others to demand retribution, to take revenge on the defeated enemy. Nevertheless, as soon as the foreign citizens were released from the siege in Beijing, immediately the peaceful call of the Tsar was heard from the heights of the Russian throne ordering the Russian troops to leave the capital of the defeated in order not to present any difficulties for the peace negotiations.

Furthermore, an entire region of China (Manchuria) was captured by the Russians, yet they are not looking to retain it for themselves according to the right of the victor, but they are already inviting the Chinese government to send their officials there now. Other nations act differently. Even if Russia wages war, it is not to capture gold and diamond mines, and not to acquire ports and coal plants, but it is either to defend itself, as in the present war with China, or to defend others who are oppressed, as in the war with Turkey. Having captured a country, Russia by all means does not eliminate the natives, but on the contrary, tries to make them part of the true Christian culture—as it is doing, for example, in Asia, for which all unbiased people pay it due tribute of respect.

And so if other nations would become more imbued with Christian principles, then wars among them would take place less and less frequently. And for that to take place, it is first necessary for everyone to become imbued with these principles of humility, meekness, long-suffering, and active love for the neighbor. It is necessary to create the Kingdom of Heaven within one's soul, and then it will come externally as well; and there will be peace on earth, good will toward men; and more and more often the angelic singing will overwhelm the rumors of war.

YEAR 1901

18. Reflection on the occasion of the arrival of the New Year (1901) and the new century (20th).

19. A sermon preached on Cheesefare Sunday.

20. A sermon preached on the fourth Sunday of Great Lent.

21. A sermon preached in the week of Antipascha.

22. A sermon on the Sunday of the Blind Man in Wilkes-Barre, Pennsylvania.

23. Suggestion (4th) regarding the opening of a "Repository of Innocent" in the city of Sitka.

24. Suggestion (5th) regarding the establishment of a "Society of Soberness" at parishes and organizing modest entertainment on Sundays.

25. A sermon preached on the 14th week after Pentecost at the consecration of a temple in the village of Vostok in Canada.

26. A sermon preached on the Feast of the Elevation of the Cross at the Sitka cathedral.

27. A sermon in honor of the 60th anniversary of the arrival of the Most Reverend Innocent in Sitka.

28. Suggestion (6th) regarding the establishment of a retirement fund for the overseas clergy.

29. A sermon preached on the Feast of the Nativity of Christ.

REFLECTION[1]

On the occasion of the arrival of the New Year (1901) and the new century (20th); in San Francisco, on January 1, 1901

USUALLY WE MEET the New Year with a certain agitation and emotional excitement. We expect from it something new, and most importantly the fulfillment of our favorite wishes and dreams for happiness. At present, this excitement is further increased by the fact that it is the eve not only of the New Year but also of a new century. Many are expecting it eagerly. Let us recall that already a year ago some were trying to prove that the new century had already arrived, and "broke pens" over it.

Meanwhile, there is quite a bit of vanity in such a passionate anticipation of the New Year and the new century.

Well, today the new century has arrived. And so? Has the day changed on account of it? Have the sky and the earth become different? We ourselves—have the young become old and the old become young? Have we become kinder, smarter, happier? No, and no again! "The thing that has been," says the wise man of the Old Testament, "is that which shall be, and that which is done is that which shall be done" (Eccl. 1:9). Life goes on at an uninterrupted pace, world events change, people are born and fade away, being overcome with the succession of the years.

Our New Year and the new century are, in fact, simple numbers that stand in our minds and memory, and they do not have the

[1] Printed in *Amerikansky Pravoslavny Vestnik*, 1901, #1, pp. 2–4.

influence on life which we sometimes attribute to them. And by all means they certainly do not bring anything new by themselves—if great discoveries, inventions, improvements take place in the coming century, they will not depend on the change of time!

We often attribute to time very much of what does not belong to it in reality. We say, for example, that the years make us old; that time heals our wounds better than anything else, makes us accept our losses, and lessens our sorrow; that time is the touchstone of our love, attachment, friendship; that it disperses darkness and brings light; that it is a great power and a mighty force; that time is money, as they often call it here. Of course, all these expressions must be understood in a figurative sense, for in them, in a poetic manner, qualities are attributed to time that do not belong to it, but rather to various other forces that only act in time.

By itself, time is only a form or an order of the succession of events, the index of change in things. Therefore, by itself it cannot produce something new; and we, reasoning with common sense, cannot demand or expect that from it.

And if this is the case, then does the coming of a new year or a new century have any meaning in our life?

Usually, when an old year ends and a new one begins, we review all the time that has passed and recall what we have done during that time, and make plans for how to act in the future. This kind of "contemplation" and introspection does bring benefit to us, since it forces us to see how far we still are from being a model (ideal) person, and impels us to strive for self-perfection.

Unfortunately, this introspection is not practiced by us often; we are occupied by external life to a greater extent, all of which passes for us in vanity, in cares for the earthly, for pleasure, riches, power, glory. "We strive to live like everybody lives," "as it is customary in the world"—in other words, we give our time to career, business matters, receptions, trips, entertainment, etc.

With a life like that, however, our soul experiences hunger. It is as if an earthly crust forms around it which dulls its receptivity to the spiritual, the lofty, the heavenly. With a life like that, says Fr. John of Kronstadt,[2] "the flesh blooms but the soul withers; the flesh is abundant but the soul is starving; the flesh is dressed up but the soul is ugly; the flesh is fragrant but the soul smells; the flesh is joyful but the soul is in trouble; the flesh is in the light but the soul is in darkness." "For what is a man profited, if he shall gain the whole world, and lose his own soul?" (Matt. 16:26).

But this is not the true life, not the "eternal life, but that which is false and temporal" (from the *kontakion* for the feast of the Beheading of St. John the Baptist). For "the kingdom of God is not meat and drink" (Rom. 14:17); it is *within us* (Luke 17:21). And the more we take care of our soul, the more often we enter the inner self, our "room," the sooner we establish it within ourselves. As a good housewife is considered not the one who spends all her time out of the house, visiting others and occupied with pleasures, but the one who takes care of the household in her own house, does not eat the bread of idleness, and gladly works with her hands, who takes care of her children and her husband (cf. Prov. 31), in the same way, in the arrangement of the inner life, a prudent master is not the one who entertains and is concerned with external, social life, but the one who, being deep amidst his thoughts and feelings, examines them and keeps an eye on them, while being withdrawn from external entertainments.

And that is why the Fathers of the Church persistently command Christians to be sober, attentive to themselves, to their thoughts, words, and deeds. "Every evening," says St. Ephrem the Syrian,[3] "enter your heart, reflect, and ask yourself, 'Have I offended God in any way? Have I spoken an idle word? Have I been negligent? Have I offended my brother? Have I judged someone? When I opened my lips to glorify God, did my soul become dispersed among worldly things? When sensuality awakened in me, did I take pleasure in it? Was I carried away by earthly cares?' If in all of these things you

---

[2] See footnote 9 on page 43.
[3] St. Ephrem the Syrian was a great Syriac Church Father of the 4th century.

suffered failure, try to make up for it; sob, cry, in order not to suffer failure again."

If we, nevertheless, as a result of concerning ourselves with and caring for numerous duties, have forgotten to act according to this saving instruction, then at least now, at the passing of years and centuries, when everywhere records are tallied up, let us review our lives according to our conscience, and fulfill what the holy Church commands us to do daily before going to bed:

1. Give thanks to the Almighty God, since He has granted you to spend the time that has passed alive and in good health through His grace.

2. Have a word with yourself and examine your conscience, going over and reviewing in detail and recalling to mind if you went to see someone, what you did, what you talked about and with whom; and all of your deeds and words and thoughts recall and examine with great care.

3. If you did something good, think that it did not come from you, but from God Himself, Who gives us every blessing; attribute that to Him in your mind and thank Him, and pray that He may strengthen you in that good, and grant and help you do more.

4. If you did something wicked, say that it arose from yourself, from your weakness, or from vile habit and will; and repent and beg the Lover of Mankind that He may grant you forgiveness in that matter, and make a firm promise that you will no longer do those kinds of things.

5. With tears talk to your merciful Creator, that He may grant the upcoming time to be quiet, peaceful, and free from temptation and sin, for the glory of His holy name.

A SERMON[4]

Preached on Cheesefare Sunday of 1901

Today's Sunday, brethren, is called "Forgiveness" or "Forgiving" Sunday. It received this name because there existed a good custom among the Orthodox Christians to ask each other forgiveness for offenses and insults on this day at Vespers. It is done for the reason that during the upcoming fast[5] we approach the mystery of repentance and ask the Lord forgiveness for our sins. But this will be given to us only if we ourselves forgive each other's trespasses: "For if ye forgive men their trespasses, your heavenly Father will also forgive you; but if ye forgive not men their trespasses, neither will your Father forgive your trespasses," as was read in today's Gospel (Matt. 6:14–15).

But they say that it is extremely difficult to forgive offenses, to forget insults. Perhaps it is indeed difficult for our self-loving nature, although it is easier, according to the saying of the holy Fathers, to forgive than to take revenge (St. Tikhon of Zadonsk, *Spiritual Treasure* 11, p. 140; same by St. John Chrysostom).[6] But as you know, everything good in us does not take place easily, but with labor, force,

---

[4] Printed in *Amerikansky Pravoslavny Vestnik*, 1901, #4, pp. 68–70.

[5] Referring to Great Lent, which begins the day after Cheesefare, or Forgiveness, Sunday.

[6] These words in parentheses are in the original text, as edited presumably by St. Alexander Hotovitzky, the editor of the *Russian-American Messenger*. St. Tikhon of Zadonsk was a beloved, well-known bishop in 18th century Russia.

and effort: "The kingdom of heaven is taken by force, and those who exert effort gain it" (Matt. 11:12).

Therefore, let us not be discouraged by the difficulty of this feat, but rather let us look for the means to accomplish it. The Holy Church offers us quite a few means to accomplish this. Among them, let us focus on the one that is the most suitable for the upcoming time of repentance.

"O Lord and King, grant me to see my own transgressions and not to judge my brother."[7] The source of forgiving the sins of our neighbors, and not judging them, is in seeing (having awareness of) our own transgressions. "Picture," says the great pastor, an expert in the workings of the heart, Fr. John of Kronstadt, "picture the multitude of your own sins and vividly imagine how the Master of your life tolerates them in you, while you do not want to forgive your neighbor even a little offense. Sigh, weep over your senselessness, and then the uneasiness within you will vanish like smoke, your thoughts will become clear, your heart will calm down, and by doing this you will become accustomed to kindheartedness as if it were not you who heard reproaches and endured offenses, as if it were some other person or your shadow" (*Lessons for a Pious Life*, p. 149).[8]

He who realizes his sinfulness, who knows through personal experience the weakness of human nature, its inclination towards evil, that kind of person will be quick to forgive his neighbor, to pardon his neighbor's offenses, and will refrain from arrogant condemnation of the sins of others. Let us recall that even the scribes and the Pharisees who brought a woman, who had been caught in adultery, to Christ were forced to leave when their conscience spoke and began to convict them of their own sin (John 8:9).

---

[7] From the prayer of St. Ephrem the Syrian, prayed repeatedly all through Great Lent in the Orthodox Church. The full prayer is: "O Lord and Master of my life, take from me the spirit of sloth, despair, lust for power, and idle talk; and grant me the spirit of chastity, humility, patience and love. O Lord and King, grant me to see my own transgressions and not to judge my brother."

[8] Again, the words in parentheses are in the original.

Unfortunately, brethren, we do not like to look at our transgressions. It seems that it would be most natural and easiest for a man to know himself, his soul, his shortcomings. But this is not the case in reality. We are ready to engage ourselves in any activity—just not in reaching deep within ourselves, not in the examination of our sins. We inspect with curiosity various things, we carefully examine our acquaintances and strangers; but when we happen to find ourselves alone, even for a short time, without anything to occupy us, we feel bored right away and try to engage in entertainment. Do we spend much time, for example, in examining our conscience even before holy confession? A few minutes, and even that once a year. Having glanced quickly at our soul and having smoothed over a few particularly striking features, we immediately cover it with a curtain of neglect until the next year, until the next time for this activity that's atypical and boring for us.

Yet we like to observe the transgressions of others in every way. Not feeling a log in our own eye, we notice the splinter in the neighbor's eye (Matt. 7:3). To engage in idle talk at the expense of the neighbor, to laugh at him, to gossip about him—we often do not even consider this a sin, but as innocent and pleasing time spent. As if we do not have enough of our own sins! As if we are appointed to judge others? "There is one lawgiver"—God (James 4:12). "Who art thou that judgest another man's servant? To his own master he standeth or falleth" (Rom. 14:4). "Prove your own selves, examine your own selves" (2 Cor. 13:5).

The champions of piousness give us a good example in this respect, for they paid attention to themselves in every manner, reflected upon their own sins, and avoided judging others. One pious elder, seeing that his brother sinned, said with a sigh, "I am in trouble, for just like he sinned today, I will tomorrow."[9]

The following is narrated about another ascetic, Abbot Moses. A monk committed a sin, and the brethren, having gathered to discuss

---

[9] This vignette is recorded in the sayings of the Desert Fathers of 4th and 5th century Egypt.

his guilt, sent someone to get Abbot Moses, but the humble elder refused to come to the council. The igumen[10] sent after him again and Moses came, but in what manner he did come? He took a worn out basket and poured sand into it and carried it with him. "What does that mean, Abbot?" the monks asked upon seeing him. "Do you see how many sins are behind me?" answered Moses, pointing at the pouring sand. "I do not see them, and yet I go to make judgment on another man?"[11]

So we, brethren, following the example of the ascetics, upon seeing the sins of others, should reflect on our own sins, see our own transgressions, and not judge our brother. Even if you have something against him, forgive him and do not hold it against him, so that the merciful God may forgive us as well!

---

[10] *Igumen* means the head of a monastery; known in English as "abbot."
[11] This story is also from the Desert Fathers.

A SERMON[12]

*Preached on the fourth Sunday of Great Lent
in San Francisco in Spring, 1901*

Set a watch, O Lord, before my mouth; keep the door
of my lips (Ps. 140:3).

THIS IS HOW the Holy Church prays on our behalf during the
present days of the fast. But we ourselves, brethren, do not realize,
it seems, the necessity to ask the Lord for this. On the contrary, we
desire and seek not a limit for our lips, but complete freedom and
absence of any restraint for our words. Yet, you know, it is said that
our word is as though an imprint of the Heavenly creative word; a
reflection of the image of God is in it. It is the greatest gift of God,
by which God distinguished man and elevated him above the other
creatures.

For what purpose is this gift given to us, other than to develop it
and perfect it? In it is our strength and power; it is the conductor of
our thoughts, feelings, needs, endeavors, and advancements. Knowledge, science, and law live and progress through words.

Is there any sense, then, to limit one's lips and restrain the word
of man? On the contrary, should we not give complete and wide
freedom to it, as to the greatest and most noble gift of God?

But the very merit of this gift itself should already dispose us to
highly appreciate and solemnly protect it—not to corrupt it, and
not to befoul it. And the fact that by his sin the man brought deep

---

[12] Printed in *Amerikansky Pravoslavny Vestnik*, 1901, #6, pp. 108–110.

discord into his nature, and that that distortion became reflected in the gift of the word as well, should dispose us even more to cautious and careful use of the gift of speech. The tongue has quite often come to serve as the weapon of sin, "full of deadly poison" (James 3:8). Lies, flattery, slyness, deceit, curse words, offenses, insults, talk full of temptation and sinful poison have started frequently coming from our lips.

Thus, along with the beneficial influence and the salutary power of the human word, a different, opposite side of it is revealed as well after the fall into sin. With our tongue we started, according to the words of the Apostle James, to "bless God; and therewith to curse men, who are made after the similitude of God. Out of the same mouth proceedeth blessing and cursing. My brethren, these things ought not to be so. Doth a fountain send forth at the same place sweet water and bitter?" (James 3:9–11).

This should not be taking place, especially since the other, opposite action of the word brought great harm and destruction into human life. "Many have fallen by the edge of the sword: but not so many," says the most wise son of Sirach, "as have fallen by the tongue. Well is he that is protected from it, who has not endured its anger; who hath not drawn the yoke thereof, nor hath been bound in its bands. For the yoke thereof is a yoke of iron, and the bands thereof are bands of brass. Its death is an evil death, and hell is better than it" (Sir. 28:18–21).

How could one after that not follow the wise advice of the son of Sirach—"make for your words a balance and a weight, make a door and a bar for your mouth" (Sir. 28:25). And how could one not exclaim with him, "Who shall set a watch before my mouth and a seal of wisdom upon my lips, that I fall not suddenly by them, and that my tongue destroy me not! O Lord, leave me not to their will!" (Sir. 22:27–23:1).

Quite often some say, what bad is in it that we allow ourselves to say an extra word, to joke, to laugh—without evil intent, of course—since we are not saints, not monks, and we live in the world, "and who is he that hath not offended with his tongue?" (Sir. 19:16). And yet the Holy Church prays to the Savior on our behalf—"drive away the spirit of idle talk!"[13] After all, we attribute an important meaning to the human word ourselves, and since this is the case, should one then use words idly, purposelessly? With our loose tongue we bankrupt our soul; we make ourselves careless, frivolous, and unstable. "He," says the most wise Solomon, "who keepeth his mouth, keepeth his life; but he that openeth wide his lips shall have destruction" (Prov. 13:3). "In the multitude of words there lacketh not sin" (Prov. 10:20); "In all labor there is profit: but the talk of the lips tendeth only to penury" (Prov. 14:23, KJV).

We should not fail to take into account the fact that our words do not disappear in the air and vanish without a trace, but they are collected and preserved for the day of the terrible judgment, when we will be held accountable for every idle word; and by our words we will be either acquitted or condemned (cf. Matt. 12:36–37).

Having said this, how can we not be careful with our words? And is it really true that there is nothing insulting for others in our jokes? Do they not contain sometimes the "adder's poison"? (Ps. 140:3, KJV) and "fiery darts" (Eph. 6:16) that strike harder than a whip's blow? (cf. Sir. 28:17). That is indeed why they cause arguments and quarrels between people who are closest to one another, and sometimes a friendship of many years is destroyed because of one word, like the whole building that goes up in flame from one spark. "Who will count," asks St. Gregory the Theologian, "all the insults caused by the tongue? If it wishes it can easily, in one instant, make one house be at enmity with another, one town with another, the people with the ruler, the king with his subjects, like a spark that sets hay on fire."

All of this forces us to turn our attention to our tongue, to think and take measures to restrain it. What measures would these be?

For the purpose of restraining the tongue, the holy champions of piousness sometimes engaged themselves for years in the practice

---

[13] From the Lenten prayer of St. Ephrem the Syrian; see footnote 7 above.

of quietude—silence in which they saw, according to the saying of the venerable John of the Ladder,[14] whom the Church commemorates today, "the preservation within oneself of fire, an imperceptible advance and a secret ascent up the ladder of virtues." In order to make themselves accustomed to the most strict restraint of the tongue, they quite often took exceptional measures. The venerable Agathon,[15] for example, for three years kept a pebble in his mouth for this purpose.

Of course, it is difficult for us to imitate these "heroes of the spirit" in our weakness. Nevertheless, let us at least learn their instructions and advice concerning restraint of one's tongue.

One monk asked an elder, "What should I do? My tongue bothers me; whenever I am with people I cannot restrain it, but I judge and condemn them even in a good undertaking." The elder replied, "This is an infirmity. If you cannot restrain yourself, run to seclusion." And indeed in seclusion there are no reasons for idle talk and a loose tongue. The necessity for seclusion was even recognized by wise men from among the heathen. One of them (Seneca) says that "every time I spend time with people, I return to myself being less humane." And we ourselves quite often have a similar experience after conversations, which are often empty and only disperse our spirit.

The Holy Fathers most often went into seclusion and isolated themselves from company for the time of Great Lent. Nothing, brethren, prevents us from secluding ourselves either, and spending in silence if not the whole fast, at least a few hours every day, devoting them to prayer, pious contemplation, introspection, and examination of one's conscience.

And the fast as well, aside from seclusion, according to St. Gregory the Theologian, helps one to restrict his tongue. It is observed that our talkativeness arises often from gluttony and especially from drinking wine, which loosens our tongue without measure. To the contrary, the fast leads us to restriction of the tongue, and suppression

---

[14] See footnote 8 on page 43.

[15] Abba Agathon was another of the Desert Fathers of Egypt.

of anger, slander, and lies, since it suppresses in us lusts which "set our tongue on fire" (James 3:6).

To succeed in restricting one's tongue, it is also necessary, according to the words of the same St. Gregory, to ask God for help. This feat is hard for a person who is inattentive and inclined to sin. And if David, and the son of Sirach, and the venerable Ephrem the Syrian, and other holy men who were strong in spirit, asked God for help in this matter, then all the more is it necessary for us, the weak ones, to pray: "Set a watch, O Lord, before my mouth, keep the door of my lips" (Ps. 140:3, LXX; Ps. 141:3, KJV).[16]

---

[16] These words are sung often in the some of the Lenten services.

A SERMON[17]

Preached in the week of Anti-Pascha (St. Thomas Sunday) in Galveston, Texas, on April 8, 1901

Grant renewal of the spirit in the hearts, and inner enlightenment, through the faith of those celebrating the holy renewal of Your temple (from the *kontakion* for the Renewal of the Temple, Sept. 13).

AT THE TIME of the renovation of every temple the Church prays to the Lord that He might not only help to accomplish the renovation of the temple through the grace of the Spirit and preserve it unshakable even unto the end of time, but also that He, the Merciful One, might not shun us who are defiled with a multitude of sins, neither break His promise because of our impurity, but overlook our transgressions and grant us the renewal of the spirit in our hearts, and inner enlightenment.

This you should especially pray for, brethren—you, who had a great misfortune befall you last summer.[18] I consider it unnecessary to describe to the eyewitnesses how your city and your temple were destroyed—you still remember it vividly. It is necessary that you have the memory of this terrible event firm and constant within yourselves and understand it in a Christian way—as a visitation of God for the purpose of bringing you to your senses, as the Lord's

---

[17] Printed in *Amerikansky Pravoslavny Vestnik*, 1901, #8, pp. 149–150.

[18] This was the Galveston Flood of 1900, caused by an unusually strong hurricane, in which some 9,000 people lost their lives.

care for you, for He "in every manner seeks to save again and reestablish what was fallen and to correct our lives" (from the *Molieben* for deliverance from floods).[19]

Perhaps someone will say that the disaster that befell your city had a natural cause, having its roots in the strong and continuous wind that drove water into the city from the sea. We do not even think to deny those natural causes, but we consider them secondary. If even in the house of a wise master nothing can take place without his being aware of it or contrary to his intent, then should this not be said even more about Nature, the great house of the Creator of the Universe? Is it not in Him that the cause of everything is? And could it be without His will that the sea breached its boundaries this time, to which He says, "hitherto shalt thou come, but not further" (Job 38:11)?

But for what reason was it allowed by the Lord for this terrible event to occur? Was it, perhaps, due to the sins of this town's inhabitants? Let us not, however, rush with our judgments, especially since the ways of the Lord are often unknown to us. So let us better draw a lesson for ourselves from the calamity that has occurred.

Once the Lord Jesus Christ said, "Or those eighteen, upon whom the tower in Siloam fell, and slew them, think ye that they were sinners above all men that dwelt in Jerusalem? I tell you, Nay: but, except ye repent, ye shall all likewise perish" (Luke 13:4–5). It seems that your devastated city and those who perished in it were not greater sinners than those who remained alive. The first and the latter sinned, but the judgment of the Lord has already fallen on some, while the others the Lord suffers, waiting if they might come to repentance (cf. 1 Peter 3:20).

The merciful Lord unceasingly and in various ways calls us sinners to repentance. The calling voice of God is heard in our conscience as well, and in the Word of God, and in natural phenomena, and in the circumstances of our life. But often we reach such a state

---

[19] These words in parentheses are in the original. A *molieben* is a prayer service for a specific purpose.

of senselessness that we do not pay attention to any of that, since we have that in front of our eyes at all times. Then the Lord, in order to awaken us from the sinful dream, and make us sober, and bring us back to our senses, uses extraordinary actions, even such as the kind of misfortune that befell your city last year.

Let us come to our senses in the light of the past visitation of God and rise from a sinful dream! While celebrating the restoration of this temple after its destruction, let us renew our hearts and our lives.

Now is the time favorable: "For lo the winter is past, the rain is over and gone; the flowers appear on the earth; the fig tree putteth forth her green figs, and the vines give a good smell" (Song 2:11–13). "Today is the springtime of souls, for Christ on the third day, shining from the tomb like the sun, has dispelled the dark storm of our sin" (Canon of Anti-Pascha 1:2, 3);[20] "You have made us new instead of old, to live worthily in the renewed life You commanded us" (3:1).

Just as the earth in the spring is washed by the rain, warmed by the sun, and becomes covered with greenery and flowers, so you, beloved, wash your soul with tears of repentance, and warm it with the rays of God's grace and feelings and intentions, which will indeed bring forth in you the fruit of the Spirit—love, joy, peace, long-suffering, meekness, and faith (Gal. 5:22–23).

---

[20] The words in parentheses are in the original. The words in quotation marks, and in the next quotation, are sung at Matins on Thomas Sunday.

A SERMON[21]

On the Sunday of the Blind Man in Wilkes-Barre, Pennsylvania, in May, 1901

WHEN A YEAR AGO the question arose concerning to whom to dedicate this temple, I offered to erect it in honor of the Resurrection of Christ. And these are the thoughts that led me to that. Last year during the days of Holy Pascha you were forced to part with your old temple; during the very same days the decision was made among you to erect for yourselves a new temple.

But aside from this external coincidence of events, there were also other, much deeper considerations for dedicating your temple to the Resurrection of Christ. Your adversaries not only had the desire to close the former disputed temple. They also thought that with the seizure of the church property from you, the local Orthodox parish would die, and the whole cause of Orthodoxy here, and in the surrounding area, would be buried. "Their hope is lost, they are cut off" (cf. Ezek. 37:11)—that was what they thought.

In the same manner, the enemies of Christ at one time desired not only His death, but they also thought that with it the entire cause of Christ would cease to exist. Nevertheless, vain and misleading were the hopes of the enemies of Christ, for His death was followed by His glorious resurrection that gave birth to His cause. Vain and misleading were the hopes of your adversaries—for the loss of the church property was followed by the acquisition of the new

---

[21] Printed in *Amerikansky Pravoslavny Vestnik*, 1901, #10, pp. 192–193.

one, and by the replacement of the temple through the building of a new one, more spacious and more splendid; and, which is perhaps far more important, [it was followed] by the uplifting and strengthening in you of the spirit of devotion to the Orthodox Church. This is how the words of Christ come true: "Verily, verily I say unto you, Except a corn of wheat fall into the ground and die, it abideth alone; but if it die, it bringeth forth much fruit" (John 12:24).

Where do the causes of animosity and anger of your enemies toward you lie? The source is rooted in the spiritual blindness which was read about in today's Gospel.[22] Christ healed a man blind from birth. "Since the world began was it not heard that any man opened the eyes of one that was born blind" (John 9:32). It is clear that the person who did this miracle was sent from God (cf. John 9:33); and the disciples of Moses, the spiritual leaders of the people, the Jewish scribes and Pharisees, should have recognized this sooner than others. In the depth of their souls they probably did realize this, but since Christ was their adversary, whom they had already decided to kill, they did not want to acknowledge an obvious miracle done by Him.

They started to interrogate those who were present at the healing of the man born blind, and the parents of the man, and the man himself, as many as three times. They asked questions with the cunning intent to distort the testimony. They asked themselves in advance, suggesting the answers that would be desirable for them. And when the healed man baldly told the truth and exposed the Pharisees, they drove him away and started looking for Christ even more in order to kill Him. Thus a blind man became able to see, and those able to see became spiritually blind.

And is it necessary to say to you that even now, in places in which we live, one comes across this kind of spiritually blind men, blind leaders of the blind? Often realizing where the truth is, they

---

[22] The Gospel reading in the Orthodox Church for Blind Man Sunday, the last Sunday in the Paschal season, is John 9:1–38, which describes Jesus' healing of the man born blind.

nevertheless do not follow it for external reasons, neither do they let those who desire it come to it (cf. Matt. 23:13). If they had not been aware of the truth, they would not have sinned; but today the sin remains on them (cf. John 9:41). Their spiritual blindness, often deliberate and intended, depends not so much on their ignorance of the truth, but rather on their unwillingness to acknowledge it and bow to it. The same thing happens to them as to a man who, unwilling to see the light, purposely covers his eyes.

And this spiritual blindness is more onerous and harmful than bodily blindness—for there one member of the body dies, but here the whole soul dies. There a blind person, being pure in heart, can see God, but a spiritually blind man is deprived of this joy for eternity.

Let us give praise to the Lord God, brethren, that He gave us light and wisdom to know the truth. And, while abiding in it, let us pray to Christ the Giver of Light that He might enlighten the eyes of our brethren—so that they might not fall asleep in eternal death.

SUGGESTION 4

Regarding the opening of a "Repository of Innocent"
in the city of Sitka; on June 20, 1901 [23]

IN SEPTEMBER of 1901 in Sitka, the 60th anniversary of the Most Reverend Innocent's arrival there in the rank of a bishop will be commemorated.

I find it timely, in memory of that event:

- to open in Sitka a "Repository of Innocent" (a museum), which should include everything that reminds us of the Most Reverend Innocent, and what is left from him and his time, such as church items that are no longer in use, books, manuscripts, letters, household items, and so on. Later on, the museum may be expanded, to include items that are generally of significance in some respect for Alaska.

- to appropriate for the museum a room in the archpastoral house which was erected during the time of the Most Reverend Innocent.

- for the Spiritual Board to offer Fr. Dean of the Sitka cathedral to make arrangements to open the "Repository of Innocent," and that he put it in print in the *Vestnik* for the Aleutian clergy to be aware of it.

---

[23] Printed in *Amerikansky Pravoslavny Vestnik*, 1901, #21, pp. 442–444.

SUGGESTION 5

*Regarding the establishment of a "Society of
Soberness" at parishes, and organizing modest
entertainment on Sundays; on June 29, 1901*[24]

F AIR COMPLAINTS are often heard that "our Rusyns[25] fill themselves with whiskey or beer," as a result of which conflicts and
fights break out among them at times.

In order to avoid these unwelcome circumstances, I would like to
recommend to our clergy:

To organize a "Society of Soberness" in the parishes (initially, perhaps, not even strict):

To serve, aside from the morning service, vespers with the reading of Akathists on Sundays, when the parishioners are free from
work, and afterwards to hold meetings at the school quarters or
the brotherhood hall. The priest or the reader may do readings of
moral-religious, historical, or common topics at these meetings;
movies might be shown with the magic lamp; and church and lay
songs of decent content may be sung. The schoolchildren may read
poems, fables. The local brotherhoods and the "Mutual Aid Societies" must provide material assistance in organizing these kinds of
meetings which pursue educational goals. They will spend less on

---

[24] Printed in *Amerikansky Pravoslavny Vestnik*, 1901, #21, pp. 442–444.

[25] "Rusyns" designates various Slavic peoples of the western borderlands of Russia—Galitsia (Galicia), Bukovina, Volhynia, and western Ukraine. They are also
sometimes known as Carpatho-Russians. The general term used by the Latin (Roman Catholic) Church for these peoples is Ruthenians.

organizing this innocent "entertainment" than on giving "help to infirm members" who are not always innocent in the cause of their illness.

Inform the clergy of this matter through the Spiritual Board by way of publishing this in the *Vestnik*.

A SERMON[26]

*Preached on the 14th week after Pentecost at the consecration of a
temple in the village of Vostok in Canada, on August 26, 1901*

BY THE GRACE of the Holy Spirit this temple has been consecrated with the name of The Holy Life-Giving Trinity. Today
Divine "Wisdom has built her house; she has set up her seven col-
umns; she has dressed her meat, mixed her wine, and spread her
table"—the Holy Eucharist. "She has sent out her servants to proclaim from the highest part of the city: 'Let whoever is foolish turn
aside to me'; and to those who lack understanding she says, 'Come,
eat my bread, and drink the wine already mixed for you; cease being
foolish and you will live; lay hold of reason, so that you will live and
advance in the way of reason and understanding'" (Prov. 9:1–6).

This summoning voice is also heard in the Holy Gospel that has
just been read. For today Christ's parable was read about a king who
gave a wedding banquet for his son and dispatched his servants to
summon people to this feast. But those who had been called did
not want to come, being occupied with their own affairs; and some
insulted and even killed these servants. Then the king became furious,
and sent his troops and destroyed the murderers; and to the servants
he said, "Those who were called were not worthy. Go to the crossroads and call all those you come upon." The servants did exactly that,
and the wedding feast was filled with banqueters (Matt. 22:1–10).

---

[26] Printed in *Amerikansky Pravoslavny Vestnik*, 1901, #19.

What does this parable mean? The king who gave the feast represents the Heavenly King, God the Father Himself. The king's son stands for the Son of God, Christ the Savior, Who enters into a nuptial union with the Holy Church. Through this union, the Kingdom of God, the highest blessedness, the spiritual wedding feast, is opened for the people.

The servants represent those who are sent by God—Prophets and Apostles—announcing to the people the coming of the Kingdom of God. Those who were called but did not want to come to the wedding celebration stand for the ungrateful and disobedient and constantly stubborn Jews. They were so mired in their devotion to what was earthly and sensual that not only did they not heed the saving voice, summoning them to the heavenly kingdom—to the Church of Christ—but they harassed even those who were calling them to it, and insulted them, beat them, threw them into prison, and sometimes even killed them.

Then the Righteous Lord punished the ungrateful people: He brought foreign troops to Judea, who devastated her; and He scattered the Hebrews through all the Earth. And in their place, into the Church of Christ, He called people from the crossroads—that is, the heathen—who came to believe in Christ, and who entered into His Church for the wedding feast.

This, brethren, is the historical meaning of Christ's parable about those who were called to the feast. But this parable also has meaning for us and for our time: the wedding feast continues to this day, since the Church of Christ will exist until the end of time. "Come to the feast!" (Matt. 22:4)—the voice of those calling is still heard today. The ones calling are those succeeding the Apostles and continuing their mission—the archpastors and pastors sent by them.

Their voice in recent years has illuminated your country, and some of those who live here have responded to the saving call. But some ignored the invitation and went their own way, one to his farm, another to his merchandise (Matt. 22:5), and some even treated spitefully those who were calling them. And indeed, how many insults, lies, and slanders the followers of the Wisdom of God have to hear sometimes here.

The followers of the Latin faith call us schismatics ("dissenters")—yet some of them themselves some three hundred years ago broke away from the Faith of their forefathers—from our common mother, the [Orthodox] Church.[27] They accuse us of sowing discord with our preaching, bringing animosity and division in the midst of those who were formerly united in faith and nationality.

But this division is not our fault; rather, it is the fault of those who for various motives do not listen to our voice, and who do not want to follow the truth. Indeed, even Christ the Savior Himself bears witness, that with His preaching He does not bring peace to the world but a sword, since He separated a son from his father and a daughter from her mother (cf. Matt. 10:34–35).

But is there not someone else, besides the people themselves, who is responsible for this?

They slander us by saying that we bring people into Orthodoxy through offering them money, buying followers for ourselves. We dare say that if this were true, we would have many more followers than we have now, since for many here the "golden calf" is an idol. All our "trade" consists of instances when we provide the poorest churches with the most needed items; and we also give a stipend to the clergy, which in many places is less than what the "reverend fathers" receive from their spiritual sheep.

They call our Church "tsar-glorifying." They say that whoever is made a member of it thereby becomes a Russian subject. They also make it up that we force people to swear allegiance to the tsar of Russia, etc.—all mindless words. And the reason behind all of this is that during the divine services, along with the local governmental authorities, we mention the name of the Russian Tsar, as the most devout Sovereign, a patron and defender of the Orthodox Church.

---

[27] St. Tikhon is referring to the Uniates in western Ukraine, who left the Orthodox Faith to come under the authority of the Papacy some 300 years earlier, through the Union of Brest-Litovsk in 1596.

In their blind malice, our adversaries do not limit their harassment to just words. There have been instances when they were ready to insult through actions the servants of Divine Wisdom who were calling them to the spiritual supper.[28]

But let us leave those who have insulted us to the judgment of God (Ps. 42:1, LXX), and turn our attention to those who have obeyed the sensible voice calling them to the bridal feast in the Church of Christ.

Among those who came to the wedding feast, it is said in the parable, there happened to be a man wearing clothes that were not festive, not appropriate for the celebration. The king ordered that he be bound, and taken from the feast to prison. Hence, those entering into the Church of Christ must wear bright, festive garments. In saying this, we of course are not referring to the clothes of the body, but rather that the soul must be clean, bright, unstained by sins. And everyone who enters into the Church receives this bright clothing, since the soul is cleansed of sins in the waters of Baptism.

But is this purity of soul—this brightness, this absence of the stain of sin—preserved forever after Baptism? Unfortunately, it is not! Christians sin too—as it is said of us all, we often sin (James 3:2); "and if we say that we have no sin, we deceive ourselves" (1 John 1:8). And yet, with our sins defiling our soul, staining our spiritual clothes, we cannot remain at the wedding feast in the Church of Christ.

What, then, is to be done? What should we do? Well, what do we do when our clothes become dirty? We wash them clean with water. So it is with our soul darkened with sins—we must wash it with tears of repentance. For this very purpose the holy mystery [i.e., sacrament] of Confession is established in the Church, in which a

---

[28] In Wilkes-Barre, in 1892, while the Right Reverend Bishop Nikolai was serving there, rocks were thrown through the windows of the church. In Old Forge [Pennsylvania], before the priest Grushko joined us, a rock was thrown through the window of the room where he was working. In the same Old Forge in 1897, the Uniates were ready to make an attack on the Right Reverend Nikolai himself as he was walking into the church [this footnote is in the original].

Christian offers to God through a priest a most sincere agonizing over his sins, receiving forgiveness of them; and his spiritual clothes once again become "white as snow" (Is. 1:18).

Therefore, brethren, in order not to be expelled from the wedding supper, it is right to wash the clothing of your soul with tears of repentance as often as possible, and come to Holy Confession for that purpose more often. "Wash yourselves and you will be clean" (Is. 1:16); and then you will be counted worthy to partake, in the spiritual supper in the Kingdom of God, of those unspeakable blessings "which the Lord has prepared for those who love Him" (cf. 1 Cor. 2:9).

And to those who are present here who as yet have not joined the Orthodox Church, who have not entered the wedding feast, the Wisdom of God calls to you through us, her humble servants: "Come, eat my bread, and drink the wine already mixed for you; cease being foolish and you will live; lay hold of reason, so that you will live and advance in the way of reason and understanding" (Prov. 9:5–6). Amen.

SERMON[29]

*Preached on the Feast of the Elevation of the Cross
at the Sitka Cathedral, on September 14, 1901*

I COME TO YOU, brethren, with this holy cross, which at one time was the property of the Sitka Cathedral and which today is returned to you. I come to you with this cross during the days when the Holy Church brings the Holy Cross out to the faithful for veneration in celebrating the Elevation of the Cross of the Lord. Therefore, my present word addressed to you will be the *word of the Cross* as well—the word about the Cross: "for I determined not to know anything among you, except Jesus Christ, and Him crucified" (1 Cor 2:2).

What does the Cross of the Lord speak of, and what does it teach us about?

Above all, it tells us that our Lord Jesus Christ, Who was crucified on the cross, accomplished the salvation of mankind. By His suffering on the cross, Christ made sacrifice to satisfy the truth of God for human sins, and reconciled humankind with God. At the same time, in the suffering on the Cross He renewed the essence of man and gave rebirth to our fallen nature, similar to a woman who in pain gives birth to her child.

Furthermore, the Cross of Christ reminds us of our cross—of the fact that according to the word of Christ we must take up a cross, since only by way of the Cross can we enter the Kingdom of Heaven.

---

[29] Printed in *Amerikansky Pravoslavny Vestnik,* 1901, #21, pp. 442–443.

Often those who preach next to us say that it is enough for a person to only come to believe in Christ for salvation. But they are under delusion, not understanding the Scripture—although they boast of its knowledge.[30]

"And they that are Christ's," says Apostle Paul, "have crucified the flesh with its affections and lusts" (Gal. 5:24). If the salvation of the *entire* human race was accomplished by the Cross of Christ, then it is necessary for *everyone*, for his salvation, to *crucify himself in a way similar to Christ*—to erect a cross in one's soul, on which to crucify his old, sinful man with his passions and lusts.

Through this, the saving power of the Cross of Christ is absorbed by a Christian, and within his soul *Christ is formed* (cf. Gal. 4:19). This kind of man can say along with the Apostle Paul about himself: "I live, yet not I, but Christ liveth in me" (Gal. 2:20); and this kind of man indeed inherits eternal life and salvation.

But aside from this "inner" cross, a Christian also has external crosses, which are sent by Christ for each one of us. These are sorrows, troubles, misfortunes, sickness, loss of those who are close to us, failures, offenses, etc. Who does not have them? Neither wealth nor nobility save anyone from them.

Why does the Lord give these crosses? Some of you know how grain is extracted from the harvested ear—it is knocked out with chains, threshed out. You have also heard that gold is purified from foreign impurities with fire. So our soul is purified through sorrows and becomes enlightened, elevated, and produces from within itself a pure grain of goodness.

A Christian also knows that here he is only a wanderer and stranger, that his motherland is in heaven (cf. Phil. 3:20). And a wanderer, as long as he remains out of his house, endures various deprivations and discomforts on his way.

We must endure them also, brethren. We must carry the cross sent from God without complaining, since only in this way will it indeed

---

[30] St. Tikhon is referring here to typical Evangelical Protestant preaching.

be for our salvation. Do not complain in the midst of misfortune, do not envy others, and do not let despair overtake you; but rather be humble, repent of your sins, and change your life for the better.

If you do not have enough strength for carrying your cross without complaining, then turn to the One Who was crucified on the Cross with a supplication for help: "the Lord hear thee in the day of trouble, and send thee help from the sanctuary" (Ps. 19:2–3, LXX; Ps. 20:1–2, KJV). "For in that He Himself hath suffered being tempted, He is able to succor those who are tempted" (Heb. 2:18).

Not only did He give us a model, an example, of how to endure afflictions without complaining. He also granted us strength for this, leaving His Cross for us, which the Holy Church glorifies as might, strength, power, firmament, a shield, and an invincible weapon.

"O thrice blessed wood on which Christ, the King and the Lord, was crucified! O most honorable and life-giving Cross of the Lord! Help us, together with the Holy Theotokos and all the saints, unto the ages of ages."[31] Amen.

---

[31] This is a hymn from Matins for the Feast of the Elevation of the Life-Giving Cross of the Lord.

SERMON[32]

*In honor of the 60th anniversary of the arrival of the
Most Reverend Innocent in Sitka, at St. Michael's
Cathedral in Sitka, Alaska; on September 27, 1901*

ONCE THE LEADER of the Jewish people, the prophet of God St.
Moses, spoke to the Jews in this way:

> If you continue to heed the voice of the Lord, your
> God, and are careful to observe all His commandments,
> the Lord, your God, will raise you high above all the
> nations of the earth. All these blessings will come to
> you in abundance: your children will be blessed, as well
> as the produce of your soil, the offspring of your live-
> stock, the calves of your herds, and the lambs of your
> flocks. Blessed will be your grain bin and your kneading
> bowl. The Lord will affirm His blessings upon you, on
> your barns, and on all your undertakings.
>
> But if you do not hearken to the voice of the Lord,
> your God, all these curses will come upon you: your
> basket and your mixing bowl will be cursed, and you
> will have defeat and frustration in every enterprise you
> undertake until you are speedily destroyed for the evil
> you have done in forsaking Me. You will be oppressed
> and robbed continually, with no one to come to your aid.
> Though you betroth a wife, another man will have her.

---

[32] Printed in *Amerikansky Pravoslavny Vestnik,* 1901, #21, pp. 443–444.

Though you build a house, you will not live in it. Your sons and daughters will be given to a foreign nation. People whom you do not know will consume the fruit of your soil and of all your labor. The foreigner residing among you will rise higher and higher above you, while you sink lower and lower. He will lend to you, not you to him: he will become the head, you the tail. The Lord will strike you with plagues and boils.

All of this will come upon you and overtake you; you shall be left small in number, whereas you were as numerous as the stars in the sky. Only a few of you will be left, because you would not hearken to the voice of the Lord, your God (Deut. 28:1–62, condensed).

This, brethren, is how Moses warned the Jews, and his words came true for them with astonishing accuracy. But do his warnings concern only the Jewish people? Do they not also concern the Christian people, and could they not come true for them as well?

Perhaps some of Moses' prophecies are being fulfilled for the local inhabitants here as well? At least, a thought of this kind involuntarily arises when one recalls the historic circumstances of this land.

Today with prayer we recall how 60 years ago on this day the ever memorable Hierarch Innocent entered this city for the first time as Bishop of the Aleutians. No more than five people are left here of those who witnessed his memorable arrival. As the years go by, the bright personality of the enlightener of this land recedes further and further from us. Fewer and fewer people are left here who heard his words and saw his deeds!

Therefore, I have determined that it is timely to establish here a repository named after Innocent, where memorable items of his time, the fruits of his hands, will be collected. In this way, these things will be preserved from the destructive action of time, and will proclaim his glorious and dear name to the future generations who do not know Innocent "from kin to kin."[33]

But, my brethren, while taking care to preserve the material artifacts relating to Innocent, we should take care to preserve his spiritual inheritance even more. You, of course, have heard how in order to spread and establish the Orthodox Faith here, the ever-memorable Innocent voluntarily left his dear homeland, a parish that provided well for him and the parishioners who loved him, and with joy departed with his family to far and little known lands on a hard and dangerous journey.

Having arrived in America, he labored here for thirty years, first as a priest, then a bishop—fulfilling his priestly duties, proclaiming the good news, translating the holy books into the local tongues, teaching by word and in writing and by the deeds of his own life, going to different islands, establishing churches, chapels, missions, and schools. We know his deeds—and his "love and service and faith and patience" (Rev. 2:19)—and that he endured much hardship in laboring for the name of God, and did not become discouraged (cf. Rev. 2:3). And the memory of the righteous one lives with praise up to this day.

The hearts of all of us are filled with love, gratitude, and reverence for this amazing hierarch. But most of all, we will prove all our kind feelings for him if we observe the heritage that he spread and left here for us—if we believe and live as he taught us: "If you love me, obey my commandments" (John 14:15). For after Christ, he could tell us this himself.

Is it necessary to remind you of this? Is it necessary to persuade you to keep Innocent's commandments? It seems so. History has preserved for us a witness of how the Most Reverend Innocent sometimes used to say to his contemporaries in Sitka a "tough word"; they must have needed such reproof to be brought to their senses. And their descendants needed it even more.

---

[33] That is, with even his own kinfolk not remembering him.

While living in Moscow, Innocent learned how, with the transfer of Alaska to the Americans, and with the lack of authority and the disorder that came with that, the lowliest of passions—which before had been held back by the strictness of the Russian authorities—burst out in Sitka. Later, in different places in Alaska, his spiritual flock began to be plundered by missionaries of different faiths. And amidst the Orthodox themselves, one could notice a cooling in many of them towards the Faith and the Church, a betrayal of the paternal traditions, and an acceptance of alien ideas and customs.

Therefore, to the former flock of Innocent one can say the same thing that God told the angel of the Ephesian Church: "I have somewhat against thee, because thou hast left thy first love. Remember therefore from whence thou art fallen, and repent and do the first works; or else I will come unto thee quickly, and will remove thy candlestick out of its place, except thou repent" (Rev. 2:1, 4–5).

And is this candlestick being removed from your land? Has something from the above-mentioned prophecies been happening to us for our sins and apostasies? Have the scarcity, and hunger, and destruction, and sickness, and boils, and plunder, and offenses from strangers prevailed over us due to our evil undertakings?

Let us fear, brethren, the righteous wrath of God directed at us. And while remembering today the ever-memorable Innocent in prayer, let us remain true to his legacy. Let us preserve the Orthodox Faith, in faithfulness and obedience to our Holy Church, that "we may lead an undisturbed and peaceable life in all godliness and honesty" (1 Tim. 2:2).

And you, Hierarch Innocent, even after departing from us, strive for us in front of the Throne of God, that we always keep this in mind (cf. 2 Pet. 1:15).

SUGGESTION 6[34]

To the clergy of the Aleutian Diocese

IN THE MONTH of April of 1899, at the meeting in Vienna of the ordained and non-ordained Church personnel serving abroad, a question was raised regarding the establishment of a retirement fund for the overseas clergy. At the same meeting, a draft of the Charter of the retirement fund was reviewed. Furthermore, the idea itself to establish the retirement fund, as well as the draft, were met with everyone's support. At the same meeting, the Board was elected as well (for the first 5 years) for the future fund.

At the end of 1899, the draft of the Charter was sent to St. Petersburg to the authorities; and, according to the information available, approval of the Charter will follow shortly. In light of this, dues and donations have already started to come to the fund—which, as of the month of July, amounted to four hundred and fifty dollars.

In the past few days the treasurer of the Retirement Fund, Fr. Deacon of the Berlin Church, N. N. Sakharov, has requested me to ask the North American clergy if they would want to take part in the retirement fund. Gladly carrying out this request, I suggest to the Aleutian Diocese to express, upon reading the draft of the Charter, their opinion on the matter in a letter addressed to the Spiritual Board.

---

[34] Printed in *Amerikansky Pravoslavny Vestnik*, 1901, #17, p. 361.

I direct that this present suggestion of mine, together with the draft of the Charter, be published in the upcoming issues of our *Vestnik*.[35]

---

[35] The Draft of the Charter of the Retirement Fund for the Orthodox Clergy of the Aleutian Diocese is presented in the *Amerikansky Pravoslavny Vestnik*, 1901, #20, pp. 429–431.

A SERMON[36]

*Preached on the Feast of the Nativity
of Christ on December 25, 1901*

O N THIS JOYOUS DAY, when the Holy Church solemnly remembers the Nativity of Christ, many of us, brethren, without a
doubt, would wish not only in thought and in heart, but with our
mortal body itself, to be transported to Bethlehem. One would wish
to fly there to the cave where Christ was born, to the manger where
He lay. One would wish to bow to Him together with the shepherds,
to bring gifts to Him together with the Magi. And some perhaps
are even ready to die by His feet, to die for Him together with the
infants who were ordered to be killed by the cruel Herod.

However, brethren, this is not achievable—we are not contemporaries of the newly-born Christ. Instead, let us be comforted by the
fact that "the Lord is at hand" (Phil. 4:5), "not far from every one of
us" (Acts 17:27). And we only need ourselves to seek Him and "draw
nigh to Him, and then He will draw closer to us" (James 4:8).

What can bring us closer to Christ? What should we do to
accomplish this? Let us look at the ones who, and for what reasons,
were brought close to Christ at the time of His birth.

His Most pure Mother, the Most Holy Virgin Mary, is the closest
to the newly-born Christ. She earned her closeness to the Lord, the
high honor of being the mother of Christ, the honor that made her
"more honorable than the Cherubim and truly more glorious than

---

[36] Printed in *Amerikansky Pravoslavny Vestnik*, 1902, #1, pp. 2–5.

the Seraphim,"[37] through her utmost purity and chastity of body and soul, deep humility, and reverential obedience and devotion to the will of God.

Further on, at the birth of Christ, the person who is close to Him is His foster-father, Joseph. The holy evangelist calls Joseph "a just man" (Matt. 1:19). And without a doubt, it is due to his righteousness, his following the Law, his fairness and honesty, coupled with his generosity (towards the Mother of God—Matt. 1:19)[38] that Joseph became worthy of the honor of being close to Christ.

After the Mother of God and Joseph the Betrothed, the Bethlehem shepherds approached the newly-born Christ before other people did. Why did the angels address them with the good news about the birth of Christ before other people? The shepherds of Bethlehem were people simple in stature (herdsmen). But, of course, it is not for that reason that they were honored with the joy of being able to approach the Lord, but for the reason that these simple folk were simple in their hearts as well as in their souls; and the Lord Himself, according to the folk saying, dwells in simple hearts.

The mysteries of the Kingdom of God, according to the words of Christ Himself, are revealed to babes (Matt. 11:25)—babes not according to years and age, but according to the state of their souls—those people whose hearts are childlike—gentle, meek, trusting, pure, and innocent. A heart like that readily and joyfully receives the words of God, and without further ado believes them, like the shepherds of Bethlehem did, who, as soon as they heard the angels' good news, immediately hastened to go to bow down to Christ.

At last, the Magi—wise men of the East and people of stature, who brought gifts to Him—approach the newly-born Christ to pay their respect. Therefore, learnedness and wealth, as well as high status in themselves not only do not distance people from Christ, but might yet bring them closer to Him—if only, as with the wise men,

---

[37] These words are from a very commonly sung hymn dedicated to Mary the Theotokos.

[38] These words in parentheses are in the original.

these things are coupled with the search for the higher wisdom of God, the acknowledgment of the vanity of earthly glory and wealth, reverence for the King of Heaven, and service to Him with one's might, talents, and wealth.

Thus, brethren, we see that the newly born Christ is surrounded by the virgin purity and chastity of His Mother, the righteousness of Joseph, the trusting simplicity of the shepherds, and the enlightened wisdom and grandeur of the Magi.

If someone has these holy virtues and noble qualities even now, let him with boldness approach the newly-born Christ. The Lord is near him (cf. Acts 17:27).

And what about us, sinners, who do not possess these virtues? No one bound by worldly desires and pleasures is worthy to approach, to draw near, or to minister to the King of Glory. To serve Him is great and awesome even for the heavenly powers. But because of "the ineffable and immeasurable love of Christ,"[39] Who clothed Himself in flesh, "Who did not send away the harlot who had come to Him in tears, neither did He reject the tax collector who had repented, nor did He refuse the brigand, nor did He abandon the penitent perse-cutor, but numbered among His friends all those who came to Him in penitence"[40]—because of this, let us not become discouraged in the matter of our salvation. While placing our hope in the unending goodness of Christ, let us approach Him—if not with the virtues, which we do not possess, then with a contrite soul and repentant prayer that He might accept us as well, in the same way He accepted the harlot, the brigand, and the tax collector.

"O Lord, the lover of mankind! You know our many errors, You know our sores and You behold our wounds. But You also know our faith, You behold my will, and You hear my sighs. Nothing is hidden from You, not a teardrop nor even part of a drop."[41] "Let our faith

---

[39] Said by the priest during the singing of the Cherubic Hymn at the Divine Liturgy.

[40] From the 9th prayer of preparation before Holy Communion.

[41] From the 7th prayer of preparation before Holy Communion.

be reckoned in place of works, for Thou wilt find no works which could justify us. But may our faith suffice instead of any deeds, may it answer for us, may it justify us, may it make us partakers of Thine eternal glory."[42] And may we also be worthy, together with the shepherds and the Magi, to bow in the cave to the newly-born Christ, the Giver of Life, without condemnation.

---

[42] From the 8th morning prayer.

YEAR 1902

30. A sermon preached at the blessing of newlyweds.

31. A sermon preached at the consecration of the chapel on the newly built battleship "Retvizan."

32. Homily addressed to the newly ordained priest, the editor of *Svet,* Fr. Benedict Turkevich.

33. A homily preached at the ordination of the teacher Michael Skibinsky, a Canadian missionary, into the priesthood.

34. Open letter to the editor of the newspaper *Svet* regarding the strike in the coal mines.

35. Suggestion (7th) regarding the distribution of icons from Athos among the Orthodox temples in America.

36. A sermon preached at the consecration of the New York church.

37. A sermon preached at the consecration of the Syro-Arabian temple in Brooklyn.

38. From the report to the Council of the All Russia Missionary Society in Moscow for 1902 on the Orthodox mission in Alaska.

39. A sermon reached on the 26th of September at the missionary school in Minneapolis.

A SERMON[1]

*Preached at the blessing of newlyweds in San
Francisco, on January 18/31, 1902*

ICONGRATULATE YOU, beloved in Christ, with a lawful marriage,
and I want at the same time to give you a few words for your
edification. With the sacrament of matrimony the Holy Church
commands that *an edifying word* be offered to the newlyweds, telling
them what is the mystery of matrimony, and how to live honestly
and in a God-pleasing way in marriage.

Quite a bit has been said about marriage and family life, especially in the past few years, but it is not always that one hears *sensible
words* about it. Therefore, it is necessary to firmly know and remember—and for you, beloved groom, as a servant of the Orthodox
Church, to teach others as well—what is the mystery of matrimony,
and how to live honestly and in a God-pleasing way in marriage.

"It is not good that the man should be alone; I will make a help-
meet for him" (Gen. 2:18), said God Himself, when our forefather
Adam was still in Paradise. Without a helpmate the very bliss of
Paradise was not complete for Adam. Endowed with the ability
to think, speak, and love, the first man in his thoughts is seeking
another being who is able to think; his speech sounds sorrowfully in
the air, and only a lifeless echo serves as an answer to him; his heart,
full of love, is looking for another heart that is close and equal to his.
His entire being desires another being similar to him, but there is no

---

[1] Printed in *Amerikansky Pravoslavny Vestnik*, 1902, #3, pp. 61–62.

such being. The creatures of the visible world around him are lower than he is and cannot be helpmates appropriate for him; and the beings of the invisible, spiritual world are higher than he is. Then the All-Merciful God, who cares about the bliss of man, fulfills his need and creates for him a helpmate appropriate for him—a wife.

But if there was a need for a man to have a helpmate in Paradise, the land of bliss, then after the Fall, in the land of tears and sorrow, such a need has become much greater. A wise man of the Old Testament rightfully said, "Two are better than one, for if they fall, the one will lift up his fellow. But woe to him that is alone when he falleth; for he hath not another to help him up" (Eccl. 4:9–10). Only a few are able to endure the burden of spiritual solitude; this is achieved through not a small labor, and "all men cannot receive this saying, except they to whom this teaching is given" (Matt. 19:11). As far as the others are concerned, "it is not good for a man to be alone," without a helpmate.

A wife is this kind of a helpmate for a man. Living primarily from the heart, a woman, with her heart's typical qualities—tender love, submissive devotedness, meekness, long-suffering, and compassion—is the best partner, friend, comforter, and helpmate for a man. In the gifts of female nature, a husband finds replenishment of the strength of his intellect, resolve, and character. And he receives support and encouragement from an affectionate wife.

There is no such hard labor, there is no such bitter lot, to which a loving wife is not able to have her husband be reconciled. Therefore, a wise man of the Old Testament says that "he who acquires a wife, acquires a helper and a pillar of rest" (Sirach 36:24); "charm upon charm is a modest wife, and no balance can weigh her value!" (Sir. 26:15). "A virtuous wife brings joy to her husband—peaceful and full is his life" (Sir. 26:1). "A gracious wife delights her husband; her thoughtfulness puts flesh on his bones" (Sir. 26:13). "With her the heart of a wealthy man and a poor one is satisfied, and his face is joyous at all times" (Sir. 26:4). "Live joyfully, my son, with the wife whom thou lovest, whom God hath given thee; for this is thy portion in this life, and in thy labor" (Eccl. 9:9).

And this lot—life together in matrimony—is pleasing in the eyes of God as well. Today in the Vespers hymns, the Holy Church glorified "the brightest life, and equal to the angels," of the Venerable Macarius of Egypt.[2] He was distinguished with virtues, especially with asceticism and prayer. Nevertheless, once this great ascetic heard a voice, "Macarius! You have not yet become equal in your perfection to two women, who live not far from you." Having heard this, the holy elder found those women and asked them how they live and how they please God. The women answered him with humility: "We are sinners and live amidst the fuss of the world; there is no goodness in us; and there is only one thing that we avoid God's anger with—that it has been fifteen years already since we married two brothers, and we live in such agreement that we have never said an unpleasant word to each other."

Therefore, this means that life in matrimony is perfect and is pleasing to God. But it is pleasing when its foundation is not some mercenary calculations and lowly motives, but rather, mutual love and devotion of husband and wife, combined with self-denial, constancy, meekness, and long-suffering, and when a husband loves and takes care of his wife, and the wife respects her husband and listens to him as the head of the family, which the Holy Church requires from a couple (cf. Eph. 5:22–29).

Furthermore, in order to be pleasing in the eyes of God, the marriage must be "in the Lord" (1 Cor. 7:39). The blessing of the Church must be called upon it, through which it becomes a mystery in which heavenly grace is given to a husband and a wife, which sanctifies and elevates their union in the likeness of the union of Christ with the Church (cf. Eph. 5:23–32), and which assists them in carrying out their mutual duties.

---

[2] St. Macarius the Great of Egypt was a very important Desert Father who lived in the 4th century. The famous *Fifty Spiritual Homilies* are attributed to him.

Sometimes, as for example some have it in this country, a Church wedding is considered unnecessary. But if we cannot do genuine good in its fullness without Christ (cf. John 15:5), if all of "our suffi-ciency is from God" (2 Cor. 3:5), if it is God Who begets in us kind desires and actions (cf. Phil. 2:13), then how is it possible that the married couple does not need the grace of God to piously carry out their high duties?

No, the true Orthodox Christian cannot be satisfied with just a civil marriage, without a Church wedding. For that kind of marriage remains without the highest Christian sanctification, since only to the marriage sanctified by the Church—this treasury of grace—is God's grace attracted. A civil marriage, for its part, places in the foun-dation and protection of the married life not creative religious-moral principles, not the spiritually beneficent power of God, but only legal obligations, which are not sufficient for moral perfection.

Your marriage union, my beloved, is blessed today by the Holy Church, and through the priest of God, God's grace has been given to you. And you, wife, at the same time, take a husband not only *in* the temple, but also *from* the temple, from the ranks of the servants of God.

We place our hope, therefore, and at the same time we pray to God, Who is glorified in the Holy Trinity, that "He may grant to you long life, well-favored children, progress in life and in faith, and perfect love. May He replenish you with all the good things of the earth, and count you worthy of the promised blessings, through the prayers of the Holy Theotokos," with whose icon I bless you today, "and of all the saints. Amen."[3]

---

[3] From a prayer from "The Service of the Crowning," before the dismissal.

A SERMON[4]

*Preached at the consecration of the chapel on the
newly built battleship "Retvizan" in Philadelphia,
Pennsylvania, on March 16, 1902*

IGREET YOU, beloved brethren, with the celebration of the blessing of your temple of God. This event is joyful and important for
your sea-faring life. As our body at times is in need of a place for
rest—and pitiful and miserable does a man look who is destitute
and homeless, who does not even have a place to rest his head—in
the same way there is no less need for our soul for a place where we
would be able to pour out our joy, cry out our sorrow, offer praise to
the Lord, and ask for His help in our needs and afflictions. A place
like that for a Christian soul is the temple of God, which is so dear to
the heart of the Russian Orthodox person—and it feels sad for our
soul to be without it and without services offered to God.

But it is especially often that this sadness visits us at sea. For
entire weeks one does not see any coastline; the eye has nothing to
rest on, being worn out by the monotonous sight of the water. Qui-
etness and stillness do not bring forth a comforting feeling; rather
they bring boredom, and a feeling of uneasiness and loneliness grows
in the soul.

And then "raiseth the stormy wind, which lifteth up the waves
thereof; they mount up to the heaven, they go down again to the
depth. Then the soul of men is melted because of trouble, they reel to

---

[4] Printed in *Amerikansky Pravoslavny Vestnik*, 1902, #7, pp. 142–143.

and fro and stagger like a drunken man" (Ps. 106:25–27, LXX); "their soul abhorreth all manner of meat, they are at their wits' end, and they draw near unto the gates of death" (Ps. 106:18, LXX).

Since no matter how big the ship is, how skillfully it is designed, yet how pitiful and insignificant it looks in the endless watery abyss! And only due to confidence "that God's providence pilots it, because God has made the way in the sea and a safe path in the waves," "therefore people trust their lives even to the smallest piece of wood" (Wisdom of Solomon 14:3, 5). Feeling their complete helplessness during the storm, "they cry unto the Lord in their trouble, and He bringeth them out of their distress"; "He maketh the storm a calm" and "bringeth them unto their desired haven" (Ps. 106:28–30, LXX).

It is not without reason that the folk wisdom says, "whoever has not gone out to sea does not pray." And what would be a better place to pray if not in the temple of God? And how useful, therefore, is the temple on a sea-faring vessel!

A voyage at sea is awaiting you, brethren, in the near future. "O Lord, our God, look mercifully upon this military vessel and by Your almighty hand, with Your heavenly blessing, sanctify it; and accompany the warriors desiring to sail in it, and send them favorable winds. And send a good angel of Your all-powerful might in order to protect and deliver them from all kinds of vicious winds, and also storms and excessive waves and drowning, keeping them healthy and safe,"[5] through the prayers of the Theotokos and Hierarch Nicholas, "good pilot of those who sail the deep."[6]

This temple is dedicated to his name, and I bless you today, brethren, with his icon, with a prayerful wish that the Hierarch Nicholas may be "a quiet harbor and a known refuge" for you as well.

---

[5] From the service for the blessing of a vessel.
[6] From the Akathist Hymn to St. Nicholas of Myra the Wonder-Worker (Ikos 7).

A HOMILY[7]

Addressed to the newly ordained priest, the editor
of Svet, *Fr. Benedict Turkevich, in Allegheny,*
Pennsylvania, on March 30, 1902

ICONGRATULATE YOU, beloved, with the grace of the priesthood. Today the desire of your heart and God's will towards you have come true, and you are called to the pastoral work. Therefore, "be strong, my son, in the grace of Jesus Christ," and as "a good soldier of Christ" (2 Tim. 2:1, 3) "take unto yourself the whole armor of God, that you may be able to withstand, having overcome everything" (Eph. 6:13). The Holy Apostle Paul lists the weapons of the spiritual soldier of Christ, with which you should arm yourself for success in the pastoral undertaking awaiting you. These weapons are: the spiritual sword of the truth, the word of God, the shield of faith, the armor of righteousness, and the helmet of salvation (cf. Eph. 6:14–17).

I will draw your attention to the first two [of these weapons], as the ones having special significance in your endeavor of proclaiming the Good News. In the second book of Ezra (Esdras), it is narrated how the wise men of old who served at the court of Darius argued that the truth is stronger than anything. "The whole earth calls upon Truth, and heaven blesses her, and all works tremble in front of her; with her there is no partiality or preference, and she does what is righteous instead of anything that is wicked." "Truth endures and

---

[7] Printed in *Amerikansky Pravoslavny Vestnik*, 1902, #8, pp. 167–169.

is strong forever, and lives and prevails for ever and ever." "To her belongs the strength and the kingship and the power and the majesty of all the ages. Blessed be the God of Truth!" (1 Ezra 4:36, 38, 40).[8] Although slowly, the Truth will gradually spread across the face of the Earth, spreading light, overcoming obstacles, and being victorious over adversaries.

You will be able to accomplish much in your undertaking, my beloved, if you arm yourself with truth. You are being sent to do just that—to testify to the truth. You should do this without resorting to cunning, without using deception and deviousness—like others do sometimes—but by revealing the truth (cf. Prov. 8:6–8; 2 Cor. 4:2). And everyone who is of the truth will listen to your voice (cf. John 18:37) and will follow you.

Carry the truth of God zealously, but use only the weapons of light for that purpose. Exhort, reason, and convince with patience, humility, and love, since Orthodoxy is the True Light and must not be spread through the ways of darkness.

Reveal and show where to "look for truth," and the truth of God will draw the hearts of the lovers of truth by itself, like the sun draws all that is living on earth to itself. At the same time, do not chase external success, such as gaining a large number of converts, but care more that those converted by you firmly know Whom they have come to believe in, so that your children will walk in truth (cf. 2 John 4).

The truth of God is revealed in the Word of God; therefore it should also serve as a weapon for you. The Apostle Paul calls the Word of God the "sword of the Spirit" (Eph. 6:17), which "is sharper than any double-edged sword and reaches the very depths of the soul" (Heb. 4:12). It is a *hammer* that crushes and softens the stony heart of man; it is a *fire* that consumes the spiritual uncleanness of people and warms our cold soul (cf. Jer. 23:29). It is good "for teaching, for

---

[8] The Bible St. Tikhon was using had these verses at 2 Ezra 4:25–31.

reproof and correction, so that the man of God may be perfect, ready for all good works" (2 Tim. 3:16–17).

Therefore, my beloved, learn the Law of God "day and night" (Ps. 1:2). Do not comfort yourself with the fact that you studied the Scriptures some time ago. Sometimes such study is narrowed to knowing who wrote a known holy book, and when, and for what reason, or to knowing a certain number of texts and being able to explain them. But of course this kind of academic and sporadic studying of the Scriptures is not enough, since in this case what is most important is very often omitted—the reading of the very "words of eternal life" and deeply absorbing their life-giving wisdom. Without this, the Word of God remains a "sealed book."

I recall that one philosopher (Shopenhauer)[9] demanded of his readers that they read his work twice, since only then would all the nuances become clear and the whole would be clearly understood. If this kind of demand is essential for the work of a human mind, then all the more is it applicable to the "Book of Life" and the words of God. And besides this, how many of those who have studied the Holy Scriptures have had the patience to read the entire Bible at least once! Make it a rule for yourself—read the Holy Scriptures daily with the most reverent attention, and the Word of God will abide in you and will make you strong (cf. 1 John 2:14).

Amidst the other spiritual weapons, the Apostle points out the shield of faith and the armor of truth. And of course it is hardly necessary to tell anyone how important and necessary it is for a pastor to have faith and to practice it in a pious life.

"O Man of God, pursue truth, piousness, faith, love, patience, humbleness" (1 Tim. 6:11), and then you will become the kind pastor who "rightly divides the word of truth" (2 Tim. 2:15).

---

[9] Arthur Schopenhauer (1788–1860) was a prominent German philosopher.

A HOMILY[10]

Preached at the ordination of the teacher Michael Skibinsky, a Canadian missionary, into the priesthood, at Holy Trinity Church in Vostok, Alberta, on April 11, 1902 (Great and Holy Thursday)

ICONGRATULATE YOU, beloved, with the grace of the priesthood. Through the providence of God you have been called to serve the heavenly meal on the very day when the Holy Church commemorates the institution by Christ of the Last Supper, the Life-giving Meal. And today Christ tells you, as He told the Holy Apostles on that day, "My friends and My beloved! Eat My body and drink My blood, and with this food and drink that are incorruptible, nourish and give drink to everyone."[11] "And you, having heard the call of the Lord to the life-giving meal, serve Christ well."[12] "Work hard with the talent you have received. Carry out the service waiting for you with cheerful heart and sober mind; avoid the slackening of your spirit and being lazy, and instead be bold; and in this way you will succeed."[13]

Perhaps you have heard complaints from some pastors in some remote areas that they have nothing to do, that they get bored and become numb from idleness. I think that for you, since you have an

---

[10] Printed in *Amerikansky Pravoslavny Vestnik*, 1902, #9, pp. 190–191.

[11] Paraphrasing Christ's words; from the "hiereisky" akathist for Holy Communion (an akathist hymn sung by priests in preparation for serving the Holy Eucharist).

[12] From the same source.

[13] From the 5th morning prayer.

understanding of the responsibilities of a pastor, having seen pastors "in weariness and toil, in watchings often" (cf. 2 Cor. 11:27), there is no need to reveal the truth that a true pastor can always find a holy undertaking—that he is more often overwhelmed with duties than lacking them.

And there is a vast field in Canada for your activity. Our cause there has just been started, and therefore much has to be accomplished in the building of temples and chapels, and in soliciting the government for land for church purposes. And it is necessary to affirm the newly converted in the Orthodox Faith, and to support the brotherhoods that have been formed there not too long ago, along with the schools and reading halls.

Quite often the parishioners will also turn to you, as an educated man, for advice in everyday matters, to which the true love of a pastor cannot be indifferent. Remember how quite often the Master of all pastors was moved with compassion towards people—how He not only taught and admonished the people, but also healed their ailments and even ordered His disciples to feed those who were listening to Him (Matt. 14:14–16).

In Canada another great and holy undertaking is awaiting you—to preach the Truth of Orthodoxy to all. There you will need, as the Holy Apostle Paul said, to have "your feet shod with the preparation of the gospel of peace" (Eph. 6:15). Some quite often cross the land and sea to make one convert (cf. Matt. 23:15); they seek the ones who do not seek them, and open up to those who are not asking (cf. Is. 65:1).

And you find yourself in more fortunate circumstances, since many from among the Uniates who live around here desire and thirst for the Truth and will willingly follow the voice of the Truth when they hear it. Their pastors often abandon them, since they find that the profit from the table of the Lord is paltry, and the labor is wearisome (cf. Mal. 1:12–13). And thus for the lack of true pastors the sheep have become dispersed and scattered, and they wander and become prey to all kinds of animals in the field (cf. Ezek. 34:4–6).

Feel pity for these lost sheep—bring them together from all sides. Find those who have gotten lost, return those who have been taken away. Treat the wounded, nourish the sick—calm them in a welcoming shelter and in a rich pasture, and tend to them, following the truth (cf. Ezek. 34:11–16). This undertaking should be especially close and dear to your heart, since you yourself come from a group of people who only twenty-five years ago were in a situation similar to that in which the Canadian Rusyns find themselves today.[14]

This missionary's cross[15] is given to you as a constant reminder of the missionary service awaiting you. When you put it on your chest, recall our Lord, crucified on the Cross, Who left the heavenly cloister and came down to earth to find the sheep who had gotten lost. "Looking unto Jesus, the author and finisher of our faith," do not "get weary and faint in your soul" (Heb. 12:2–3), "but with boldness come to the throne of grace to obtain timely help from Him" (Heb. 4:16) Who was tempted and is able to help those who are tempted! (cf. Heb. 2:18).

---

[14] Fr. Skibinsky was from the province of Lublin in southeastern Poland. For "Russins," see footnote 25 on page 68.

[15] A special cross worn by missionaries was given by St. Tikhon to the newly ordained Fr. Skibinsky at the time of his ordination.

AN OPEN LETTER[16]

To the editor of the newspaper Svet *regarding the strike
in the coal mines, in San Francisco, on July 9, 1902*

THE STRIKE is still going on, our parishioners endure everything
and become poorer; and it is not known when there will finally
be an end to this onerous situation. But the saddest part of it is that
even if an accord is reached (between the group of capitalists and
the representatives of the workers), still it will only bring temporary
calm and satisfaction.

Without a doubt, in the future, life will become more expensive;
supplies and goods will increase in price, while wages will remain
the same and therefore will be insufficient. This means, with the way
things are around here, it will again become necessary to resort to a
strike, and suffer again, and continue to live in poverty.

In these circumstances it is necessary to come to help the needy.
Why not establish a special fund specifically for the purpose of helping during strikes?—since many of our parishioners now work in
factories and, not taking part in the present strike, have a certain
income. It would be sinful not to remember the needy and suffering
during the well-to-do times! Likewise, when the needy attain what
they want, why should they not set up at least a small reserve for a
"rainy day" in the future?

How to pay the dues in order to establish the fund, how and
to whom to distribute funds from it—the brotherhoods themselves

---

[16] Printed in *Amerikansky Pravoslavny Vestnik*, 1902, #14, pp. 306–307.

can discuss these things at their meetings. The fund may be opened under the patronage of the Board of the Mutual Aid Society, which could contribute to this cause from its funds.

To start this good undertaking off, I am sending 100 dollars from myself to the Board of the Society. May God grant that it will be successful!

SUGGESTION 7[17]

To the North American Spiritual Board regarding the distribution of icons from Athos among the Orthodox temples in America

ONE PIOUS "Russian dweller of the Holy Mountain," who is taking the needs of the Orthodox mission in America close to his heart, has sent to me 19 icons of the Mother of God "The Akathist" (*Akafistnaya Zagrafskiya*). These icons are the "gratuitous gift of the Russian inhabitants of the Holy Mountain," and are sent "as a blessing from the holy Mt. Athos—the earthly domain of the Queen of Heaven"—to the Orthodox parishes in America that were formed by former Uniates.

All the icons have particles of the relics of the Unmercenaries Cosmas and Damian[18] embedded in them (and securely closed up), along with pieces of cotton soaked in holy oil from the inextinguishable lamps that are in front of the miraculous icon of the Mother of God in the Zographou Monastery, and in front of the icons of the 26 venerable martyrs of the Zographou Monastery who were torched on October 10, 1276, by those of the Latin faith for refusal to accept union with Rome and to submit to the Pope. (The narration about the invasion of the Holy Mountain by the followers of the Latin faith is included in the Kholmsk calendar of 1886.)

---

[17] Printed in *Amerikansky Pravoslavny Vestnik*, 1902, pp. 354–355.

[18] Saints Cosmas and Damian were twin brothers born in Arabia who both were doctors and treated patients without charge—hence their epithet, "Unmercenaries." They both died as martyrs in about 287.

The icons are blessed with holy water from the Jordan River that God was baptized in, and from the spring of St. Panteleimon in Nicomedia. Enclosed with the icons are several Mt. Athos publications—"Selected sayings of the holy Fathers in honor of the Most Holy Theotokos," "Glory to the Mother of God," "The heavenly protection of the saints above us," and others.

I suggest to the Spiritual Board to make arrangements to send the holy icons and books to the following churches: Minneapolis, Streator, Marblegate, Cleveland, Charleroi, Allegheny, Phillipsburg, Buffalo, Hartshorne, Shepton, Wilkes-Barre, Old Forge, Bridgeport, Kuskokwim, Troy, Passaic, Wilkeson, and to the chapels in the town of Edmonton and in the province of Manitoba (in Canada).

Upon receiving the icons, cases must be made for them with glass. Then, on the first Saturday, before the all-night vigil, a *molieben* for the blessing of the water is to be served, the icons and the worshipers are to be sanctified with the holy water, and the Akathist to the Mother of God is to be read at the all-night vigil. And on Sunday after the Liturgy, a *molieben* is to be served to the Mother of God, along with the chanting of "Many Years" to the "Russians of the Holy Mountain," with an appropriate exhortation.

The feast of the Holy Zographou Icon must be celebrated annually on the Sunday that is closest to October 10th according to the Old Calendar.

A SERMON[19]

*Preached at the consecration of the New York
church on November 10, 1902*

IGREET YOU, Russian Orthodox people, with the celebration of
the consecration of your temple. The present day is just as joyful
for you as once the day was joyful for Israel when instead of the tabernacle the temple of God was erected during the time of Solomon.

And indeed up to now it is as if we have had in New York only
a tabernacle. As the tabernacle was taken from one town to another,
we, in the same manner, moved here from one place to another with
our temple. And as David at one time felt discomfort that he lived
in a cedar house while the Ark of God was under the cover of a tent
(cf. 2 Kingdoms 7:2, LXX; 2 Sam. 7:2 in the Hebrew OT), so did
we lament many times that our temple was poor and crowded and
uncomfortable.

Today the end has come to those lamentations; and our heartfelt
sighs that a temple worthy of the Russian people, and in conformity
with the greatness of the Orthodox Faith, should be erected in this
great city have been heard by the Lord!

Although in its riches our new temple is inferior to many temples
of the great Russian land, it has, just as the temple of Solomon, a
missionary significance to make up for it. We hope that those of
other faiths will also hear about it, and will come to it, and will pray
here, and will raise their hands to our God!

---

[19] Printed in *Amerikansky Pravoslavny Vestnik*, 1902, #14, pp. 306–307.

Let us give thanks to our Lord, Who is beneficent to us, Who compelled the kind, Russian people to give alms for the construction of this temple, and Who has sanctified it with the grace of His All-Holy Spirit today!

Having tasted that the Lord, Who has helped you to erect this magnificent stone temple, is gracious (cf. 1 Peter 2:3), you yourselves as well, brethren, according to the word of St. Apostle Peter, "as lively stones, are built up into a spiritual house" (1 Peter 2:5). In other words, form from among yourselves a church community that is just as firm and sound as your temple.

Up until now, while you have not had this temple, while you only have had a temporary accommodation for it, it has seemed to others, and you yourselves thought at times, that perhaps the entire cause of the Orthodox Church is only temporary here. Today, with the establishment of this temple, these fears are dispersed.

"I will build My Church; and the gates of hell shall not prevail against it" (Matt. 16:18); "I am with you always, even unto the end of the world. Amen" (Matt. 28:20). We believe and hope that these promises of Christ concern our cause here as well, and therefore approach this temple without fear, with boldness, gathering around it and forming a close family, bound by a union of faith and love. You know that the way we have it in Russia is that the temple and the parish are closely tied together. May it be the same with you. Love your temple and visit it often.

The Russian people are known since olden times as God-loving and as lovers of God's holy churches—Holy Russia stands adorned with its temples. Unfortunately, some Russian people, having found themselves abroad, are embarrassed to preserve here the good customs of the Faith of their homeland due to a weak spirit; and by denying these customs, they hope to gain for themselves the respect of the foreigners. A bitter and sad delusion—no one respects an apostate! Not to say anything about what our Lord said about that kind of person: "Whosoever therefore shall be ashamed of Me and of My words in this adulterous and sinful generation, of him also shall the Son of man be ashamed, when He cometh in the glory of His Father with the holy angels" (Mark 8:38).

You, however, are different. Stand firm in the Orthodox Faith, preserve the customs of your homeland, and love the temple of God.

While uniting around the temple, erect among yourselves "a spiritual house" (1 Peter 2:5), in order to devote yourselves, your soul, your life to the service of God. Do not forget that just as your temple, your community has a missionary significance: "Ye are a chosen generation, a peculiar people" to proclaim the wonderful light of Orthodoxy to those of other faiths (1 Peter 2:9).

In one of the wonderful prayers during the consecration of the temple, we ask the Lord that the newly erected temple serve us for the "directing of life, for pious living, and for the fulfillment of all truth." Therefore, at the blessing of your temple I find it timely to entreat you with the words of the Apostle Peter which closely relate to us as well:

"Dearly beloved, I beseech you as strangers and pilgrims, abstain from fleshly lusts which war against the soul; and have your conversation honest" among those of other faiths, so that "they may by your good works, which they shall behold, glorify God" and your Church. "For so is the will of God, that with well-doing you may put to silence the ignorance of foolish men." "As free, yet not using your liberty as a cloak for maliciousness, but as servants of God," "be subject to your masters," "honor all men, love the brotherhood, fear God." "And above all things have fervent love among yourselves: for 'love shall cover a multitude of sins.'" "Be you all like-minded, compassionate, loving your brother, merciful, friendly, wise in humility." "As every man has received the gift, even so minister the same one to another, so that God in all things may be glorified through Jesus Christ, to Whom be the praise and dominion for ever and ever. Amen" (1 Peter 2:11–12, 15–18; 4:8; 3:8; 4:10–11).

A SERMON[20]

Preached at the consecration of the Syro-Arabian temple in Brooklyn, New York, on October 27, 1902

I GREET YOU, Orthodox Syrians, with the celebration of the bless-ing of your temple.

On this present joyous day I recall how four years ago I entered your former temporary temple for the first time, and how then the most honorable Fr. Raphael, your rector, on meeting me was express-ing sadness regarding the smallness and poorness of the temple you had at that time. To comfort him, I told him that the King of the world Himself was born in a den and laid in a manger; that He spent thirty years in obscurity in a small town in Nazareth in the poor family of the carpenter Joseph; that at first Christianity only had the poor, the lowborn, those of no social status as its followers; that they arranged their temples in simple living rooms and sometimes even underground (in catacombs); and that the holy ascetics as well often started their holy cloisters somewhere in the wilderness and in great poverty. And afterwards, all of that grew, becoming great and famous. Therefore, I said then that the Lord, in His great and rich mercy, will not pass over you either—as long as faith and love for Him do not diminish in your hearts.

And now the merciful Lord has not put to shame our hope in Him. "Ye are no more strangers and foreigners" (Eph 2:19), and there is no longer a need to rent small and uncomfortable quarters for

---

[20] Printed in *Amerikansky Pravoslavny Vestnik*, 1902, #22, p. 468.

prayer and other kinds of meetings. For from now on you have your own *house of the Lord*. You have created it using your own meager means and with your own righteous labor. And now this splendid temple has been blessed with the grace of the Most Holy Spirit. Indeed "This is the day which the Lord hath made; we will rejoice and be glad in it" (Ps. 117:24, LXX). "Your joy is full" (1 John 1:4). But your joy, brethren, is also *our* joy, and we Russian Orthodox rejoice in your joy.

We rejoice for the reason that we are your brethren in faith. We have with you "one Lord, one faith," one communion (cf. Eph. 4:5), and here (in America) one clerical authority.

We rejoice also for the reason that just like in your homeland of Syria the Russian people assist you in the preservation of the Faith and of your ethnicity, it is the same way here—for they helped with the construction of your temple. This includes a donation by our most pious Tsar; and there is also a mite from the spiritual authorities and the local Russian people.

Therefore your temple is close and dear to us as well. And may today's celebration of its consecration bring us even closer, and tie us with unbreakable bonds of faith and love for Jesus Christ, for the great glory of the Orthodox Faith and for our mutual benefit.

THE ORTHODOX MISSION IN ALASKA (NORTH AMERICA)[21]

From the report to the Council of the All Russia Missionary Society in Moscow in 1902

THE NORTH AMERICAN DIOCESE embraces parishes on the mainland of North America (in the States and Canada) and in Alaska (the former Russian territories in North America). The Orthodox mission in Alaska is under the patronage (since 1900) of the All Russia Missionary Society. It comprises 16 parishes (Sitka, Killisnoo, Juneau, Nuchek, Kenai, Kodiak, Afognak, Unga, Bielkovsk, Unalaska, St. George Island, St. Paul Island, Mikhailovsky Redoubt, Kvikhnah, Kuskokwim, and Nushagak). Last year the number of parishes increased by one—namely, priest Nikolai Risev (who previously resided on St. Paul Island), following a request, was appointed by me to the church of the Unga settlement (which has been attached to Bielkovsk up to this day), for whose support the Bielkovsk parish psalmist's pay (600 rubles in gold) was reallotted.

There are 17 churches in Alaska (including one in a private home—a *krestovaya*,[22] in Sitka), as well as 60 chapels and prayer houses. Construction of a new church in Nushagak (instead of the old, dilapidated one) has been completed during the reporting year; a

---

[21] Printed in *Amerikansky Pravoslavny Vestnik*, 1903, #3, pp. 34–37.

[22] A *krestovaya* church was a church arranged in the private quarters of the home of a Russian priest. Usually a separate room with an altar and a small iconostasis would serve as the *krestovaya*.

grant of 195 dollars (290 rubles) was issued for its construction from the funds of the Missionary Society.

Also, a new church named after St. Sabbas of Serbia[23] was constructed in Douglas (near Juneau) by the Serbs who work in the gold fields. Two thousand dollars were raised by them (4000 rubles) for this purpose. The icons were provided free of charge for the new church at my request by the Holy Synod, and the vestments and vessels were donated by the diocesan authorities.

Construction continues on the churches in Kuskokwim and Afognak in place of the old decrepit ones; 100 dollars (200 rubles) was allotted by me from the funds of the Missionary Society for the one mentioned last. Construction of a chapel, or at least a prayer house, in the settlement of Hoonah (in the area of the Juneau mission) should be started in the near future, for which the Orthodox people of the Kolosh tribe who live there have been asking already for several years.

There are 17 priests in Alaska (including 3 hieromonks), 1 deacon (who is not on staff), and 12 psalmists. The activities of the parish clergy include conducting liturgical services and religious rites, activities related to school, directing the life of the parish and the brotherhoods in accordance with the Orthodox way, visiting chapels and settlements (which in many places is a very difficult undertaking),[24] and enlightening the heathen (in whatever places they reside) with the light of the Orthodox Faith in Christ.

There are 11,758 Orthodox parishioners in Alaska—namely, there are 87 Russians, 2257 Creoles, 2147 Indians, 2406 Aleutians, 4839 Eskimos, and 22 persons of other ethnicity. The number of parishioners increased by 305 persons versus last year (11,453) in part due to birth, in part due to joining of the Orthodox Church by

---

[23] St. Sava of Serbia (1174–1236) served as the first archbishop of the newly-founded and organized Serbian Orthodox Church. He is the patron saint of Serbia.

[24] The Kuskokwim missionary Priest Pavlov, for example, almost died from hypothermia during Christmastide on his way to the Venisarn Settlement [this footnote is in the original].

new members. 140 persons joined—100 from heathenism, 33 from Protestantism, and 7 from the Latin faith.

There are 45 church schools in Alaska. Two of them are in Sitka and Unalashka; they are 2-year missionary schools. There are 5 orphanages—in Sitka, Unalashka, Nuchek, and two in Kodiak: one for boys and one for girls. The need for the latter one has been felt for a long time, and therefore its opening was met with great enthusiasm by the local population. There are up to 760 students attending the schools, and 65 children live in the orphanages. The classes are taught by the members of the parish clergy, but the missionary schools have special teachers; and in Kodiak there is a teacher/caregiver as well.

Readers teach at the schools that function as chapels. The missionary schools are maintained by funds provided by the Holy Synod, and the Kodiak girls' orphanage by funds from the Missionary Society. 800 rubles were released by me from the funds of the Missionary Society during the reporting year to the priests for rewarding the hardest working teachers and readers in the grammar schools.

Aside from schools, the educational activity for the Natives has consisted of offering locally (in Unalashka, Kodiak, Kenai, and on St. George Island) talks and readings for adults, and publishing and the free distribution of the Gospel of St. John, the Acts of the Apostles (translated by Priest I. Shayashnikov[25]) and the *Brief Exhortation* in the Aleut dialect (by the deceased champion of the Faith, Metropolitan Innocent).[26]

As for the material well-being of the inhabitants of Alaska, this was aided to some extent by the brotherhoods, which are established at almost all the parishes (help is provided by the parishes themselves as well). This aid, however, cannot be very substantial since the Native population in Alaska is poor almost everywhere due to

---

[25] Fr. Innocent Shayashnikov (1824–1883) served in Unalashka between 1848 and 1883. Fr. Innocent made a great contribution to translating the holy Scripture into the Aleut language. He translated the Gospel of St. Luke and the Acts of the Apostles.

[26] The full title of this remarkable work by St. Innocent, Apostle to America, is *Brief Exhortation about the Way into the Kingdom of Heaven.*

the depletion of means of sustenance, and it is in great need. Thus, according to the report of the priests, last year it was necessary to send from the funds of the Missionary Society 100 dollars to the Aleksandrovskoe settlement for food, and to the Aespamsh settlement for clothing.

The state of the Orthodox mission in Alaska is not the same everywhere. Things are at their best in the Aleutian district (Aleutian Islands). The local population—Aleuts—are distinguished by their devotion to the Orthodox Church, their love for the temples of God and the liturgical services, and their respect for and obedience to their spiritual pastors. The Aleuts are all Orthodox and are not influenced by the propaganda of other faiths. Missionaries of other faiths are no longer trying to lead adult Aleuts astray, yet they do not leave the children alone. They gladly take orphans, and children of mixed marriages, and those who are poor, to their orphanages. When they take children they promise not to prevent the children from remaining in the Orthodox Faith, yet they do not keep their promises, and they bring up those in their care in a purely sectarian spirit. To counter this evil, orphanages for boys have been established by us as well; and as of the end of 1902, in Kodiak, thanks to the help of the Missionary Society, an orphanage for girls (12) has been opened also, in memory of the venerable Elder Herman, a Valaam monk, who struggled near Kodiak and who taught children there during his life.[27]

The Sitka District is inhabited by Kolosh people. They are not as distinguished by long-suffering and meekness the way the Aleuts are. On the contrary, they have always been known to be quick-minded, brave, and freedom-loving; they are not strangers to pride, animosity among themselves, and inconstancy. They are not always steadfast in their faith and devotion to the Orthodox Church. It happens that they respond sometimes to the flirting of the Presbyterian Mission, which tempts them with material bribes, such as providing them

---

[27] This is St. Herman of Alaska, who was glorified as America's first saint in 1970 by the Orthodox Church in America (OCA).

with paid positions with the police, promises of "civil rights," etc. Many of them, though, return back to the Orthodox Church, and in general the sympathies of the Kolosh are on the side of the Orthodox Church. Some of the Orthodox Kolosh brethren even are voluntary missionaries and spread Orthodox ideas among their acquaintances of other faiths.

In the north of Alaska—among the Eskimo—the state of our affairs is worse than in other places. The north is too far away. Those in authority have almost never reached there, and they have not been aware of the sad truth for a long time. It is enough just to point to the fact that in the northern missions two to four thousand persons were reported as parishioners, but in reality there are only 500 to 700 people. One hundred year olds, who already have long departed to the next world, were entered in the number of the faithful. Some of our missionaries led a way of life there that was "questionable," and sometimes even "dubious"; they rather engaged themselves in trade than in preaching. They visited only settlements closest to them; those that were far off they promised to come to but did not visit for entire decades.

Priest Pavlov, who is the present Kuskokwim missionary, arrived at one of those settlements last year. He was trying to convince the residents to build a small prayer house in which he would be able to conduct liturgical services in the future. In response, he heard these bitter but truthful words: "We have been deceived constantly. How many times did they promise to come here! People would gather from the tundra, and all in vain. And here you are saying that you will come again and will teach about prayers, that you will come every year, but instead you will leave now and will never come back."

Having made such a note in his travel diary, the priest reasonably adds that "the words here are irrelevant; instead it is necessary to prove them with deeds." It is not surprising after all of this that the Eskimo, who were baptized but left without pastoral care, in quite some numbers are being half-Christians—with heathen beliefs, signs, customs, and way of life. They believe in shamans, pray to God rarely, even hide sometimes from priests, do not care about the mystery of Confession, and do not want to marry in a Christian manner. They do not consider debauchery, idleness, and other amusements to be sin.

The Eskimo in general made a very dismal impression on our missionaries who were newly appointed there in regard to their moral-religious state. But the propaganda of other faiths had an even more disheartening effect on our missionaries there.

"Among our missions in the north," they write to me, "missions of other faiths are stationed in many places. The most dangerous, threatening, and powerful enemy from among them for us is the Jesuit mission. Its strength is particularly great compared to ours. In the main nest of it, in the Kozyrevsk settlement, they have a school-orphanage where 80 boys and 60 girls are being brought up, mostly children of Orthodox parents, who became orphans during the epidemic. There are also 18 nuns here under whose direction there are several novices from among the female Natives, 4 monks, and 4 Jesuit priests who permanently reside there. And altogether there are 12 Jesuit priests with assistants accompanying each one of them in our area.

"Aside from the numerical strength of these fanatical servants, the Jesuit mission possesses also vast resources. This allows it to lure the Natives, as well as Orthodox who are not firm in their faith yet, and orphans, those of weak health, and the elderly. Presents and promises from the Jesuits also serve as a lure for those who are healthy and able to work, but who are lazy and careless, which almost all of the local Natives are by nature.

"With that, the dangers for Orthodoxy do not end—for with the baseness and arrogance typical of the Jesuits, they commit terrible abuse of the Orthodox and humiliate Orthodoxy here, especially in places that are distant from civil authority, which already looks the other way from the deliberate actions of the Jesuits."

Further on [in his report], instances are provided where Jesuits sometimes baptize children of the Orthodox against their will, take them to their orphanage, force them to marry against their will, rip off Orthodox icons and crosses, call Orthodox temples the houses of "Satan," say that the Russian churches will soon be repossessed and sealed, that soon there will be no "Russian" faith left anywhere, and other mindless words.

These are the forces of the Jesuits, and this is how great the danger is from them for Orthodoxy in the North.

Dean Kedrovsky writes regarding these reports of the missionaries that "indeed the state of Orthodoxy in the North of Alaska is far from comforting, but the main reason for that is not due to other faiths that are growing there, but due to our missionary-pastoral activity that has not been in order there. It is true that the material means of the Catholic mission are enormous, and that their mental strength and devotion to the cause are great, 'but the Lord is not in the strength but in the truth' (cf. Ps. 20:7, KJV). On our part, a selfless devotion to the cause of God is necessary for the support, strengthening, and development of Holy Orthodoxy there, or at least that the earthly concerns be secondary. It is important and necessary to have not so much an increase of the workers in the vineyard of God in quantity, as to have good quality in the workers themselves as well as in their labor—for which a start, most likely, has been given, and Glory be to God for that!"

This is true indeed, but one cannot but wish that along with the improvements in the work of our missionaries, there be an increase in their numbers as well. Our missionaries number only four people, while the areas for mission work are enormous. And as for the missionaries of other faiths, there are swarms of them! In light of this, in 1901 the Mikhailo-Redoubt Mission was separated by me into a special mission independent from the Kvikhnah Mission, which without a doubt will bring benefit for the cause of Orthodoxy.

But an even greater benefit would be brought by the establishment in the North, at least in the Kvikhnah Mission, in the Ikogmiut settlement,[28] where there are two churches and two church houses available, of a cenobitic missionary monastery. In this way, several of the monk-missionaries would be able to travel to missions, and the others would stay at the church to conduct services and to teach classes at schools. An orphanage could be organized for poor children, and a monastic household would be established where it would be easy to give work and sustenance for many Natives.[29]

If only God would place in the hearts of some of the kind Russian monks a good thought to come to Alaska to serve the Holy Orthodox Church there and the salvation of lesser brethren!

---

[28] This is where St. Jacob Netsvetov established his headquarters as he labored among the Eskimo peoples of the Yukon and Kuskokwim River Basins in the 1840s and 1850s. Often it is referred to as Russian Mission.

[29] Sadly, such a monastery was never established there.

A SERMON[30]

On visiting the local missionary school, at St. Mary's Church in Minneapolis, Minnesota, on September 26, 1902

LAST YEAR on this day I was greeted far away from here, in Alaska, by the Sitka Orthodox Missionary School. Now on the same day, through All-Merciful Providence, I am brought to you, to your missionary school troop. I would wish to see in this a coincidence that is not random. Is it not shown to me in this manner that it is timely and necessary to remind the students of the local missionary school, as well as the future missionaries, the helpers of the Lord, of the principles which the great missionary and theologian, who is glorified today, St. Evangelist John, used to guide himself and others? Those principles are Truth and Love. Having learned the truth in the Person of Christ, St. John indeed preached what he had seen and heard and touched with his hands (cf. 1 John 1:1), and he had no [greater] joy; he persistently convinced his followers to preserve truth and turn away from the antichrists—false teachers.

And you, the nurslings of our school, having acquired the truth, and having learned it in the Orthodox Church, remain in it at all times, and lead others onto its path. Preach the truth to those who are not aware of it, and defend it from false teachers who attack and condemn Orthodoxy out of ignorance, which happens occasionally, as well as out of anger, which happens frequently. And in your personal life beware of worshiping idols, since unfortunately there still

---

[30] Printed in *Amerikansky Pravoslavny Vestnik*, 1902, #21, pp. 441–442.

remains much that is heathen and idolatrous in the circumstances of our daily life.

Another principle which St. John the Theologian used as a guide was Love. "Children, love one another" (cf. 1 John 3:18)—this was his constant instruction and teaching. Recall the incident known to each one of us about a young brigand who was won over and steered to the right path by the highest love of St. John.[31]

May you be clothed in love as well. Come to love one another, and come to love with all your heart the pursuit to which you have been called and those people to whom you will preach the ways of Orthodoxy. Feel sorrow and compassion for them, as at some times Christ and His disciples showed compassion. And then success will crown your work, since, according to St. Tikhon,[32] love will whisper the words of persuasion and will find a way of conversion. And without love, our preaching is the ringing of brass and the clanging of cymbals (cf. 1 Cor. 13:1).

May the Apostle beloved by the Lord Jesus (cf. John 21:7) hasten to our help, and may he teach us Christ's love!

---

[31] This dramatic story appears as Chapter 42 in Clement of Alexandria's *The Rich Man Who Finds Salvation*, and in Eusebius of Caesarea's *Ecclesiastical History*, Book 3, section 23. It also is printed as an epilogue in David C. Ford's *Wisdom for Today from the Early Church* (South Canaan, PA: St. Tikhon's Monastery Press, 2014).

[32] This is St. Tikhon of Zadonsk (1724–1783), a greatly beloved Russian bishop and writer.

YEAR 1903

40. A sermon preached on the Sunday of Orthodoxy.

41. A sermon preached at the blessing of the Orthodox temple in Chicago.

42. A sermon preached upon visiting the Mayfield parish.

43. Suggestion #8 regarding the establishment of a seminary.

44. A sermon preached at the funeral service of the Right Reverend Bishop Markell (Popel).

A SERMON[1]

*Preached on the Sunday of Orthodoxy in San
Francisco, California, on February 23, 1903*

THIS SUNDAY, brethren, is called the Sunday of Orthodoxy or
the Triumph of Orthodoxy, since on this day the Holy Orthodox
Church solemnly remembers its victory over iconoclasm and other
heresies, and glorifies all who have struggled for the Orthodox Faith
"with word, writing, teaching, suffering, and pious living."[2]

Those who celebrate the day of Orthodoxy, the Orthodox people,
must themselves preserve the Orthodox Faith solemnly, standing
firmly in it. It is for us a rich treasure—we were born and brought
up in it. And not only all of the important events in our lives are tied
to it, but it also hastens to give us a blessing and help in every need
and in every good undertaking, no matter how insignificant it may
seem. It brings to us strength, joy, comfort, purification, and salvation.

The Orthodox Faith is also dear to us because it is the Faith of
the Fathers. The holy Apostles suffered afflictions and labors for it,
confessors and martyrs suffered for it, venerable fathers and ascetics
shed tears and sweat for it, pastors and teachers fought for it, and our
forefathers defended it, commanding to us to guard it better than the
apple of the eye (cf. Ps. 17:8).

And what about us—their descendants? Are we keeping the
Orthodox Faith, are we abiding by its Good News? At one time the
Prophet Elijah, the great defender of the glory of God, lamented that
all of the sons of Israel had abandoned the commandment of the

---

[1] Printed in *Amerikansky Pravoslavny Vestnik*, 1902, #21, pp. 441–442.
[2] From a prayer from the Rite of Orthodoxy celebrated on this day.

Lord, and had deviated from it to the heathen gods. But the Lord revealed to His prophet that there were still fully seven thousand among the Israelites who had not bent their knees in front of Baal (3 Kingdoms 19, LXX).

Without a doubt there exist true followers of Christ nowadays. "The Lord knoweth them that are His" (2 Tim. 2:19). Even we have happened to meet sons of the Church who are obedient and compliant with its instructions, who honor spiritual pastors, who love the temple of God and its splendor, who diligently attend church services, who are striving to lead a pious life, who recognize their human weaknesses and sincerely repent of their transgressions.

Yet how many of those are among us? Rather are there not more of those in whom "the thorns of vanity and passion make the evangelical gospel bear little fruit in some places, and to be fruitless in others; and who, following the increase of iniquity, oppose the truth of the Gospel, abandon Your heritage, and reject Your grace"?[3] "I gave birth and brought up children, and they have rebelled against Me" (Is. 1:2), God said about Israel in the ancient times. There are quite a few of those at present whom the Lord has given birth to, and has brought up and elevated in the Orthodox Faith, who reject the Faith, are not attentive to the teaching of the Church, do not listen to the spiritual pastors, and are cold towards the services and the temple of God.

And how some of us in this country of many faiths and many nationalities little by little do lose the Orthodox Faith! They begin their departure with things that in their opinion are insignificant. They consider it to be "outdated," and "not accepted among educated people," to pray before and after a meal, even in the morning and in the evening, to wear a cross, to have icons in the house, to observe Church feasts and fasts.

And they do not stop there. They go further—they rarely visit the temple of God, and at times do not do that at all, since on Sundays

---

[3] From a prayer in the Service of the Triumph of Orthodoxy.

"it is necessary to get a break from work" (in a saloon). They do not observe the fasts, they do not practice confession, they do not marry the way the Church requires, they delay the baptism of their children. This is how they tear the ties with their native Orthodox Faith!

To justify their apostasy, they use the naive reasoning that "it is not the old land here, but America, and therefore it is impossible to observe everything that the Church requires." As if the word of Christ is only suitable for the old land and not for the entire world! As if the Church of Christ is not catholic! As if the Orthodox Faith did not "establish the universe!"[4] "Ah, sinful nation, a people laden with iniquity, a seed of evildoers, children that are corrupters, you will forsake the Lord and will provoke the Holy One of Israel" (Is. 1:4)!

If you no longer keep the Orthodox Faith and the commandments of God, then at least do not incline your hearts to wicked words to come up with excuses for your sins (cf. Ps. 140:4)! If you do not honor our rules and our rituals, then at least do not judge and mock what you do not know and do not understand! If you do not accept, as is necessary, the motherly care of the Holy Orthodox Church for you, then at least realize that you do not act properly, you sin, you are unworthy children! Then, perhaps, the Orthodox Church, as a loving mother, will forgive you, your coldness towards her, and your insults, and will accept you, like a lost child, into her motherly embrace.

While solemnly preserving the Orthodox Faith, revering it wholeheartedly, the Orthodox people must take care to spread it among those of other faiths. Christ the Savior said that having lit a candle, do not put it under a bushel but place it on a candlestick that it may give light to all (cf. Matt. 5:15). And the light of the Orthodox Faith was not lit up to shine for a small circle of people. No, the Orthodox Faith is catholic—it remembers the commandment of its Founder: "Go ye into all the world and preach the gospel to every creature"

---

4 From the service of this day.

(Mark 16:15). We must share our spiritual heritage, our truth, our light, and our joy with others who are deprived of these blessings, but who are often seeking and desiring them.

At one time the Apostle Paul had a vision—a man appeared to him from Macedonia, asking him and saying, "Please come to Macedonia and help us," and after that the Apostle immediately went there to preach about Christ (Acts 16:9–10). A similarly calling voice is heard here. We live surrounded by those of other faiths; and amidst this sea of heterodoxy our Church is a saving island, the place to which some of those who swim in the sea of life direct themselves. "Come, hurry, help" we hear quite often from the heathen in far-off Alaska, and more often here, from brethren not only in the flesh but at one time in the Faith.[5] "Accept us into your communion, give us your kind pastor, send us a priest to serve on feast days, help us build a temple, establish a school for the children so that they will not lose their faith and national character in America"—these are the cries that are often heard here, especially in recent years.

And so? Are we going to remain deaf and insensitive to them? May God spare us from this kind of insensitivity! Otherwise a great misfortune will fall on us, because we, having taken the keys to the Kingdom of Heaven, do not enter it ourselves, and shut it in front of those trying to enter it (cf. Luke 11:52).

But who should care about spreading the Orthodox Faith, about multiplying the sons and daughters of children of the Orthodox Church? Pastors and missionaries, you will say. Yes, of course, they should, but should it be just they alone? The Apostle Paul wisely compares the Church of Christ with a body, and every member takes part in the life of the body (1 Cor. 12:12–27). This is how it should be in the Church life as well, "fitly joined together and compacted by that which every joint supplieth, according to the effectual working

---

[5] Here St. Tikhon is referring to the Uniates—the Byzantine Rite Catholics whose ancestors shared the Orthodox Faith up until the Union of Brest-Litovsk in 1596.

in the measure of every part, the great body" of the Church "maketh increase unto the edifying of itself" (Eph. 4:16).

In the early days there were tortured not pastors only, but laymen as well—men, women, and even children—and heresies were fought by lay people as well. Accordingly, the spread of the Faith in Christ must be a matter that is dear to, close to, and cherished by each Christian; every member of the Church should take part in this actively and wholeheartedly.

It is comforting that there are examples of this among our laymen. Thus the members of the Indian brotherhood in Sitka conduct missionary activity among their fellow countrymen. One zealous brother intentionally went to another settlement (Killisnoo), and with his explanations and persuasions greatly assisted the local priest in protecting the simple and trusting children of the Orthodox Church from the enemy's lies. In the same manner, in the States in many places, those who have turned from the Unia to Orthodoxy show to those close to them where the truth is, and dispose them to joining the Orthodox Church.

Of course, not every one of us will find opportunity and ability for a personal feat of spreading the Good News. In this case, I will point out to you, brethren, what may and should be done by everyone for spreading the Faith of Christ. We often find indications in the letters of the Apostles that, when the Apostles departed to preach, the faithful then helped them in that endeavor with prayers and donations. The Apostle Paul turned to the Christians for this kind of assistance especially often.

Therefore we can express our sympathy towards the matter of spreading the Good News with prayer to the Lord that He may take this matter under His Almighty protection, granting those who preach to carry out their service honorably, helping them to overcome hardships and dangers related to this matter, not allowing them to succumb to despondency or weaken in holy zeal; and that He may open the hearts of the non-believers to hearing and accepting the Good News of Christ, "instructing them in the word of truth, revealing to them the Gospel of righteousness, and uniting them to His Holy Catholic and Apostolic Church";[6] that He may strengthen, multiply, and comfort His Church and preserve it undefeated for ages.

This is what we pray for, but more often only with our lips, for it is rare when we do it with our hearts. Do we not often hear, "What are these *ektenias*[7] for the catechumens for? There are none like that in these days, you know, other than in some wild corners of Asia and America. Let that prayer be prayed there, where they are present"; and, "We only have our services, that are long already, get longer because of this." Oh, the unreasonableness of our people! Oh, the carelessness and negligence!

Along with an earnest prayer for the success of the preaching about Christ, we can express our sympathy towards this holy undertaking and help it with material donations. This is how it was in the earliest Church, and the holy Apostles accepted offerings for the matter of evangelizing in love, seeing in them an expression of love and zeal by the Christians.

In our day, these kinds of offerings are especially needed, since due to a lack of them the matter of preaching often stalls. Now there is nothing to send the preacher with, then there is no means to support one; now there is nothing to build the temple with, or start a school, then there is nothing to help the needs of the newly converted. Funds are required for all of this, and others manage to find them.

You may say that the others are wealthier than we are. True, but even great means are made up of smaller portions. And if each one of us gives as much as he can for this undertaking, it would add up to substantial funds for us as well.

Thus, let us not be discouraged by the modest size of our donation. If you do not have much, give as much as you can. But give, do not

---

[6] From a prayer in the Divine Liturgy for the catechumens (learners who are preparing to be received into the Orthodox Church).

[7] An *ektenia* is a litany of brief prayers.

pass up a chance to help the matter of the conversion of your neighbor to Christ, since in doing so, according to the word of the Apostle James, you will save your soul and cover a multitude of sins as well (cf. James 5:19–20).

Orthodox people, celebrating the Day of Orthodoxy, love the Orthodox Faith "not with word or tongue, but with deed and truth" (1 John 3:18).

A SERMON[8]

*Preached at the blessing of the Orthodox temple
in Chicago, on March 16, 1903*

God is with us, understand all ye nations (Is 8:9).

THESE WORDS of the Holy Prophet Isaiah involuntarily come to my mind, beloved brethren, at today's blessing of this holy temple. Ask yourselves, what was here a year ago? Nothing, an empty space. And now this splendid temple has been already erected. I will also ask you, what did we have and how many of us were here several years ago?

Today is the tenth anniversary since the World Exhibition took place in this great city, and a Congress of representatives of various churches was even held here on that occasion.[9] But how many people could represent us here then? At that time in Chicago there was only a small handful of Russian Orthodox people. Through the wise and fatherly care of the then Orthodox bishop in America, the Most Reverend Nikolai,[10] this handful was gathered into an Orthodox parish, a small room was rented for church services, and clergy were appointed for that purpose.

This was how a start was given to the undertaking, the undertaking was good, and therefore God Himself was with it, blessing it

---

[8] Printed in *Amerikansky Pravoslavny Vestnik,* 1903, #8, pp. 113–115.

[9] This was the Chicago World's Fair of 1893. A worldwide "Parliament of Religion" was held there simultaneously.

[10] Bishop Nikolai (Ziorov) was the ruling hierarch of the Russian Missionary Diocese in America from 1891 to 1898.

with success. The parish began to strengthen, to grow. Our brothers in the flesh—and at one time in Faith and motherland (the Uniates)[11]—having beheld the true light of Orthodoxy, were drawn by the grace of God to the ancestral Faith of Vladimir, the Equal to the Apostles,[12] and started to return to their native Church, under its motherly roof. Due to that reason, our old temple here became cramped and uncomfortable, and a need arose to establish a new one.

Good deeds, nevertheless, are accomplished through labor, and the Lord often tries the patience of His faithful servants, in order to strengthen and temper them in love and faith in Himself even more. This is how it was here as well. When the lot of land for the church had already been acquired, when the money for the construction of the temple was especially needed, the Lord allowed the local parishioners to become poor, and they, as the righteous Job at one time, were deprived of all their savings in one day.

"Doth Job fear God for nought? Hast not thou made a hedge about him and about his house and all that he hath on every side? But touch all that he hath; will he praise You then?" (Job 1:10–11). This is how the devil lied about Job, but Job managed to remain in his righteousness and spoke wonderful words: "The Lord gave and the Lord hath taken away; blessed be the name of the Lord" (Job 1:21); and the enemy, the devil, was put to shame. The enemy's slander was heard from unkind people during your misfortune and losses as well, and I think they are still in your memory.

But through the mercy of God you, as well, have emerged from temptation pure, and you have withstood, and stood fast in your devotion to the Orthodox Faith and the Church. Then you were poor in means, but rich in your faith in the holy cause of Orthodoxy and in setting hopes on kind people and their help. And your hope was

---

[11] The Uniates (Byzantine Rite Catholics) came from the same lands as many of the Orthodox immigrants to America. Their ancestors shared the Orthodox Faith until the Union of Brest-Litovsk in 1596.

[12] St. Vladimir, Grand Prince of Kiev, converted to Holy Orthodoxy, and led his people into the Dniepr River to be baptized, in 988.

not put to shame. The Lord has solemnly revealed once again that "the Lord is with us!"—that our cause here is God's cause, it is holy, it is righteous.

Your pastor of souls[13] turned to the sons of Holy Orthodox Russia, which has loved the temples of God from the olden days and has donated generously for them, with a request to help your temple. And the Lord turned the hearts of the eager benefactors to be good donors to our needs here as well. More donations were collected here than we had expected, and it became possible with those funds to begin the construction of the temple. And so, it has not even been a year since we laid the cornerstone of this temple, and now it has already been completed and blessed. Indeed, God is with us!

But, my brethren, knowing that God Himself is behind us and our undertaking should dispose us in such a way that we work on this great endeavor with fear and trembling, as on a cause that is holy and godly. The Lord told Moses at one time from the burning bush, "put off thy shoes from off thy feet, for the place whereon thou standest is holy ground" (Ex. 3:5). And righteous men (such as Isaiah, and the Apostle Peter) were consumed with reverential trembling, when sensing the Lord was near to them.

And do we realize that the Lord places on all of us a great mission to be the bearers of Orthodoxy in the non-Orthodox world, to be the light for the local people? And even if we realize this, do we live, then, in such a manner that others, seeing our good deeds, may glorify our Mother—the Holy Orthodox Church? Or perhaps, due to our way of life, the very name of the Orthodox is slandered among the non-Orthodox? Perhaps we mix in our own calculations with the holy cause of Orthodoxy, bring in our own divisions, darken it with our own inventions? Every time, the "Glory of Orthodoxy" should lead us to reflect whether we "walk worthy of the vocation" (Eph. 4:1)

---

[13] The priest of the Chicago parish beginning in 1895 was Fr. John Kochurov, who returned to Russia before World War 1, and became the first clergyman to be murdered by the Bolsheviks. He was glorified as a saint by the Russian Church in 1994.

of Orthodox Christians, and whether the kingdom of heaven might not be taken away from us and given to others—those who are worthier and who bring forth fruits (cf. Matt. 21:43).

Brethren! The judgment of God, according to the word of God, "begins at the House of God" (1 Peter 4:17)—in other words, with the children of the true Church of Christ. Remember that, and "work out your own salvation with fear and trembling" (Phil. 2:12). Amen.

A SALUTORY SERMON[14]

Preached upon visiting the Mayfield Parish on May 3, 1903

Christ is Risen!

"Peace be unto you" (John 20:21).

My first visit to you, beloved brethren, coincides with the days when the Holy Church joyfully recalls the appearance of the risen Lord to His Disciples. It was evening, on the first day of the week, when the risen Christ, having appeared to the Apostles for the first time, spoke to them His first word: "Peace be unto you" (John 20:21).

And with this holy greeting I address you as well, brethren: "Peace be unto you."

Christ the Savior, with His suffering, reconciled all things (Col. 1:20); He reconciled us with God. "By annulling the curse, He bestowed a blessing; by destroying death, He has granted us eternal life."[15] "There is, therefore, now no condemnation to them which are in Christ Jesus" (Rom. 8:1). It is God that justifieth; "who is he that condemneth?" It is "Jesus Christ that died, yea rather, that is risen again" (Rom. 8:33–34). This is our "righteousness and peace" (Rom. 14:17).

May the peace of Christ be among you as well, brethren. Peace to you and blessing from your Mother, the Holy Orthodox Church. Your forefathers were Orthodox and struggled for the Orthodox

---

[14] Printed in *Amerikansky Pravoslavny Vestnik*, 1903, #9, pp. 134–136. This was St. Tikhon's first visit to the Mayfield parish in northeastern Pennsylvania.

[15] From the *troparion* of the Feast of the Nativity of our Most Holy Lady, the Mother of God and Ever-Virgin Mary.

Faith, but you have only recently returned into the fold of the Orthodox Church. As at one time the Apostle Thomas, having touched the risen Christ, came to believe in Him and exclaimed, "My Lord and my God" (John 20:28), in the same way, with your eyes and ears, you now have become convinced of the truth of the Orthodox Faith. In the Orthodox Church you have come to know your own Mother. In its priestly hierarchy you have recognized true and lawful pastors and teachers, and you have acquired peace for yourselves in union and love with them. Therefore, brethren, stand fast in the Orthodox Faith and preserve it as a great treasure.

Peace be unto you and a blessing from the Russian Holy Synod,[16] which having accepted the news from me regarding your return to the Orthodox Church, with a feeling of gratitude to God and joy, is sending you a letter of blessing.

Peace be unto you and a blessing from my unworthiness. With your joining the Orthodox Church you have filled our heart abundantly with jubilation and joy, having given us the comfort to see that the Lord blesses our undertaking here and multiplies the children of His Church. As a blessing, accept from me an icon of the holy patron of your temple, John the Baptist of the Lord. He was a burning and a shining light (John 5:35); he testified of the Light, and having loved the truth of God rather than the truth of man, "he endured great suffering for the Truth with joy."[17] He prepared the way of the Lord. To Him he directed your path as well, and as the Preacher of Light, he also illuminated you who honor his memory in this temple.

Walk, then, in the light of the Orthodox Faith and, lovers of truth, make the Lord's paths straight (cf. Matt. 3:3).

May you have peace with your pastor,[18] with whom you have entered into the fold of the Orthodox Church and who in this day

---

[16] This was the highest ecclesiastical authority in the Church in Russia in the years when the Patriarchate was abolished (1721–1917).

[17] From the *troparion* of St. John the Baptist.

[18] At that time the priest of the Mayfield parish, who brought the entire parish into Holy Orthodoxy from the Unia, was the hieromonk (monk-priest) Arseny Chagovtsov—the one who founded St. Tikhon's Monastery in South Canaan,

teaches you the truth "in speech and in his conduct" (1 Tim. 4:12). For his labor, the Holy Synod is awarding him a holy cross. Keep him in your love for his work for your benefit.

May peace be among you yourselves. There are several brotherhoods that exist in your parish, and the memory of the holy "proto-teachers" of the Slavs, Cyril and Methodius,[19] is especially revered. May all of this be not only in name but "in deed and in truth" (1 John 3:18). Live among yourselves in a brotherly manner in peace, love, and concord, the way the holy brothers Cyril and Methodius did. Help one another and instruct one another in faith and love.

May the God of peace "establish and strengthen you" (1 Peter 5:10) in this with His grace.

Pennsylvania, along with Archbishop Tikhon, just two years later.

[19] Saints Cyril and Methodius were Greek brothers from Thessalonica, Greece, in the 9th century, who as missionaries in the Slavic state of Moravia developed an alphabet for the Slavic language and undertook translating liturgical, Scriptural, and Patristic texts from Greek into Slavonic.

SUGGESTION 8[20]

*To the attention of the North American Diocese regarding
the establishment of a seminary; on August 5, 1903*

IN THE PAST YEARS the number of students at the Minneapolis school has continuously been increasing, and many have to be
denied entry due to lack of accommodation. There is, therefore, a
need to expand the building of the Minneapolis school.

But, on the other hand, this is not the first time that a wish has
been expressed by many to have in America something of a kind
of seminary which would prepare not only psalmists but priests as
well. The Congress of the Clergy of the Eastern States, which took
place at the end of last year, acknowledged that opening a seminary
is a matter that is not only desirable but necessary as well, and the
Cleveland parishioners expressed readiness to give for a seminary a
building of a Latin women's monastery purchased by them, and to
donate 1555 dollars on top of that.

In light of this, I acknowledge it useful and timely to establish
a commission consisting of Archpriest I. Nedzelnitski, Priests A.
Nemolovski, K. Popov, and I. Kapanadze, and teacher A. Kuku-
levski, and to entrust it with the preliminary review of the questions
regarding:

- what type should the future seminary be—should there
  only be theological courses in it, which those who have
  finished public or church schools would take; or should

---

[20] Printed in *Amerikansky Pravoslavny Vestnik*, 1903, #18, pp. 309–310.

it represent itself as something comprehensive—for example, as a kind of church-teachers' school;[21]

- in which location is it better to have the seminary—Minneapolis, Cleveland, or another city; and in the latter cases, should the Minneapolis school be preserved as a preparatory one for the Seminary;
- how many teachers are necessary for the Seminary;
- what type of funds would be necessary for that, and similar types of questions.

The commission should start reviewing them without delay. And the rest of the clergy are invited to speak on the issue.

---

[21] This type of school in Russia prepared teachers for parish schools.

A SERMON[22]

*Preached at the funeral service of the Right Reverend
Bishop Markell (Popel), in St. Petersburg, Russia*

Lord, now lettest Thou Thy servant, O Master, depart in
peace, according to Thy word: for mine eyes have seen
Thy salvation (Luke 2:29–30).

THESE WORDS of the holy God-Receiver Simeon the deceased
hierarch applied to himself already 25 years ago when he was
leaving the hierarchical cathedra in Kholm.[23] Even at that time,
already he considered the main task of his life fulfilled, and himself
ready to depart to another world. But it is only now that through the
will of God he has been taken away from our midst, and the Spirit
speaks to him as well: "Blessed are the dead who die in the Lord: Yea,
that they may rest from their labors, and their works do follow them"
(Rev. 14:13).

What sort of cause is connected with the name of the deceased
hierarch?

This capital city[24] knew the Right Reverend Markell little,
although he lived in it for close to 15 years. He arrived here in the
twilight of his life; and with an old man's infirmities, he led a life here
that was secluded and solitary. Yet without hesitation we can say that

---

[22] Printed in *Amerikansky Pravoslavny Vestnik*, 1903, #21, pp. 369–371. St. Tikhon was traveling in St. Petersburg, Russia, in late 1903.

[23] A city in northwestern Russia.

[24] This sermon was delivered in St. Petersburg, Russia.

today we bury a laborer of significance in history, a hierarch whose name is indelibly written in the annals of the newest history of our Church and Motherland. He belonged to the chosen ones of God, to whom it was given to do great deeds.

The Right Reverend Markell was born in Galitsia.[25] That land is Russian, but it does not belong to the Russian state, and its inhabitants have to defend their Faith and national character from enemy assailments seeking to wipe the first and the latter off the face of the Galitsian land. And the deceased hierarch toiled in his native Galitsia in the field of struggle for the Russian Faith and national character, when he was a teacher and a priest there. His labor was so zealous and fruitful that when similar proponents were needed for Kholm, Russia, as well, he was one of the first to be invited there (in 1867) by the Russian government.

Right at that time an awakening of the Russian national character began in Kholmshina and Podlyashie. That land from the olden time was inhabited by Russian Orthodox people. But, being on the border with a foreign nation, although of the Slavic race, but of a different faith, the Russians fell under the authority of the more powerful Poles, who thought of remaking them to the Polish liking. Knowing that the Russians draw their core strength for the preservation of their national character from the Orthodox Faith, the Poles encroached on this holy inheritance and thought up a Unia for the Russians, a union with Rome, and imposed it with all sorts of coercion.[26]

The Orthodox people fought against the ill-starred Unia for a long time, but were overpowered for a time. The Unia was accepted, and a gradual but steady destruction of the Russian Faith and national character started taking place in Kholmshina. The church services started to become closer to the Catholic kind. Iconostases began to be thrown out of the temples, statues were introduced, and Latin images and organs began to be used. It was suggested to the Uniates

---

[25] This area (also spelled Galicia) was part of the Austro-Hungarian Empire in the 19th century; today it is part of western Ukraine.
[26] This occurred at the Council of Brest-Litovsk in 1596.

that their faith and the Latin one are the same—that they, to satisfy their spiritual needs, could easily turn to *ksendz* in *kostels*.[27] Their very churches were often rented out to the Jews. And this kind of work for the destruction of the Russian national character continued for three centuries! It is not surprising after that, that if the Russian Faith and national character survived in Kholmshina, it was only in the form of a spark barely alive and ready to die out.

And then it was decided to blow this dying spark (after the revolt of 1863 in Poland) into a bright flame. A noble intention emerged to liberate the Russian people from the Polish oppression, to awaken in them Russian self-awareness, to restore the ritual, customs, and language. It was for this gratifying but very hard work that the workers were called from Galitsia, and Fr. Markell was among them. Here he quickly advanced along with the others, and he was entrusted with the important and crucial matters of pacifying discord, and explaining to the Uniates the necessity to reestablish the former ritual.

Soon he was placed in charge of the Uniate clergy and appointed to be the administrator of the Kholm Uniate Diocese. When accepting this important appointment, Fr. Markell stated that "hard labor and numerous afflictions await him in the upcoming field of service; but, in spite of that, he enters this path with a cheerful spirit and readiness to bring all his strength to the altar of the Church and the Motherland." And God blessed his labors with such success that in a short time, not only the Unia liberated itself to a great degree from the Latin-Polish infusions, but even in many places the thought arose to leave the Unia entirely and join the Orthodox Church.

The movement toward Orthodoxy skillfully and firmly directed by Fr. Markell began to grow more and more, and in 1875 resulted in close to two hundred thousand Kholm Uniates joining the Orthodox Church. At that same time, Fr. Markell was tonsured a bishop. He lived in Kholm for four more years, strengthening those who

---

[27] Meaning that they could turn to the priests in the Latin-rite parishes.

rejoined the Orthodox Faith. Altogether he lived in Kholm for 12 years.

This was the best time of his life and work. He himself spoke about it in this manner:

> Twelve years of earnest and indefatigable labor, twelve years of fears depressing to the soul, and of rosy, enlivening hopes; but, through the mercy of God, the labor was crowned with success, the fears passed by, and the hopes came true. The centuries-old delusion of my flock dispersed in front of the light of the truth; the Unia, introduced through force and cunningness, vanished, as any matter of deceit vanishes. Kholm, Russia, began to believe again as its ancestors used to believe. 'Now lettest Thou Thy servant depart, O Master, according to Thy word, in peace: for mine eyes have seen Thy salvation.'

It is exactly this reunification of the Kholm Uniates that is indeed the great undertaking accomplished by the Right Reverend Markell, which gained for him a grateful remembrance from generation to generation, which will write his name into the history of the Russian Church and state.

And afterwards the Kholm, Podolsk, and Polotsk dioceses, in which the Unia was present at one time, were entrusted to the Right Reverend Markell to administer. And in the Holy Synod itself, where he was a member for the past fifteen years, he took an especially active part in the confessional matters of the western dioceses. In this way, to his last days he remained faithful to the once chosen and beloved pursuit of enlightening the former Uniates.

We do not recount the other archpastoral labors of the deceased hierarch, his cares to develop the missionary work, church singing, schools, and brotherhoods. The good fruits of these efforts are preserved to this day in those dioceses where he labored. Likewise, a good memory lives in them about the simple, heartfelt attitude of his towards the pastors and the flock; about a warm, sincere participation in their needs; about ardent love and constant help to the relatives and people who were close to him.

A kind and sympathetic heart was beating in him, although in his appearance the deceased elder did seem reticent and reserved. But did that very reticence not proceed from his realization that the pursuit set for him by God had been accomplished by him—and that he, as he used to express himself, was a citizen not of this world, but seeking the city that is coming in a different world?

Today he has been called to a different world...

Let us pray then, brethren: may the Lord give peace to the deceased Hierarch Markell in the dwelling places of the righteous; may He absolve all his transgressions voluntary and involuntary, for there is no one who lives without sinning. And in such great and difficult pursuits which the deceased accomplished, it is not easy to avoid mistakes and transgressions. But we hope for the deceased according to the word of the Holy Apostle: "he who converteth the sinner from the error of his way shall save a soul from death, and shall hide a multitude of sins" (James 5:20).

May the Lord God remember his archpastorship in His kingdom, now and ever and unto the ages of ages. Amen.

YEAR 1904

45. A sermon preached at the presentation of the hierarchical staff to Bishop Innocent of Alaska.

46. A sermon preached at the New York Cathedral upon returning from a trip to Russia.

47. A sermon preached on the week of the Prodigal Son in Yonkers, New York.

48. A homily addressed to the newly ordained priest, Fr. Mikhail Potochny.

49. A sermon preached at the presentation of the episcopal staff to the Most Reverend Raphael, Bishop of Brooklyn.

50. A sermon preached on the birthday of Tsar Nicholas II; in San Francisco.

51. A response to His Holiness Meletius, Patriarch of Antioch.

52. A letter of the most humble servant to Tsar Nicholas II, April 29, 1904.

53. Resolution on the occasion of establishing the Alaskan Vicariate.

54. Resolution on the occasion of establishing the Syro-Arabian Vicariate with a cathedra in Brooklyn.

55. A sermon preached at the vespers service on the eve of the blessing of the side chapel at St. Nicholas Cathedral, New York City, in honor of the Nativity of the Mother of God.

A SERMON[1]

*Preached at the presentation of the hierarchical staff
to the Most Reverend Bishop Innocent of Alaska*

MOST REVEREND BISHOP INNOCENT, beloved brother in Christ! As your closest co-servant and co-worker in the field of the Lord, I present you this staff, the symbol of your new high service, and with all my heart I congratulate you with the grace of the episcopacy.

In this present, truly great event in your life, my thought involuntarily pauses on the remarkable fact that you are ordained a bishop in the very temple,[2] on the very day [of the week] and almost on the very date when and where 63 years ago (December 15, 1840) the ever memorable Innocent was ordained as Bishop of the Aleutians, who later became the Metropolitan of Moscow. At the time of your tonsure into monasticism, you were given the same name as this hierarch. And today you receive Alaska into your care, where Innocent was the archpastor; and you will pray in the temple and live in the house which were erected through his labors and care. All of this certainly disposes you to imitate this great enlightener. Let God help you to continue his work and be successful in your undertaking there.

You, beloved brother, who devote yourself a great deal to pastoral matters, are aware of what is required of us to make our pastoral labors successful. For that, it is necessary to be merciful to people and

---

[1] Printed in *Amerikansky Pravoslavny Vestnik*, 1904, #2, pp. 22–23.
[2] This church was the Cathedral of the Kazan Icon of the Theotokos in Moscow.

love those whom you are a pastor to, in the likeness of the Master of all Pastors—Christ. "I feel pity for these people," Christ the Savior used to say; and He taught people, cured their ailments, and miraculously fed them (Matt. 15:32; Mark 8:2). And the hierarch Innocent was filled with love for the ones in his care, having pity for the "sweet and kind Aleutians." He admonished them in the faith of Christ, and arranged their external way of life.

At present, they need to be loved and cared for—they know little about faith, although they desire to know. Sometimes they become abandoned by their own missionaries and get taken away by missionaries of other faiths. They often suffer oppression and offenses from trade companies and businessmen; they often go hungry and have little clothing.

How can one not feel pity for them? I trust, beloved brother, that you will love them and feel pity for them, that they will be close and dear to your heart. I feel confident in that, since you, knowing all the needs and hardships of life in Alaska, nevertheless are exchanging your present calm and secure life for them.

I do not think that the honor of the high position that you have received today plays a significant role in this case, since in America, more than anywhere else, the episcopacy, according to the word of Saint Isidore of Pelusium,[3] is hard work and not luxury. It is a responsible service and not an irresponsible dominance; it is fatherly care and not an overwhelming autocracy.

Therefore, receive this staff not only as the symbol of archpastoral authority, but also as a staff of a wanderer, upon which not just one time you will have to lean when being tired from difficult travels in the northern tundra. Receive it as a pastoral staff which the kind pastor uses to protect his flock from predatory beasts, and which you will use to protect your spiritual flock from "wolves that destroy it," from assaults and kidnappings of various missionaries who love to "build their house on somebody else's foundation" (cf. Rom. 15:20).

---

[3] St. Isidore of Pelusium, in Egypt, was a Church Father of the early 5th century.

But do not be discouraged by this, my brother! God is with us, and you are given the grace of God today. Therefore follow your path; rejoice that the Lord again leads you to the land where and for which you received the monastic tonsure and gave vows of self-denial. Rejoice that today you go there invested with twice the grace and the power, and can bring more good to those whom your soul already has known and loved for a long time.

Give now your first hierarchical blessing to the faithful standing around you, and in your mind send it to the Orthodox sons of Alaska who are far away in distance, but close to your heart.

A SERMON[4]

Preached at the New York Cathedral on his first Sunday upon returning from Russia, on January 18, 1904

I GREET YOU, BRETHREN, with the arrival of the New Year. Almost every one of us associates the meeting of the New Year with the expectation of something new. And may God bless our heart if this expectation is the thirst for the renewal of our inner being, if with this hope we encourage ourselves in the rejection of the old person! But if it is not these most noble aspirations, but simply the desire for novelty and variety that guides us in the moment the New Year arrives, then may we recall that it is not the symbolic change of time that renews the flow of our lives, but it is because of the Lord that the footsteps of man become redirected, and the new in our life depends on the will of the eternal God.

May indeed our search not be directed to the repudiation of the old commandments, sanctified by centuries; but may it be our concord with the eternal truth of Providence that our earthly journey be blessed with. If even our own, dear, *everyday* olden ways happen to be so sweet and close to our hearts, then may the holy, olden ways *of our Faith*, the practices of the Church—of ancient Christianity itself as proclaimed by Christ, and of the Orthodox way of life—be for us a hundredfold more precious.

Having entrusted my earthly path into the hands of God also, I rejoice that in the New Year it is destined for me to walk in my old

---

[4] Printed in *Amerikansky Pravoslavny Vestnik*, 1904, #3, pp. 42–44.

field of service, and that I am among you again, after eight months of separation. But though absent in body, I have always remained with you in spirit, and my connection with the flock did not become interrupted. For in Russia I was taking care of matters connected with you, I interceded for your needs, and in the services I constantly sent up prayers for you, the flock given to me by God. I have gratifying evidence that you did not forget me in my absence.

And now our communion has extended to these days of the New Year. We are together again; and today, as before, we have exalted the name of the Lord together. Let us further pray, labor, and tend to our salvation, carrying each other's burdens! Is it not in support of this former, old way of Church life—this, so to say, spiritual "conservatism"—that the deeply edifying words of today's reading from the Apostle call us to as well?—"but continue thou in the things which thou hast learned and hast been assured of, knowing from whom thou hast learned them" (2 Tim. 3:14).

This is how the holy Apostle Paul wrote to his disciple Timothy, convincing him to be unswerving and faithful in proclaiming the good news of the truth of Christ. It was already then that false teachers and deceivers had appeared; but their eloquent, new words ought not to seduce Timothy—he always sought to remain faithful to what he was taught first by the Apostle Paul.

And the Holy Orthodox Church preserves the apostolic commandment. Having vanquished the assaults made against Her by Her enemies during the long flow of the centuries, She has preserved and keeps unto this day the Holy Faith in the form in which the Holy Apostles and Teachers passed it to further generations.

Those fond of innovations often accuse Her of stagnation and lifelessness for that. Who of us has not heard these kinds of reproaches? But do they not return back upon the accusers themselves? Does it not happen to us, who live here, to often see how people of other faiths, fed up with constant innovations in faith, are drawn to the Orthodox Ecumenical Church and strive to find in Her firm and immovable foundations upon which their restless spirit may find peace?

Inspired by the fire of the right Faith, our motherland Orthodox Russia stands firm also. And we are pleased to witness how it is adorned with splendid temples as before, how these temples are not vacant but filled with those worshiping, how the people thirst to hear the word of God! Although the enemy sows his tares in that field as well—false teachers are appearing in Russia as well—the Russian folk always remember that throughout the duration of their thousand-year history their land has been Orthodox. And at the call of the Apostle, it remains faithful to what it had been taught originally.

These age-old fundamental qualities of the Russian nation—its love for the Orthodox Faith, for the holy temples and service of God—are inherent also to the Russian people outside of the motherland, here, abroad. What else, other than that, has caused the construction of many of our temples in America? What else, other than that, has led the founders and the flock of this magnificent cathedral, under which roof the Bloodless Sacrifice has been offered now?

Having become used to the temple of God from childhood, a Russian person experiences grief and emotional distress when being away from it, being abroad. But what great joy his heart becomes filled with when through the mercy of God he succeeds in erecting in the foreign land as well even a small temple, dear to his heart! In it is the main bond for the Russian people here. If the Russian people do not lose their national character far from the motherland, living among other more numerous people, then it is thanks to the native Faith and the holy temples, binding the Russian people together!

And we, brethren, here are surrounded by people foreign to us, people of other faiths and religions strange to us. There may be quite a few found among them who would like to be uninvited patrons or enlighteners for you, and draw you into their nets. You, nevertheless, like Timothy, remain firm in the Faith that you were taught—and which, as a sacred pledge, was bequeathed to you by your fathers.

The same way, in the New Year and unto the end of our days, and from generation to generation, may the Lord God be glorified through our lips and our lives, through the confession and observance of His eternal truth!

May the blessing of the Lord be upon you through His grace and His love for mankind always, now and ever, and unto the ages of ages. Amen.

A SERMON[5]

*Preached for the week of the Prodigal Son at
the Yonkers church, on February, 1904*

NOW A PARABLE has been read, brethren, from the Holy Gospel about the Prodigal Son.

A person had two sons. Their life flowed in complete contentment and calm under the parental roof. But for the younger son, who was youthful and who did not have a bitter experience in life, who had not tasted disappointments, this quiet and serene life seemed boring.

In truth he is not in need of anything; he does not have heavy burdens to provide for himself. But to live being dependent on another person, although it is one's father, to do what you are told, to strictly abide by the established order of things, when you are full of vigor, when you want to put it to use, show your worth, show off your boldness and wealth, to live on your own! So then the younger son comes to the father, asks him to apportion to him his part of the inheritance, and to let him go from the house. Without a doubt the father tried to talk him out of it, warning him that nothing good will come of it. But the youth often do not want to listen to the wise advice of the elders and consider themselves smarter. With grief does the father let the disobedient son go from the house; and the latter rejoices, that he finally has received his freedom; and he hurries to get away from the family home as quickly and far as possible.

---

[5] Printed in *Amerikansky Pravoslavny Vestnik*, 1904, #4, pp. 61–63.

And now the untrammeled life begins. Money is plentiful, and wherever it is present, there are many friends also, those fond of eating and drinking at the other person's expense! Constant entertainment, pleasures, feasts, wine, women—how much fun all of it is! And how could one even compare this with the former boring and monotonous life!

There is only one problem: the money keeps vanishing, and there is less and less of it. You are forced to cut partying, and at times to be in need. Seeing this, the drinking pals abandon you. And at last, they are gone. And help is nowhere to come from. And you still have to eat and drink!

Look for a job? But what kind of labor is he familiar with? He is not accustomed to it and does not know any trade. And here a famine strikes this country on top of it. And now the prodigal son gets hired to tend to the swine—he, the son of a wealthy father, who used to throw big parties, eat delicacies, be surrounded by joyful youth. And now he is among the swine, hungry, willing to satisfy his hunger with what the swine eat—and even that is not given to him!

You can no longer live this way. What should the prodigal son do? Wait for death from hunger?—or perhaps, return to the father who even has his servants living well off. So the prodigal son, hungry, ragged, but with enlightened soul, with contrite and humble heart, falls before the father; and the latter, a merciful person, does not remember former griefs for the sake of the joy that his lost son is found, that his beloved child is with him again!

The state of a person who is a sinner is depicted in the parable of the Prodigal Son. In his spiritual blindness he does not want to live in the home of the God of heaven, does not feel the sweetness of the peaceful, pious life according to the commandments of God. He wants to fulfill his own will; he is drawn to the expanse of sinfulness. So he departs from the heavenly Father into the area of sin and spiritual darkness. And there, living in the passions of his heart, he wastes his strength and gifts, loses his innocence and purity of conscience, destroys his health, reaches spiritual poverty, and stands on the brink of perishing.

But the parable of the Prodigal Son becomes true not only in each one of us sinners, but in entire human communities, religious and civil. There are instances, as you brethren know yourselves, when a few people sometimes do not like the order that has been established from long ago in a known community—for amidst the lawfulness that rules there, no room is left for willfulness. But they would like to have themselves be noticed, to show off, to make everybody talk about them. And then they look for supporters for themselves; and with their help they become ringleaders of the entire community to do whatever they want.

Realizing that there is power in money, they demand for themselves, similar to the prodigal son, the part of the household due to them, and often take what is not due to them at all. They try to rouse the community against the lawful authority, and tear it away from the parental house where it was given birth and brought up. Having rid themselves of the lawful authorities, they invite imposters as leaders for themselves—people who are complacent, who act entirely on their orders. Along with them, they make others go astray altogether, lead others wherever they please, get them involved in various adventures, squander wealth spiritual as well as material, lead others to poverty, to ruin, and then usually abandon them, and vanish themselves, hiding, saving themselves from the righteous human wrath. And for those people who were abandoned and cheated by them there is only one way left—similar to that chosen by the prodigal son: to return under the fatherly roof, having been abandoned by them so thoughtlessly.

Without a doubt, all of us, brethren, are moved by the end of the story of the Prodigal Son: the picture of how he returns home with a contrite heart; and how the merciful father, having caught sight of him from afar, hurries to meet him, throws himself on the neck of the younger offspring, and not only forgives him his faults, but pours on him all of his love, gives orders for him to be adorned, throws a feast in his honor. It is not always, though, that things end up so happily—some prodigal sons do not return to the fatherly home at all, but perish once and for all.

Would it not be better, therefore, to not repeat the story of the Prodigal Son—to never depart from the fatherly home, and like the older son in the parable to work all one's days for the Lord and not trespass His commandments (cf. Luke 15:29)?

And would it not be better to have in front of our eyes another, not less touching scene—of how a young child is holding tightly and persistently onto his mother; and if it happens for her to step away from her child even for a minute and leave him among strangers, then he immediately starts crying and stretching his baby hands to the mother, grabbing onto her clothes.

All of us, brethren, are children, and the Church is our mother. And if we will not love the Church and hold onto Her tightly, like children holding on to their mother, then we will not enter into the Kingdom of our heavenly Father, since, according to the patristic saying, "those for whom the Church is not a mother, for them God is not the father."[6]

---

[6] Written by St. Cyprian of Carthage (mid-third century), in *On the Unity of the Church.*

A HOMILY[7]

Addressed to the newly ordained priest, Fr. Mikhail Potochny, in the Russian Cathedral in New York City, on February 15, 1904

ICONGRATULATE YOU, good priest Mikhail, with the grace of the priesthood. Something truly great and mysterious has taken place in your life today. Both your descent and your situation did not suggest that in time you would become a pastor of the Orthodox Church. Could you yourself possibly have thought this some ten years ago? But the merciful Lord leads each one of us through unknown, most wise paths.

Desiring to better arrange your future—to find happiness—you came here from the Old Country, but you found here something more valuable than external well-being. Here you perceived the True Light and acquired the right Faith. Since becoming Orthodox you have come to love for your new Faith—which, however, had been the Faith of your ancestors—and you have become bound to it. It has become for you a valuable treasure, the precious evangelical pearl, for which you have forsaken many other earthly treasures (cf. Matt. 13:45–46).

You desired to become a humble servant of the Orthodox Church; and so, for ten years, with love, zeal, and patience, you have been a reader, cantor, and catechizer at our church in Streator [Illinois]. And now, because of this, you hear the voice of the Lord your God, "Well done, thou good and faithful servant: thou hast been faithful

---

[7] Printed in *Amerikansky Pravoslavny Vestnik*, 1904, #4, pp. 78–79.

over a few things, I will make thee ruler over many things: enter thou into the joy of thy Lord" (Matt. 25:21). Today the Lord elevates you to a spiritual height, and makes you a servant of the Mysteries of God. So love the Lord your God Who protects you—love Him with all your heart, serve Him with all your might, and be true to Him until death.

You have received the grace of the priesthood on this important day of the "Triumph of Orthodoxy." Today the Holy Church remembers Her victory and triumph over Iconoclasm and other heresies, and honors all those who have stood up for the Orthodox Faith. But our sacred duty is not only to glorify these holy champions of faith, but to follow their example in standing and fighting for the holy Orthodox Faith.

For the earthly Church of Christ is a Church militant at all times. She is a ship attacked by the waves of the sea—not only during ancient times, but also at the present time. Up to this day She suffers afflictions from slanderers,[8] and from relatives, and from false brothers; She endures persecutions and insults from different sides. There is no need to tell you, for example, about how many insults, lies, and slander which we, the servants of the Orthodox Church, have to hear. Perhaps not just one time you yourself have had to take abuse and all kinds of angry words that slandered the Orthodox Church. And of course, the solemn duty to protect the Orthodox Church, to stand up for the Orthodox Faith, to take care to spread the Truth, lies above all upon the pastors of the Church. For it is not in vain that they are called the watchmen of the house of God (cf. Ezek. 3:17; 33:1–9). And here you are added to their ranks today.

And as earthly warriors receive a weapon for the fight, so you are given a spiritual weapon—this holy cross. The Cross is our strength, firmness, power—our shield, victory, and confirmation.[9] As you place your cross on your chest, repeat the words of the Holy Church which

---

[8] Literally, "tongues."

[9] These words describing the Cross of the Lord are taken from various hymns for the Elevation of the Holy Cross (September 14).

we hear often these days: "Invincible, incomprehensible, divine power of the true and life-giving Cross, forsake not us sinners."[10]

---

[10] Sung during Great Compline in Great Lent.

A SERMON [11]

Preached after the liturgy at the presentation of the episcopal staff to the Most Reverend Raphael, Bishop of Brooklyn, at the Syro-Arabian Orthodox temple, at St. Nicholas Syrian Orthodox Cathedral in Brooklyn, New York, on February 29, 1904

THE MOST REVEREND BISHOP RAPHAEL, beloved brother in Christ! I greet you upon this joyful and great event in your life. "Today everything is filled with light and joy here" [from the Paschal *troparion*]. The American Church rejoices for you, since with your tonsure as a hierarch the number of workers that are so longed for in the field of the Lord increases. Your relatives and your fellow countrymen, the Orthodox Syrians, rejoice, since today they receive what they may only have dreamed about. Your heart leaps up with joy as well, since today you are called to the highest service in the Church of God, the symbol of which is the hierarchical staff that you receive from my hand. But while rejoicing and thanking God, Who showed His favor to you in this manner, grasp with your mind and heart that although you are vested with high authority, yet its symbol that is given to you is simple and modest—a staff that reminds us of the staff of a shepherd.

Christ, the head of all pastors, told His disciples, "the princes of the Gentiles exercise dominion over them, and they who are great exercise authority over them. But it shall not be so among you: but whosoever will be great among you, let him be your minister; and

---

[11] Printed in *Amerikansky Pravoslavny Vestnik*, 1904, #6, pp. 97–98.

whosoever will be chief among you, let him be your servant: Even as the Son of Man came not to be ministered unto but to minister" (Matt. 20:25–28). Therefore spiritual authority represents service to others, those who are lower in status; and the "hierarchical service is not an irresponsible dominion, not a repressive autocracy, but fatherly care."

This fatherly care for people is most often presented in the Word of God with the image of a shepherd tending his flock, which is why the shepherd's staff is its symbol. Christ Himself calls Himself the Good Shepherd (John 10:12); and in the Old Testament the Lord Adonai says this: "As a shepherd seeketh out his flock in the day when there is thick darkness and cloud, among the sheep that are scattered, so will I seek out My sheep and will deliver them out of all places where they have been scattered in the cloudy and dark day. And I will bring them out from the people, and gather them from the nations, and will bring them to their own land; and I will feed them in a good pasture; their folds shall be there, and there they shall lie down and rest in perfect prosperity, and in fat pasture. I will seek that which is lost, and bring again that which was driven away, and will bind up that which was broken, and will strengthen that which was sick, and will guard the strong" (Ezek. 34:12–14, 16).

Here is the example for you to imitate as well, beloved brother, and even more so, since much of what has been said above is applicable to your flock also. Your own Syrians, driven by need, have arrived here from a faraway native land to seek happiness. But how many "cloudy and dark days" do they have to see here as well! Like sheep without a shepherd, they are scattered over the face of this land. Simple-hearted, trusting like children, they have often become prey of the "beasts of the land" (Ezek. 34:28); and they did not have someone who "seeks and brings back" until your very arrival here. From now on, better times are coming for them also: scattered among different places, they gather into parishes, churches are built for them, and pastors are found that tend to them in "good pasture."

And now, for the further success of this pastoral effort, you are vested with the Hierarchical [i.e., bishop's] power as well.

Beloved brother! A pastor tends to his sheep with a staff in his hands; with it he leads them to the pasture; with the help of it he seeks the lost sheep and rescues the stolen one. As a good shepherd, accept this staff of kindness as well (Zech. 11:7), and with it tend to the flock entrusted to you in the pasture of Christ.

A SERMON [12]

Preached on the day of His Majesty Emperor's birth, in the San Francisco Cathedral, on May 19, 1904 (May 6, os)

TODAY WE, BRETHREN, celebrate the birthday of our Sovereign. The day of birth is important in the life of every man, and a joyful day it happens to be. "A woman when she is in travail hath sorrow, because her hour is come: but as soon as she is delivered of the child, she remembereth no more the anguish, for joy that a man is born into the world" (John 16:21).

Life is a precious gift of God, the greatest good, which opens for man a number of other blessings—in nature around him; in his own being, spiritually and bodily; and in the society of people that surround him. Nevertheless, after the fall of our forefathers, there is no complete and perfect joy on earth. "Which earthly joy is not related to sorrow!" [13]

In the life of each one of us there happen to be quite a few sorrows and sufferings, and they are the lot of all born on earth. And since, according to the word of the most wise Solomon, the tsar himself is a mortal person as well, similar to all, and equally with everyone else has a common entrance into life and the same going out; and having been born, the first voice he reveals is crying, similar to all (cf. Wisdom 7:1–6). Then, of course, there are sorrows and sufferings in the life of our beloved Sovereign.

---

[12] Printed in the *Amerikansky Pravoslavny Vestnik*, 1904, #10, pp. 181–183.

[13] From a hymn in the Orthodox funeral service, composed by St. John of Damascus (8th century).

May it not seem strange, brethren, that on this joyful day of our Sovereign's birth, we speak of his sorrows and sufferings. An excuse for this may be found also in the fact that the birth of the Sovereign falls on the day when the Orthodox Church remembers the Long-suffering Job. Of course, this coincidence perhaps seems random to some. But there is nothing that is random to the eye of the believing man. And even more so in such important events as the birth of rulers, whom God Himself raises up, the right ones for the time (cf. Sirach 10:4). Therefore, it is not a random but rather a mysterious coincidence of the birthday of our Sovereign with the day of remembrance of the Long-suffering Job.

The Holy Righteous Job: who has not heard how this "opulent man, abounding in wealth and cattle, was shorn of riches and glory; he who had many children is childless and homeless; he who was formerly on the throne is now naked and covered with sores" (from the Canon of St. Andrew of Crete). Through the permission of God, terrible afflictions overtake this righteous man, and blow after blow strike him. One after another, the messengers come to him with sad news about the loss of his entire estate; and "while he was yet speaking, there came also another" (Job 1:18) telling about the death of all of his children and servants; and after some time he himself is stricken with a terrible disease (leprosy).

Was it easy for Job to endure all of this? Was his flesh of brass, and was his strength the strength of stones? (cf. Job 6:12). If one weighed his grief, it would surely be heavier than the sand of the sea (cf. Job 6:2–3). And yet Job courageously endures the misfortunes that have befallen him: "in all of this he did not sin with his lips" (Job 2:10); and he does not grumble against God.

But there still are wounds that await him, more painful than the external misfortunes. Three friends of his, who came to visit him in his misfortune, instead of comforting him, started accusing him of various vices, since they thought that the Lord was punishing him for his sins. "Is not thy wickedness great?"—this is how one of them speaks—"and thine iniquities infinite? For thou hast taken a pledge from thy brother for nought, and stripped the naked of their clothing. Thou hast not given water to the weary to drink, and thou hast withheld bread from the hungry. But as for the mighty man, he had the earth. Thou hast sent widows away empty, and the arms of the fatherless have been broken!" (Job 22:5–9, KJV). These kinds of reproaches they threw at him of whom the Lord Himself spoke that "there is none like him in the earth—a perfect and an upright man, one that feareth God, and escheweth evil" (Job 1:8).

How could Job not say to his friends, "How long will ye vex my soul, and destroy me with words? These ten times have ye reproached me: ye are not ashamed that ye make yourselves strange to me" (Job 19:2–3). "Do you imagine speeches of reproof? Ye fall on the orphan, and ye dig a pit for your friend" (Job 6:26–27). "Shall vain words have an end?" (Job 16:3). "Have pity upon me, O ye my friends: for the hand of God hath touched me. Why do ye persecute me as God, and are not satisfied with my flesh?" (Job 19:21-22).

Let us bring ourselves, brethren, from the ancient times to the present days—from "the greatest of the sons of the east" (Job 1:3) to the Supreme Leader of our motherland. Great is our land, and it is endowed with generous gifts from the Lord. It is called Holy Russia, and it is inhabited by people whose faith is known throughout the world; its tsars are called "the most pious" ones, and not in name only, but according to their lives.

But according to the unknown designs of God, lately misfortunes strike various places of our vast motherland. To our Tsar, as at one time to Job, one after another word has come—now of harvest failure, now of destruction due to earthquake, avalanches, now of floods. And in very recent days a war has joined all of it, with all its horrors, losses, victims—a war that was forced upon our Most Peace-Loving Tsar. And is it easy for our Tsar to bear all these misfortunes? Does he not suffer pain for his native land?

But even more painful wounds are inflicted upon his heart. Just as Job was not understood by his friends, and suffered terribly from that, in the same way the Russian people and their Crown-Bearing Leader until this day cannot gain proper estimation from other nations. The best of their intentions are met with mistrust and suspected of insincerity; terrible designs are attributed to them; the most honorable of their undertakings are misinterpreted, twisted, laughed at. Everything that is good is met with silence, and their shortcomings are blown exceedingly out of proportion and announced for the whole world to hear. Our country is presented as being the most uneducated, while some Asian nations, like Japan, are said to be far more culturally advanced than we are. Our government is, supposedly, the most ineffective, which only the Russian people can tolerate.

Let us not enumerate further these mindless words—they are already well-known to all of us who live abroad.

"Plead my cause, O Lord, with them that strive with me: fight against them that fight against me" (Ps. 34:1). And to our beloved Tsar, together with the well-being of Moses, the courage of David, and the wisdom of Solomon, give the "patience of Job" as well. Help him and the whole of the Russian nation to believe in the truth of Christ, in the righteousness of their cause, and to adhere to the right paths of the Lord as before, no matter what our ill-wishers say. Then the Lord will not abandon us, but will help and uphold us with the right hand of His righteousness, and all they that are incensed against us shall be ashamed and confounded (cf. Is. 41:10–11).

"Ye have heard of the patience of Job and have seen the end of the Lord" (James 5:11). The Lord returned the losses of Job and gave him twice as much as he had before, and blessed the latter end of Job more than his beginnings (cf. Job 42:10–17). We believe and hope that today the Merciful Lord, "having punished us with a brief visitation of sorrow, will fill exceedingly our hearts with joy and cheer."[14] Amen.

---

[14] Source unknown.

A RESPONSE[15]

*To His Holiness Meletius, Patriarch of
Antioch, in the Summer of 1904*

YOUR BEATITUDE, Most Blessed Kir Meletius, beloved Father
and Archpastor in Christ!

The Paschal greeting and fatherly embrace of Your Holiness again
has filled our hearts with joy because of the mercy shown by the
Lord to the sons and daughters of the glorious Antiochian apostolic
see who were cast to this overseas land long ago. And here, through
the love of the Most Holy Ruling Synod of All Russia and the generosity of the Orthodox Russian Sovereign, they have gained for
themselves an Archpastor in the person of the like-minded pastor Fr.
Raphael, who previously had labored for their spiritual salvation as
well. We thank Providence, Who has blessed the sincere prayers and
the daring petitions of our unworthiness for this.

It is with satisfaction we testify that in the election, confirmation,
and consecration of this valiant man, we were guided by the confidence that the most honorable Fr. Raphael, who is so pleasing to the
heart of Your Holiness and your co-workers, has never interrupted
the closest spiritual tie with his mother-Church of Antioch, and has
always remained in love and devotion to the most worthy angelic
primate of this glorious Patriarchate, even though the Lord determined for him to succeed in the feats of apostolic service, in the role
of a humble pastor and in the high rank of the Archpastor, not in

---

[15] Printed in *Amerikansky Pravoslavny Vestnik*, 1904, #12, pp. 225–226.

his homeland, but among the workers of another great and glorious branch of the true vineyard of Christ, the Russian Church.

Responding with heartfelt gratitude to the cordial message of Your Holiness, we pray that there may be no diminishing of Your hierarchical love and prayerful remembrance of our American flock, which holds in its bosom the sons of all Orthodox nations, and guards here the holy testaments of the truth of Christ from temptations and false teachings with which this country, rich with material blessings but distant from spiritual perfection, is abundant. We hope that Your Benevolence will not deprive the newly ordained Bishop Raphael of the necessary guidance and advice on all the paths of his difficult mission. And we believe that this care will be received by this most beloved brother of ours as the best and the most pleasant greeting from the East, from his motherland, and by us as the pledge of that blessed unity which alone can lead the work of all Orthodox nations and Churches to the desired end, bypassing the differences in tongues and nations, and bestowing a mutual brotherly embrace to all those who carry the commandment of Christ.

Having entered now the days sanctified by the celebration of the Descent of the Holy Spirit on the Apostles, and with remembrance of the all-potent action of the grace of God, with which this small company of disciples of Christ, firm in unity of heart and mind, was moved to accomplish the great feat of bringing the Good News to all nations and countries, we pray to the Almighty and humbly ask Your prayers as well, that the Lord may count us among that company also, and may exceedingly establish our unworthiness for this feat, along with our co-workers, in the holy endeavor here. And may this country, which has seen the most glorious Orthodox episcopal tonsure in Bishop Raphael's consecration for the first time, be worthy to see this mystery many times in the times to come, for the return of our own lost sheep, as well as those who do not belong to it, into the bounds of the True Church.

Always exalting the name of Your Beatitude along with our hierarchs in our earnest prayers, we entreat Your Holiness not to leave us without a blessing and prayers, which aid every undertaking that is good and pleasing to God. Christ is in our midst; and He is and forever shall be.

With filial devotion to Your Beatitude, Tikhon, Bishop of the Aleutians and North America.

A LETTER[16]

*Of the most humble servant to Tsar Nikolai
Aleksandrovich, on April 29, 1904*

Your Imperial Majesty!
Most merciful Lord!
In this war with Japan that has befallen the Russian State at this
time, the subjects of Russia who have been cast to far-off America,
in their thoughts and feelings are entirely present in the native land,
and they take keenly to heart what is taking place in the Far East.
We mourn here the Russian losses also, and rejoice at the valiant
display of courage and self-sacrifice of the Christ-loving troops. And
just as in the temples of holy Russia, prayers are offered here as well
to the God Who is "firm in battle," that He may give victory over
the enemy, and that He may bring closer the end of the war, forced
upon the Most Peace-Loving Leader of the Russian people. These
feelings are completely shared with us by the parishioners of various ethnicities in the North American diocese, and in particular the
Russian immigrants from Austria, in common with us in blood, who
have become in common with us in the Orthodox Faith also. Being
inspired with these feelings, all of us—the clergy, and the brotherhoods, and the parishioners also—ardently wish to express our love
in action for great Russia, and to help it at least in something in
this present war. For this purpose, we dare to present, through the
mediation of Mr. Ober-Procurator of the Holy Synod, our first mite

---

[16] Printed in *Amerikansky Pravoslavny Vestnik*, 1904, #13, pp. 245–246.

for the benefit of the Red Cross and for the strengthening of the Russian Navy. My Lord, our mite is small compared to the large donations being received in Russia. But may the fact that there are few Orthodox people in this country—and often they themselves "require mercy and help"—be an excuse for us. Yet they are rich in love for Russia, in sincere compassion for it in this present war, and in ardent desire for its fortitude and success, and for a glorious reign of long years for its Sovereign.

Your Imperial Highness Most Merciful Lord's most loyal servant, and an earnest solicitor of God, Tikhon, Bishop of the Aleutians and North America.

San Francisco, April 29, 1904.

RESOLUTIONS[17]

1. On the occasion of establishing the Alaskan Vicariate, #729

DECEMBER 4, 1903. Thanks be to God and the Authorities who care for the needs of the Orthodox inhabitants of Alaska. I am confident that they will receive the news about the establishment of a vicariate in Alaska with the most lively joy. And I am nurturing the hope that they will themselves gladden the Archpastor, who is closest to them, with their devotion and obedience to the Orthodox Church, and with their piousness.

[I hereby stipulate] For the Alaskan clergy to honor the name of the Most Reverend Vicar Bishop at prayer services after the name of the Diocesan Hierarch [i.e., Bishop Tikhon]; and to bring, as of January 1, 1904, all matters that this latter one has previously dealt with directly to the Most Reverend Vicar, who is given the right to appoint, move, and dismiss upon request priests, psalm singers, and teachers in Alaska, and to have immediate supervision over all of the Church-related matters there.

—Bishop Tikhon

2. Resolution of His Eminence, #730

December 4, 1903. To print in the *Amerikansky Pravoslavny Vestnik* regarding the establishment of a vicariate in Alaska, and about the appointment of Archimandrite Innocent as Bishop of Alaska.

---

[17] Printed in the *Amerikansky Pravoslavny Vestnik*, 1904, #2 (page is missing).

And for the Spiritual Board to inform also the Office of the Russian Imperial Embassy in Washington and in Sitka, and also to require:

- For the Alaskan clergy to honor the name of the Most Reverend Vicar Bishop at prayer services after the name of the Diocesan Hierarch [i.e., Bishop Tikhon]; and to bring, as of January 1, 1904, all matters that this latter one has previously dealt with directly to the Most Reverend Vicar, who is given the right to appoint, move, and dismiss upon request priests, psalm singers, and teachers in Alaska, and to have immediate supervision over all of the Church-related matters there.

- For the Dean of the Sitka Cathedral to make it his concern to provide an accommodation for the Most Reverend Vicar at the Sitka Hierarchical house.

The position of the Dean of Sitka is terminated as of January 1st. From the parishes of his deanery, to place the Seattle parish under the authority of the Spiritual Board, and the Sitka, Juneau, and Kilisnoo parishes under direct supervision of the Most Reverend Vicar as the ones closest to him; and to transfer the rest to the Unalashka Deanery, which in that case may more likely be called the "Alaskan Deanery."
—Bishop Tikhon

3. On the occasion of establishing the Syro-Arabian Vicariate with a cathedra in the city of Brooklyn[18]

February 18, 1904. The Russian Spiritual Authorities have always paid attention to the needs of the Orthodox Syrian Arabs, and the establishment of the Brooklyn Vicariate in North America is a further confirmation of this attention.

---

[18] Printed in *Amerikansky Pravoslavny Vestnik*, 1904, #5, p. 78.

I greet from my heart our Orthodox Syrian Arabs with the fact that in the person of Archimandrite Raphael they receive their national bishop. All of the Orthodox Arabs in America are under his direct supervision, and the name of the Bishop of Brooklyn is to be honored at prayer services along with the name of the Diocesan Hierarch [i.e., Bishop Tikhon] in all Syro-Arabian parishes in North America.

The naming of Archimandrite Raphael will take place February 28/March 12 at the New York Cathedral, and the tonsure on February 29, the third Sunday of Great Lent, at the Brooklyn Syro-Arabian church.

Fr. Raphael is relieved of the duties of the censor of the *Amerikansky Pravoslavny Vestnik* upon his ordination into the rank of a bishop, and the Diocesan Authorities announce an acknowledgment to him for his work as censor. The censorship of the *Vestnik* now is entrusted to a member of the Censorship Committee, Priest John Kochurov.[19]

—Bishop Tikhon

---

[19] This man will become the first clergyman to be murdered by the Bolsheviks; he was proclaimed as St. John Kochurov, Protomartyr of the Soviet Yoke, by the Church of Russia in 1994.

A SERMON[20]

Preached at the Vespers service on the eve of the blessing of the side chapel in honor of the Nativity of the Mother of God at St. Nicholas Cathedral in New York City, on October 21, 1904

A<small>T</small> V<small>ESPERS</small>, in the first *paremia*[21] a Biblical narration was read, brethren, about how at one time Jacob had to flee from the wrath of his brother Esau, leave his paternal home, and go to a land far and unknown to him. Not just once on his way did unpleasant thoughts come to his mind: What awaits him ahead? How will he live in the foreign land? With these uneasy thoughts he falls asleep one time, and he sees in a dream a ladder, which rests with its lower end on the earth, and with its top it reaches the sky. Upon it the angels descended and ascended, and at the top of it God Himself was sitting. And Jacob hears the voice of God: "I am the God of Abraham and Isaac, your father. Do not be afraid. The land whereon thou liest, to thee will I give it; and thy seed shall widen out from here to the sea, to the north and to the east. I will keep thee in all the places whither thou goest, for I will not leave thee" (Gen. 28:13–15; condensed).

I find something similar to this Biblical narration in your life as well, brethren. Due to various reasons you left your dear homeland, your fatherly home, and went to a faraway country, unknown to you, over the sea, at the other end of the world. It was not just once along

---

[20] Printed in *Amerikansky Pravoslavny Vestnik*, 1904, #21, pp. 409–410.

[21] In the Orthodox Church, a passage from Scripture that is read on feast days.

the way that thoughts troubled you as well about what awaits you in a foreign land, how would you live among strangers, how would you do without God's temples, with which Holy Russia is so rich and which are so loved by the Russian people.

And so? Does the voice of God not sound in you as well? "I am the God of your fathers, the God of the Russian land; do not be afraid. I will preserve you in all your paths, and will multiply you and spread your seed in this land."

And do we not see how the Russian Orthodox people multiply and are strengthened here? Recall, brethren, how not long ago there were only a few of you in this city, only a few dozen, and how at first you did not have a temple at all. Then for several years you had to pray in a cramped house of strangers; and now you have a capacious, splendid temple. Now there are no longer dozens of you, but whole hundreds and thousands.

It is the same in other parts of this country—the number of the Russian people keeps growing, and the number of our temples is increasing on the face of this land "from the north and the sea, from the east and the west";[22] Holy Orthodoxy is growing and being strengthened here. If only the Russian people will remain faithful to the God of the Russian land, and keep the Faith of their fathers, the Orthodox Faith, then the Merciful God will not withhold His blessings here.

And our advocate in this, the intercessor for us sinners, is the Most Holy Theotokos—whom, according to the interpretation of the Holy Fathers, the ladder seen by Jacob prefigured. She connects heaven with earth, God with people; and She sends down the mercies of God upon mankind, and upon the Russian people in particular. The Most Holy Virgin has been the Most Pure Mother of the Russian region from long ago, the triumphant leader of the Russian nation, throughout almost a thousand years of the history of our motherland. It is not just one time that She saved it from an invasion

---

[22] This phrase appears in Ode Eight of the Paschal Canon.

of foreigners, from inner strife, from hunger and devastation. And here today we celebrate in honor of the icon of the Mother of God of Kazan; and we recall how 300 years ago, through the intercession of the Mother of God, the punishment of our homeland was superseded with mercy, and the capital city of Moscow was liberated from the enemies, the Poles.[23]

And we did wisely, brethren, when we entrusted our Brotherhood here in this foreign land to the protection of the Most Holy Theotokos, the zealous intercessor of the Russian people, and named it in honor of the Nativity of the Theotokos. In commemoration of the Birth of the Theotokos Brotherhood of yours, which tried to have a church here from the very beginning, and which supports it with its offerings, and beautifies it, we dedicate this chapel also in honor of the Nativity of the Theotokos, which "proclaims joy to the whole universe, since today is the beginning of our salvation, since the intercessor for our life is born, the annulment of the curse, bestowing the blessing" (from the festal hymn).[24] Therefore the Holy Church calls out—"This is the day of the Lord, rejoice in it, O people!" (cf. Ps. 118:24, KJV).

Rejoice as well, Russian Orthodox people who live here! The Theotokos Herself is your Guardian and Intercessor. And while glorifying Her most glorious Nativity, pray to Her earnestly, that She may deliver you from every need and sorrow!

---

[23] The expulsion of the Poles from Moscow in 1612 marked the end of the terrible Time of Troubles for the Russian people.

[24] From the Great Vespers service on the Feast of the Nativity of the Theotokos (September 8).

YEAR 1905

56. Homily addressed to the newly ordained priest Fr. Michael Andreades, March 25th, 1905.

57. A sermon preached on the anniversary of the holy crowning; March 14, 1905.

58. A sermon preached on the 14th of August, 1905, on the occasion of the relocation of the hierarchical cathedra from San Francisco to New York.

59. A sermon preached at the presentation of the staff to Archimandrite Sebastian (Dabovich).

60. A sermon preached at the first service at the New York Cathedral, on September 25th, 1905.

61. Opinions on the issues proposed for discussion at the Pomestni Council of the All-Russia Church.

62. A sermon preached on the Feast of the Nativity, December 25th, 1905.

63. Notable remarks.

64. Added notes.

HOMILY[1]

Addressed to the newly ordained priest, Fr. Michael Andreades,
at Holy Trinity Cathedral, San Francisco, on March 25, 1905

ICONGRATULATE YOU, beloved in Christ, Priest Michael, with the
grace of the priesthood. Through the Providence of God you have
become a servant of the Word of God[2] on this important day when
the Holy Church solemnly remembers how "The one without beginning begins, and the Word becomes flesh" (cf. John 1:14).[3]

"Today is the beginning of our salvation,"[4] and you are called
today to promote the salvation of your spiritual children. Remember
this remarkable coincidence, and draw from it edifying lessons for
yourself in your new ministry.

Today you received the Grace of the Holy Spirit—and this
gift, according to the word of the Apostle, you must stir up within
yourself (2 Tim. 1:6). How? By which means? The example of the
Most Holy Virgin will show you. For when the Archangel Gabriel
announced to her that she would conceive a child by the Holy Spirit,
she said, "I am the handmaid of the Lord; be it unto me according
to thy word" (Luke 1:38). With these words she expressed great faith
in God. How could the Most Holy Virgin not be in doubt when she

---

[1] Printed in *Amerikansky Pravoslavny Vestnik*, 1905, #9, pp. 164–165.

[2] Literally, "hypostasis of the Word."

[3] "Today He who knows no beginning now begins to be, and the Word is made
flesh" (hymn for Matins for the Nativity of our Lord; *Festal Menaion*, p. 286).

[4] These are the opening words of the *troparion* for the Annunciation.

heard the strange words of the Archangel? How could she give birth to a child without a husband?

Well, her relative, Zacharias, doubted the words of the same Archangel—even though he was a priest, and even though there are examples in the Old Testament of what was announced to him would happen.[5] But the Mother of God did not doubt. She believed in the omnipotence of God, in the fact that "when He wills, the order of nature is overcome."[6] And although she did not know how this birth without a husband would take place, she believed that God was able to make it happen. And therefore she answered the Archangel with faith, "Be it unto me according to thy word."

You, beloved, will always be involved with the depths of God. Who can perceive the mind of God? His ways are unknown and His judgments are unsearchable (cf. Rom. 11:33). And of course, in order to teach faith to others you yourself must first surrender to the fact that God is incomprehensible. "The world is amazed at how the unchanging God could become perfect man, and how the Virgin could give birth";[7] and you, being amazed by the mystery, exclaim in honesty, "I believe, Lord; give and multiply faith in me" (cf. Mark 9:24).

With the words "I am the handmaid of the Lord" (Luke 1:38), the Most Holy Virgin also expressed deep humility. She was given the highest honor to become the Mother of God; through this she is elevated not only higher than all men, but she becomes greater than the heavenly forces, "more honorable than the Cherubim and more glorious beyond compare than the Seraphim."[8] And yet, at the same time, how far even a shadow of self-exaltation is from her! She is the Queen of Heaven and the Mother of God; yet in her humility, she calls herself "the handmaid of the Lord."

---

[5] That is, that his barren wife would conceive a child; such examples in the Old Testament are Sarah, the mother of Isaac; Rachel, the mother of Joseph and Benjamin; and Hannah, the mother of the Prophet Samuel.

[6] From a *stikheron* for Great Vespers for the Annunciation.

[7] An adaptation of part of a hymn for Great Vespers for the Annunciation.

[8] From a very frequently sung hymn to the Theotokos.

You, beloved, have been clothed today in glory and honor. You are a priest of God the Highest, a pastor of souls, a servant of the mysteries of God,[9] of which the angels themselves wish to partake. You are given power that even they do not have. But do not take pride in that. Remember that this is not because of your deeds, and not on account of your merits, but it is because of the grace of God, because of the mercy of the Incarnate Son of God. All of our well-being is from God, and we should not even think of ourselves. Do not dare to elevate yourself above your flock, or to consider it lower than yourself; do not dream with pride about your future influence on it; and most of all, do not ever say with contempt, "Cursed are these people, since they do not know the law of God." No, consider yourself the slave of God, lower than others, to whom you have been sent by God to serve—and not to be their master, to exercise authority over them (cf. Matt. 20:25–28).

The Most Holy Virgin expressed complete obedience to the will of God with her words, her submission, and her devotion, which she displayed throughout her entire earthly life. And a pastor must not pursue his own ways, carry out his own will, and please himself; rather, he must please God. Let it be "according to thy word." Let Thy will be done, Lord. "It is no longer I who live, but Christ lives in me" (Gal. 2:20). "Listen, breathe, and see, and incline your ear and forget the home of your father" (cf. Ps. 45:10; Ps. 44:10, LXX).[10] This is how a pastor should think. And so, you—forget yourself, and fall in love with your flock, which is presented to you by God, to which you have become engaged today. And having rejected your pride, be indifferent to your personal life, and give yourself entirely to your new calling, which is high and holy.

Today is not only a religious holiday, but for the Greeks it is also a civil one. Today their liberation from the Turkish yoke is remembered.

---

[9] Probably referring to the Holy Eucharist.

[10] This psalm is interpreted in the Orthodox Tradition as referring to the Theotokos.

Being a Greek by birth, you are not indifferent to this holiday.[11] But for a true Christian, spiritual freedom—freedom from sin, from serving passions—is more valuable than freedom from external slavery, since "in Christ there is neither Greek nor Jew, neither slave nor a free man" (cf. Gal. 3:28). However, it sometimes happens that after arriving in this country, the sons of free Greece fall into spiritual slavery, serving mammon and passions; and having forgotten God, they become indifferent to their Faith. May God spare us from this kind of "freedom-slavery." We are called to freedom according to the word of the Apostle (cf. Gal. 5:1), but our freedom cannot consist of pleasing ourselves and our flesh.

Grow firm in these thoughts, and teach your flock the same. Then you will save yourself, and you will save the spiritual flock entrusted to you.

---

[11] March 25, 1821, was the day the Greek Revolution against the Ottoman Turks began; hence, March 25 is celebrated every year by the Greeks as Independence Day—as well as the Feast of the Annunciation.

A SERMON[12]

*Preached at the New York Cathedral on the anniversary
of the holy crowning; on May 14, 1905*

TODAY, BELOVED COMPATRIOTS, we remember the Holy
Crowning of our Sovereign, and on this day I consider it appropriate to talk to you about the autocratic power which is distinctive
of the Russian tsars.

We who live far from the motherland, in a foreign land, among
people who know little or nothing at all about our country and its
regulations, quite often have to hear criticism, censure, and ridicule
of the institutions that are native and dear to us. These kinds of
attacks are most often directed against the autocracy, which is one
of the foundations of the Russian State. To many here it seems to be
some sort of a "scarecrow," an Eastern despotism, a tyranny, an Asian
thing. All of the failures, shortcomings, and disorderliness of the
Russian land are attributed to it. Russia, they say, will always remain
a colossus with clay feet until it introduces in its land a Western-style
constitution, order based on law, and a constituent assembly. And
following the words of these kinds of faultfinders, our homegrown
politicians have started to yell lately in Russia, "away with autocracy."

We cannot dissuade all those who wish to remain under delusion—those whose eyes do not see and ears do not hear. But on you,
who live abroad and love your native land from this faraway place,

---

[12] Printed in *Amerikansky Pravoslavny Vestnik*, 1905, #10, pp. 184–186.

lies a special duty to explain and acquaint the local honest thinkers with what the autocracy in Russia really is.

Autocratic power means that this power does not depend on any human power; it does not draw anything from the latter, is not limited by it, and has within itself the source of its being and strength. And for what purpose does it exist? The Jews asked the Prophet Samuel for a king for themselves so that he might judge and protect them (1 Sam. 8:5, 19–20). And the psalm singer David prays for his son Solomon, "Give the king Thy judgments, O God, and Thy righteousness unto the king's son, that he shall judge Thy people with righteousness; he shall judge the poor of the people, he shall save the sons of the needy and humble the oppressor; he shall rescue a poor one from a mighty one and a needy one who has no helper" (Ps. 72:1, 2, 4, 12; KJV).

This means the tsar's power must guard the law and righteousness, protecting the subjects from violence and especially those who are destitute and crippled, who do not have any other intercessors and protection. And for this reason it has to be autocratic and independent, not limited by either the powerful or the rich. Otherwise, it could not fulfill its purpose, since it would have to constantly tremble for its fate. For in order not to be deposed, it would have to please the rich, the powerful, and the influential, and to serve the truth in the way it is understood by the latter, to deliver the judgment of men and not of God.

It is this kind of autocratic power that exists in our motherland, which arrived at it by way of long suffering from the internal strife of the princes and from the heavy yoke of non-Orthodox enemies. The tsar in Russia possesses power and freedom of action in such a measure as it is possibly allowed for a man. Nothing and nobody restrains him—neither the claims of the parties, nor the benefits of any class at the expense of another. He stands immeasurably higher than any party, any titles, and any fortunes. He is impartial and unbiased; ingratiation, servility, and mercenary motives are foreign to him. He does not have any need for any of that, since he is standing at the height that is inaccessible, and nobody can add or take anything away from his majesty. "He does not accept favors from the hands of his subjects, but on the contrary gives them gifts himself."[13] He cares not for his personal interests, but for the well-being of the people, so that "everything is well arranged for the benefit of the people entrusted in his care and for the glory of God."[14] The rights and the interests of all his subjects are equally dear to him, and each one of them has in him a protector and benefactor.

The tsar is the "*batiushka*"[15] for the people; this is how the people lovingly call him. Autocracy is based on the feeling of fatherly love for the people, and this love removes any hint of despotism, enslavement, and mercenary possession, which some are trying to attribute to the Russian autocracy.

And how would it not be shameful to talk about the despotism of the tsar's power when its bearers—let's take the sovereigns who have reigned closest to our time: Great Tsar Liberator Aleksandr ii, Wise and Righteous Tsar Aleksandr iii, and Meek and Kind Nicolas ii—are the cause of amazement and admiration of sensible people even outside of Russia! Is it not strange to speak about the tyranny of the tsarist power when a Russian person imbibes love for his tsar with the "milk of his mother," when he then nurtures within himself this love until it reaches exalted adoration, when he displays complete obedience and loyalty towards his tsar, when our own troublemakers even deceive him and incite him to rebellion using the name of the tsar, when he is always ready to give his life for the tsar? No, despots and tyrants are feared and trembled at, but are not loved.

But they say, and especially frequently lately, that the tsarist power is only autocratic in theory, since in practice the autocracy is in the hands of the bureaucratic officials, who rule everything, who rule poorly, who create a dividing wall between the tsar and the people, so that the voice and the needs of the people do not reach the tsar ("The

---

[13] Source unknown.

[14] From the service of the Holy Crowning.

[15] "*Batiushka*" is a term of endearment that means *dear father* in Russian.

Lord is too high and the tsar is too far").[16] The people know their needs better than the officials or the tsar, and better understand their own benefit and usefulness; and therefore the people themselves should be in charge of all of that and rule, as is done in other states.

Indeed, the tsarist power has its own agencies, and these agencies are run by humans who are not deprived of shortcomings and imperfections, and who arouse fair criticism against themselves sometimes. But let us ask if there is a place where this does not happen? Let somebody show us this blessed land! We, here, live in a state where people rule themselves and choose their officials. Are they always up to the mark? And has serious abuse of power never taken place here?

They say that under tsarist power this type of abuse is more common since with it there is a great opportunity for bureaucracy, which has seized all the reins of government into its hands. The bureaucracy is especially attacked these days, although bitter historical experience shows that the criticizers of bureaucracy become just as bureaucratic, and sometimes even worse, as soon as they receive power into their hands.

The bureaucracy, however, is not associated with the essence of the autocratic power; and the tsar, apart from it, enters into "direct" contact with the people. He listens to the voice of the people regarding the "questions of the state organizational improvement," and he receives representatives even from the "strikers" (which does not always happen even in the republics). And in tireless caring about the well-being and improvement of the state, "he draws upon the most worthy persons who are invested with the trust of the people, selected from the folk to take part in the preliminary formulation and discussion of legislative proposals."[17]

And as far as people's government that is so pleasing to them is concerned, it is a complete delusion to suppose that the people

---

[16] This is an old Russian proverb.

[17] From an edict issued by Tsar Nicolas II to the Minister of the Interior A. G. Buligin in 1905. This edict laid the ground for the calling of the parliament, the Duma, that met in that same year.

themselves rule the state. It is supposed that all of the people in public meetings work out the laws and elect the officials, but this is only according to theory; and this just might be possible only in the smallest of states, consisting of one small town.

In reality, this is not the case. The masses of people, burdened with cares to provide the means for daily life and not familiar with the preeminent goals of the state, do not use their personal "autocracy"; rather, they transfer their rights to a few favorite people, those who are elected. The way the elections are held, what kinds of methods are used in order to become elected, there is no need to tell you; you have seen it here yourselves.

So the people do not rule, but those who are elected rule. And since they are not elected by all of the people but only a part of them (the majority), by a party, so then when they rule, they express the will not of all of the people but only of their party (and sometimes even purely their own will, since they even forget about the promises which they had poured out before their elections), and care only for the well-being and interests of their own party. And the opposing party they treat in a despotic manner, oppressing it in every way and pushing it out of power.

And this kind of imperfect state some want to introduce even in our country—often only for the reason that other people, who are more knowledgeable than we are, have it. They forget, however, that every people have their own special qualities and their own history, and what might be good for one turns out to be unsuitable for another. Only those institutions are sound and valid whose roots are established deep in the past of a particular nation, and which have emerged from the qualities of its spirit.

The rule of law (constitution, parliamentarianism) has these kinds of roots in some western nations. But in our country, Russia, autocracy emerged from the depths of the people's spirit and is most common to it. Everyone must consider this. And to experiment with changing the order of the state is not a trivial matter; it could disturb the very foundations of the state instead of improving things and fixing some shortcomings. May he who has ears, hear!

As for us brethren, let us pray to the Lord that He further preserve the Autocratic Tsar for Russia and grant him wisdom and power to judge the people in truth, and that He preserve the Russian state in peace and without sorrow.

A SERMON [18]

*Preached at the farewell liturgy in San Francisco
on the occasion of the relocation of the archpastoral
cathedra from there, on August 14, 1905*

WITHOUT A DOUBT, for all of you, brethren, it is well known how our Lord Jesus Christ during His earthly life traveled through the cities of Judea, taught the people, healed the sick; and how people followed Him everywhere, sought Him to spend time in their place, to stay with them for some time longer. But Christ responded to those requests by saying that it was necessary to bring the Good News to other cities as well (cf. Mark 1:38). And in the same manner the Holy Apostles, having stayed several months and sometimes even years in a certain country or town, went on to preach about Christ in other places, although they were asked to stay longer in those places (cf. Act 18:20). And in place of themselves, they left presbyters and disciples.

I remind you of this because the needs of our Diocese and the benefit of the faithful compel us as well to leave this city—this time, not for visiting other places and then returning back here, but to permanently move from here, along with our Consistory,[19] to another city (New York), and to come here only during the summer months.

Many of you probably wish that the Bishop would continue to stay here, since you are used to this order of things, and the Hierarchical

---

[18] Printed in *Amerikansky Pravoslavny Vestnik*, 1905, #17, pp. 331–333.

[19] The Consistory was the bureaucratic team of the Diocese.

service is more splendid also. Yet it is more beneficial if I move from here to another place.

This parish is the oldest in the States. It has been 35 years since the Bishops started to live in San Francisco; and at the time when they moved here from Alaska, this parish was the only one in the States. But then through the Providence of God for His Holy Church, ten to fifteen years ago parishes started being established in other places also. And since the wave of Slavic and Russian immigration to this country, and especially to the eastern states, has been increasing more and more, our churchly undertakings there have grown as well. The numbers of the faithful have grown, churches have been erected, brotherhoods established, and schools opened. All of this requires direct stewardship and care by the Bishop—and therefore, his immediate presence in that place, since this work is still new.

As far as your church community is concerned, as I said, it is the oldest one and has already become an established one. Therefore, it can be left in the care of the presbyter, whom you are well familiar with, as he is with you.

Of course, sadness steals into your hearts at the thought that San Francisco is losing its status, so to say, with the move of the Hierarchical cathedra. But I will point out to you, brethren, an example of how one should treat this kind of "diminishment." Here is the Forerunner of Christ, John the Baptist. The whole of Judea and the whole area of Jordan came out to him and were baptized, confessing their sins to him. He has many disciples, and he tells the truth to anyone without fear; people honor him, and King Herod himself fears him.

But then comes Christ and everybody goes to Him; and John is abandoned even by some of his disciples. John, however, does not have a place for sorrow and ill-wishing when this happens; as he says, "A man cannot take upon himself anything except it be given to him from heaven; I am not the Christ, but I am sent before Him; he that has the bride is the bridegroom, but the friend of the bridegroom, who stands and hears him, rejoices greatly because of the bridegroom's voice; this my joy, therefore, is fulfilled. He must increase, but I must decrease" (John 3:27–30).

Likewise you, brethren, should not be saddened by the diminishing of your city's status, but rejoice about the elevation of the other city. Christ said, "Both he that soweth, and he that reapeth, may rejoice together" (John 4:36). It happens often in the spiritual, divine world that one person sows but the fruits are reaped by another. But if the first person is a true Christian and acts for the sake of God and goodness and not for his own personal glory, then he rejoices even though the fruits of his labor are reaped by another. And here you have sown the seed of Orthodoxy in this country, you have given a start to the churches in the States, you have provided a residence for the Bishop in your place here. Now already, others are calling him to their place; and you should not be saddened, but rejoice, that you have served for the benefit of other parishes.

And so, brethren, let us go in peace. We leave you peace as well. Let the peace of God settle in you. I beg you, along with the Holy Apostle, in the name of our Lord Jesus Christ, that you be like-minded, that no divisions take place in your midst, and that you be united in one spirit and in one judgment (cf. 1 Cor. 1:10).

At the time of the Apostles, the Christians in Corinth were divided into parties according to the names of their teachers, so they would say, "I am of Paul, I am of Apollos, I am of Cephas" (1 Cor. 1:12). With us, the division into parties is according to nationality sometimes: "I am Russian, I am a Serb, I am a Greek, I am a Syrian." And some wish to bring this division into parties, where there ought to be no place for it—the Church of Christ. The holy Apostle Paul asks, "Is Christ divided? Was Paul crucified for you? Or were ye baptized in the name of Paul?" (1 Cor. 1:13).

Likewise, you, brethren, should remember that in Christ there is no Greek or Jew, no slave or free man, but Christ is everywhere and in everyone. We all have one faith, one baptism, and one God—and therefore, not discord, not division, not a proud laudation, not the striving to prevail, influence, and dominate others, but single-mindedness, love, humility, and readiness to serve others must adorn the church community.

There will soon be for you an opportunity and an occasion to express love, concord, and union in deed—I mean, the construction of your new temple. King David felt at times uncomfortable that he lived in a house of cedar while the Ark of the Covenant was in a simple tent—the Tabernacle. And he intended to start construction of the Temple. You and we, as well, I think, not just once also felt uncomfortable that our cathedral temple is located in a house, and is more like a simple Hierarchical "home-church"[20] rather than a cathedral temple.

It was not just once that repairs were made to improve it, but nevertheless in its external refinement it was far from the usual kinds of churches. And here now, with the relocation of our cathedra from here, an opportunity presents itself to replace the present temple with another, although not big in size, but more splendid in appearance, separate from the house, and such that anybody who passes by will see that this is the holy Church and not a private house.

You, perhaps, have already heard that a suitable place has been purchased for this purpose, and we intend to start construction of the temple there in the near future. And thus, you should indeed unite yourselves in this great and holy undertaking, come together, and, under the stewardship of your pastor, erect a temple for the glory of God and for the salvation of your souls.

May the Lord help you in this undertaking! I will also endeavor as well, upon my departure from you, to remember you, that you may excel in faith and piety. And today I call the blessing of the Lord upon you through His grace and His love for mankind. Amen.

---

[20] The words used in the text are "*krestovaya tserkov,*" which means a church located in the home of a metropolitan or a bishop where the owner can appoint the time of the service and add or reduce prayer services.

A SERMON[21]

Preached at the presentation of the staff to Archimandrite
Sebastian (Dabovich) in Chicago, on September 18, 1905

IGREET YOU, Reverend Father Archimandrite Sebastian,[22] for your ordination into the order of Archimandrite, and your appointment to be the head of the Serbian mission in America. As a native Serbian, you were previously entrusted by the Diocesan authority[23] to be in charge here of one Serbian parish or another. Today, though, you are called to a higher service—you are entrusted with the care of all the Serbian churches of our vast Diocese, and the spiritual needs of all the Serbian people who reside in America.

You know how many of them are scattered here; how often they wander as sheep without a pastor; how they end up in the stranger's "yard"; how, having arrived here to earn money and to enrich themselves, some fall into spiritual poverty and lose, in this non-Orthodox country, the great spiritual treasure of the old land—the holy Orthodox Faith, and love for the Slavic people, and adherence to the good customs of the fathers. Our highest Church authority,[24] which cares for our welfare, which is always concerned with the needs of the

---

[21] Printed in *Amerikansky Pravoslavny Vestnik*, 1905, #19, pp. 373–374.

[22] This is Archimandrite Sebastian Dabovich (1863–1940), the first American-born Orthodox priest, who was glorified as a Saint by the Church of Serbia in 2015.

[23] Referring to the authority of the Russian Missionary Diocese in America.

[24] St. Tikhon is referring here to the Holy Synod of the Church in Russia.

Slavs who are of the same blood as we are, has compassion for these people too, and calls you today to lead the local Serbs spiritually.

Guide them according to the commandments of Christ with all diligence and earnestness. Lead them from the temporary to the eternal, from the earthly to the heavenly—just as Moses, who, having taken the staff from God, led the people of Israel from the labor of Egypt to the Promised Land. You ought to strengthen your brethren not with the staff of wrath and violence, but with words of humble counsel, and with the example of your holy life. Tend to the flock given to you by God like a father tends to a child, showing equal love to all, comforting the faint-hearted, strengthening the weak and healing the sinful, reforming them with a spirit of meekness.

As for those who do not follow the Church rules, but act against the clerical authority and are a temptation for others and confuse them, do these things unfailingly and wisely: according to the occasion, admonish them at a proper time; and always reproach, forbid, and plead with utmost patience.

As a symbol of your spiritual rule, this staff is given to you today from us. It is not a sign of worldly dominion, something to be proud of, with which to elevate yourself above those entrusted to you; but it is like the helm with which the helmsman guides the spiritual ship that sails amidst the abundantly storm-filled sea of this life. It is a staff that is of a true pastor, not a hired man, with which he is not to harm the sheep, but to protect and preserve them from the wolves that pillage the spirit.

Accept this staff, then, and strengthen your flock with it, and rule so that you may answer to our God for it on the day of judgment.[25]

---

[25] These words are from the "*Chinovnik*"—in the Russian Orthodox Church, a book that contains hierarchical church service texts (i.e., for services with a bishop presiding).

A SERMON[26]

*Preached at the first service in the New York
Cathedral, on September 25, 1905*

THIS PRESENT VISIT of mine to you, beloved brethren, is somewhat different from those in the past. Up until now I have come
to you for relatively short periods of time, rather as a guest. Now,
however, compelled by the needs of the Diocese and for the benefit
of the missionary undertaking here, I am moving, along with the
Consistory, to you to reside here. And so, at this time, at the first
service in this temple as a cathedral, my thoughts rest on Christ's
parable about the talents read here from the Gospel.

A certain man while departing to another country called his servants and gave gifts to them—talents: five to one, two to another,
and one to the third person; and upon his return he demanded from
them a report of what each one of them did with his gift. Every
one of us, brethren, according to the mercy of God, receives talents,
gifts from the Lord, one more, the other one less, each according to
his ability (cf. Matt. 25:15); and everyone must exert diligence and
effort so that these gifts develop and multiply. Whoever does not
care about this, whoever buries his talent in the earth, will have his
gift taken away, and he himself will be condemned to suffer. He that
has ears to hear, let him hear (Matt. 11:15).

The transfer of the archpastoral cathedra to your city and temple has recently been added to the gifts abundantly poured on your

---

[26] Printed in *Amerikansky Pravoslavny Vestnik*, 1905, #19, pp. 372–373.

parish from the Heavenly Tsar and the earthly Tsar. And this is given to you according to your ability. Your city is second in the world and first in this country. Which nationality is not present here? And how many temples are there of all sorts of faiths! Why should a representative of the true Orthodox Catholic Church not be present here? It is befitting also for the Russian hierarch to live precisely at this parish, which among all parishes is the most Russian. And your temple, which is the biggest and most splendid in our Diocese, should precisely be the cathedral temple.

But while accepting this gift of the Hierarchical cathedra being transferred to you, according to the parable about the talents, you should yourselves care that this gift will not turn out to be useless for you, that it may not be buried without bearing profit, but that it will be useful in your church life, and will be for your benefit.

From now on your parish becomes the first among other parishes, and it should be like this not in word but in deed also. For this purpose you should exceedingly, more than others, love the Orthodox Faith and the temple of God, come to it diligently and care for beautifying it, be obedient to your pastors, live in brotherly love among yourselves; care for the poor, those who are without work; and care for the Christian upbringing and education of children, and for your own personal enlightenment.

May God indeed help you in all of these good undertakings, and may the Lord's blessing be upon you through His grace and love for mankind, now and ever and unto the ages. Amen.

OPINIONS[27]

*On the issues proposed for discussion at the Pomestni[28] Council
of the All-Russia Church; written on November 24, 1905*

1. On the issue of the division of the Russian Church into metropolitan provinces.

B Y THE DECISION of the Holy Synod as of March 18–25, 1905,
it was suggested that the office of the Patriarch be reinstated in
Russia. This would not only reflect the significance and grandeur of
the Russian Church, but it would also move its governance closer to
the order outlined in the Canons.

The desire to follow that order calls for another reform in our
Church—its division into metropolitan provinces. As is known, we
already have metropolitans at the present time—but they only differ
from other bishops by titles, and not by rights. However, according
to the canons, the metropolitan is "the head of the area," and the
bishops in each region must treat him as the head and do nothing
that exceeds their authority without his consideration.[29]

---

[27] Printed in *Amerikansky Pravoslavny Vestnik*, 1905, #23, pp. 460–466. This document was written by St. Tikhon in response to the request of the Holy Synod made to every bishop of the Russian Church, asking for personal input concerning various issues of reform within the Russian Church. This was part of the preparation that led to the Great Council of Moscow in 1917 and 1918.

[28] The word *"pomestni"* means *local* in Russian.

[29] Most likely, St. Tikhon had in mind here Canon 34 of the 85 Apostolic Canons, which states, in part: "The bishops of every nation must acknowledge him who is first among them and account him as their head, and do nothing of consequence

Aside from canonical reasons, practical considerations speak for the division into metropolitan provinces. The Russian Church is too vast, and the highest Church authority is burdened with an abundance of matters, many of which may be transferred to the provinces. It is quite reasonable to agree with the thought expressed in the suggestion of Mr. Ober-Prokuror[30] as of June 28, 1905, #100, that "it is impossible to deny the existence of unique tasks in various territories of the Empire which require Church administration and which serve as a vital reason for the establishment of regional and district self-governing bodies (as for example in the western region, in the eastern provinces, and in the Caucasus)."

At the same time, there are no valid reasons to fear that the division into metropolitan provinces would contradict the principle of state unity. These provinces are only parts of one and the same Church, whose highest administrative body is located in the capital of the Empire. In spite of some local peculiarities, the common Faith nevertheless remains in the provinces, and its unity already in itself is the solid moral cement that binds the multinational population into a single family.

As far as the division itself of Russia into metropolitan provinces is concerned, it is, of course, unfeasible to base it upon one single principle—such as, for example, geography or ethnography. In some cases it would be necessary and quite natural to use the first of these two as the basis for the division, and in other cases, the second; and in yet some other cases it would be necessary to take into consideration the prior history of the Orthodox nationalities that make up the Empire.

In accordance with this, the division of Russia into the following metropolitan provinces might not seem unreasonable:

---

without his consent."

[30] The *Ober-Prokuror* was the government official who presided at every meeting of the Holy Synod of Bishops of the Church of Russia during the period in which there was no Patriarch (1721–1917).

1. Novgorod Province, which would include all the northern provinces with the exception of Petersburg, where the Archbishop of Petrograd, the Patriarch of all Russia, would reside;

2. Vilno Province for the Western region (the former Uniate diocese);

3. Kiev Province for the South-Eastern region;

4. Moscow Province for central Russia;

5. Kazan Province for the eastern provinces and the Volga region;

6. Tbilisi Province for the Caucasus (the Exarch of Georgia ought to be called *Catholicos*);

7. Tomsk (or Tobolsk) Province for Western Siberia, along with the Turkestan region; and

8. Irkutsk Province for Eastern Siberia, where it might be possible to include the Chinese and the Japanese Orthodox Churches.

And the North American Diocese should be reorganized into the Exarchate of the Russian Orthodox Church in North America. The fact is that its members include not only different nationalities but also different Orthodox Churches—each of which, within the unity of the Faith, has its own peculiarities in canonical structure, in liturgical order, and in parish life. These peculiarities are dear to them and are quite tolerable from the common Orthodox point of view.

Therefore, we do not believe we have the right to encroach upon the national character of the local Churches. On the contrary, we are trying to preserve it in them, giving them an opportunity to be under the direct authority of a superior of their very own nationality. Thus last year the Syrian Church here received her own bishop (the Most Reverend Raphael of Brooklyn), who is considered to be the second vicar to the bishop of the Aleutian Diocese,[31] but is almost independent within his area—and the Most Reverend bishop of Alaska is in the same position.[32] The Serbian parishes now are subject directly

---

[31] Referring to the North American Diocese of the Russian Church; the full name of the diocese was the Diocese of the Aleutian Islands and North America.

[32] This was Bp. Innocent, consecrated as the Bishop of Alaska, first vicar bishop to Archbishop Tikhon, in 1903.

to a special superior who still remains in the rank of archimandrite,[33] but he might be elevated to the order of a bishop in the near future. And the local Greeks would like to have their own bishop, regarding whom they are petitioning the Athens Synod.[34]

In one word, an entire exarchate of Orthodox national Churches might form in North America, with their own bishops headed by an Exarch—a Russian archbishop. Each one of them would be independent in his own area, but matters common for the entire American Church would be dealt with by way of sobor[35] under the chairmanship of the Russian archbishop. Through him the connection of the American Church to the All-Russia Church is preserved, along with a certain dependency on her.

At the same time, one should not lose sight of the fact that life in the New World compared to the Old has its own peculiarities, which the local church has to take into consideration as well. And therefore a greater degree of autonomy (autocephaly) should be granted to the American Church than to the other Russian metropolitan provinces.

Within the structure of the North American Exarchate that is being planned, the following might be included:

1. The Archdiocese of New York, which would have all the Russian parishes in the United States and Canada under its authority;

2. The Diocese of Alaska, which would include the churches of the Orthodox inhabitants of Alaska (Russians, Aleuts, Indians, Eskimos);

3. The Diocese of Brooklyn (Syrian);

4. The Diocese of Chicago (Serbian); and

5. The Greek diocese (?).[36]

---

[33] This was Archimandrite Sebastian (Dabovich), the first person born in the "Lower 48" to be made an Orthodox priest, when he was ordained in San Francisco in 1892.

[34] This was the Synod of the Church of Greece, centered in Athens, Greece.

[35] Meaning through conciliar meetings (*sobor* means "council" in Russian).

[36] This question mark is in the original. Here St. Tikhon is acknowledging that it was not certain in his day if and when the Greek Orthodox in America would consent to be a part of this system, or if the Church of Greece and/or the Patriarchate

In order to resolve the issue of the division of Russia into metropolitan provinces, we do not consider it excessive to say that the bishops of prominent cities, although subject to the metropolitan, might bear the title of archbishop, especially those who have vicars.[37] Regarding these, however, it is preferable that they be aides to the bishop, and be independent in those cities and areas that they bear the title of and reside in, in as many cases as possible. In general, it is necessary to define the position of vicar bishops and give them more rights than they have presently.

2. Regarding the reform of the diocesan administration and court.

The Diocesan administration also requires reform. At the present time the main organ of this administration is the chancery, which draws many reproaches from the laity as well as from the clergy. The Statutes of the chancery are outdated and are imbued with extreme formalism, which extinguishes the "spirit of life."[38] There is a need in the revision of these Statutes that the chancery be brought closer in its spirit to the "council of elders" (presbyters) which existed under the bishops in ancient times. It should not serve as a "divider," separating the bishop from the clergy along with the flock. The Right Reverend Bishop of Volyn writes in his review,

> The fewer matters that the bishop refers to the chancery, the better it would be for the Church. Thus, assignments to places of duty, transfer of clergy, and various decisions concerning liturgical matters must be dealt with outside of the chancery and be referred to it after such matters have been decided upon. The bishop must

---

of Constantinople would ever allow them to become integrated into this system.

[37] Meaning vicar, or auxiliary, bishops placed directly under them.

[38] No doubt St. Tikhon has in mind here 2 Corinthians 3:5–6: "for our sufficiency is from God, who also made us sufficient as ministers of the new covenant, not of the letter but of the Spirit; for the letter kills, but the Spirit gives life."

use the existing administrative bodies as little as possible and must himself deal directly with those appealing to him.

Rather, the chancery should deal with "household" and financial matters, as well as be a judicial body. We do not find it necessary and agreeable with the canons of the Church to separate the Church court from the chancery, and making it into a separate organization, regarding which many wrote in the '70s of the last century.

But this does not mean that the chancery court is not at all in need of reforms. On the contrary, they are necessary regarding its composition and the scope of judicial matters it is to deal with, and regarding the order of legal procedures. The staff of the "court table" in the chancery, aside from a person appointed by the bishop, should include two clergymen, elected from the clergy at the Diocesan convention.

In regard to the electoral principle, we have to deal with two extreme opinions. Those of the first opinion are ready to see salvation from every kind of evil in the electoral principle, and so they promote it in places where there is no particular need for it. And those who hold the second of these opinions reject the electoral principle as being completely defective, seeing in it an expression of "parliamentarianism," the spirit of the republic.[39]

But in the true Church of Christ, where there should not be any worldly possessiveness and dominance of one group, with another group protesting and struggling—and where, on the contrary, all should be seeking the common good, uniting in amicable, harmonious work—the electoral principle might be applied not without benefit in many areas. Thus it can be allowed in the selection of spiritual judges, and in the selection of a dean (if he is regarded not only as an organ of the archpastoral power, but also as the one who expresses and tends to the needs of the clergy and the churches of his

---

[39] In our day, we would say, perhaps, the spirit of *democracy*.

area before the Diocesan authorities—needs that a bishop cannot personally identify in many dioceses).

As far as the issues for the chancery court are concerned, divorce cases should be excluded from it in favor of the civil court, while preserving for the Church the right to acknowledge or disagree with the decisions of the civil authorities in these cases, and to determine herself who might be allowed to enter into a second marriage after a divorce. Clergy accused of disturbing the public peace and order, of insulting someone, of disorderly conduct, etc., must be tried by the civil court as well. Often when the guilty one is tried for these types of offenses by the spiritual court, he becomes subject to punishment that is less severe than it would have been had he been tried in the civil court. This in turn results in criticism, with the clergy themselves becoming less disciplined.

Disapproval of the procedures of the chancery court is expressed as well. They should be reformed also, according to the latest methods of legal proceedings. In particular, improvements in conducting the so-called "investigations" of the clergy are much to be desired, since even if they end in an acquittal of the accused clergyman, they greatly undermine his authority in the eyes of his parish. Here, more rights should be given to the bishop to replace such investigations with a private probe.

Speaking of reforms and improvements in the Diocesan administration, one might also wish for changes and improvements in the way the Diocesan councils of the clergy are organized. They first appeared for the purpose of identifying the means to satisfy the material needs of the spiritual-educational, missionary, and charitable organizations in the Diocese. But should the clergy always "leave the word of God and serve the tables" (Acts 6:2)? Why should their right to gather and have discussion about service to the Word of God—about issues of the spiritual life, of pastoral guidance, of missionary work, of the struggle against heresies, and so on—not be recognized? Nowadays in some Dioceses these matters are discussed at the "flock meetings."[40]

The scope of the work and the issues under the authority of the Diocesan councils ought to be expanded everywhere by putting on their agenda all matters that concern all aspects of the church-parochial life: matters of faith, education, deaneries, and almsgiving. And as far as material, financial, and "household" issues are concerned, for their discussion, the representatives of lay folk must be invited without fail, especially the parish presidents [*starosta*] and the members of the parish councils. Indeed, the parishes pay all sorts of dues, and it is not surprising that the parish presidents do not want to pay the dues established by the [diocesan] council, since nobody consulted them at the time the dues were imposed.

With the participation of laymen in the Diocesan councils, the councils themselves might be conducted in the manner of church conventions that are practiced in America—by Episcopalians, for example. They have joint sessions of clergy and laymen, as well as private sessions of only clergy that concern purely spiritual matters. This type of lay participation would bring into Church life a more pronounced "churchly" character,[41] and would promote its rejuvenation.

3. Regarding improvements in the parish.

Along with the diocesan administration, the life of the parish needs improvement. It is undeniable that in many places in Russia the life of the parish is very stagnant. The connection between the parish and the Church [as a whole] is weak; it is expressed only in parishioners attending the needed ceremonial services and attending church only on feast days. Educational and charitable institutions in places like

---

[40] Perhaps these were open parish meetings, such as the annual parish meeting held in many of our parishes today.

[41] In the Russian, "*tserkovnost.*" This language suggests that with more lay participation in the Church's administrative life, the Church would become more like She is meant to be ontologically.

that are absent; the voice of the priest is rarely heard, and few take it into account.

Very much has been written about all of this recently. Loud voices are heard regarding the revival of the life of the parish, and the rebirth of the ancient significance of the parish—regarding not only allowing the parochial community to take care of the material needs of the parish, helping the needy, and providing education, but also the very selection of the candidates for priesthood. It is hard to object to the recognition of the parish as a legal entity which has the right to private property (this has not taken place yet, and therefore it is necessary to make changes in our legislation in this respect, as well as regarding the issue of the acquisition of property by the churches, monasteries, and the clergy in general). It is also hard to object to the parochial community, with its priest at the head, along with the elected council members, being able itself to manage and be in charge of what is in its possession. Of course, none of this would be done without the knowledge and control of the Diocesan authority.

This is exactly how things are dealt with in most of the parishes of North America. Here the churches constitute the property of the congregation (parish); and even where the deed is in the name of the bishop, they are maintained by the parish itself. Usually there is an annual meeting of parishioners (*rochny meeting*),[42] where the church *uryad*[43] is elected—the parish administration (the parish president, treasurer, and parish council); at this meeting a report is presented on the income and expenses for the whole year. In some parishes, the report is done semi-annually, or even monthly. The parish council has the responsibility to collect from the parishioners *rochnoe*[44] (an annual contribution of five dollars or more), and to do *collecta*[45]

---

[42] We see here an interesting inclusion of the English word "meeting" into the Russian language!

[43] This word means "official position," or "position of authority."

[44] This word means an "annual contribution."

[45] This is another English word incorporated by the Russian-Americans into their native language; they gave it the specific meaning of "donations" (that which is *collected*).

(collect donations). The parish not only maintains the church building, but also pays the salary of its priest and its *diakouchitel*[46] (the amount varies in different places), according to a mutual agreement between the priest and the parishioners. Also at the meeting, fees are agreed upon for ceremonial services. All of this is recorded in *statuti*,[47] which are approved by the bishop.

If there is no parish house, then the parish rents an apartment (with furniture, light, and heat) for the priest, and accommodation for the school—and in some places for the reading hall. There is a brotherhood in each parish (and in the populous parishes there are several brotherhoods). The brotherhood always has a religious character—it selects some saint (or feast) as a protector (patron); from its income it makes contributions for the upkeep of the church, for the priest, for the school, and for refurbishing and beautifying the temple. Aside from this, it also pursues charitable goals—it gives *zapomogi*[48] to its members in cases of sickness, injury, and unemployment. And within the brotherhood there is sometimes a benevolent[49] court for its members.

In general the brotherhoods here are very popular. Together with the "Orthodox Mutual Aid Society," with which they unite, and which also by itself helps with the construction of churches and the education of the people, the brotherhoods contribute much to the enlivening of the church-parochial life.

But even here in America there is no election of priests, and thus far we consider it untimely to institute it. This should be said about Russia even more so. In itself, the principle of the election of clergy is legal, its introduction is desirable, and it is necessary to strive to implement it. But to set out to introduce it everywhere and right away, and to start restoring the ancient order of things in the parish,

---

[46] This is a coined word, taking words for "deacon" and "teacher" and making them into a compound word; hence, "deacon-teacher."

[47] Meaning "statutes"; another English word incorporated into Russian by the Russian-Americans.

[48] Meaning material assistance; literally, "help".

[49] In the Russian, *"polyubovny"* (literally, "loving").

would mean, according to the vivid expression of The Right Reverend Bishop of Volyn, "to offer a severely sick patient lardy, coarse food, which would be useful for a workman, but mortal for an ill person." In his notes, The Right Reverend Bishop reveals the disease of the contemporary parish community in detail, which renders it not ready to have the right to elect a worthy pastor. Our spiritual schools [i.e., seminaries], which have almost monopolized the right to produce candidates for the priesthood, also present difficulties for the introduction of the elective principle.

Here we approach this issue:

4. On improving the theological-educational schools.

The foremost shortcoming of our theological schools is that they pursue two goals which in themselves are quite respectable, but in practice they do not always agree with each other. The theological schools exist, firstly, for the purpose of educating the children of the clergy,[50] and secondly, to prepare candidates for the priesthood. But not only the children of clergy might become these candidates, but also from other social groups. Meanwhile, although people from other social groups are accepted into the theological schools, this is in very limited numbers, which in effect restricts the flow of fresh forces from the lay folk into the clergy.

On the other hand, it is not all of the children of the clergy who wish to join the priestly rank, and they are forced to do so against their will, since there is almost no other option available for them

---

[50] During the Synodal Period of the Russian Church (1721–1917), when the Church was subjected to extensive government control as a kind of "Department of Religion" within the State, the clergy had become a kind of caste unto itself. Sons of clergy were almost all sent to the theological schools, where tuition was free, and the expectation was that they would all be ordained upon graduation, whether or not they had a clear calling from the Lord for priestly ministry. As we can see from St. Tikhon's words about the theological schools, he very much wants this system to be reformed, so that the schools would be oriented towards receiving people of any social background who had a sense of calling to the priesthood.

upon graduation from the seminary. And this is where the constant dissatisfaction, grumbling, and insurgencies of the seminarians start from. Wishing to calm them with something, the faculty introduces various leniencies into the order of the seminary life, trying to bring a civil character to the seminaries, which causes direct damage to the achievement of their other goal—that of preparing candidates for the priesthood, servants of the Holy Church. As a result, the ranks of clergy are joined not only by those who do not wish to be priests, but also by those who are most undesirable for this. Who and what benefits from this order of things—or to say it better, *disorder* of things?

It seems that the most natural way out of this situation is that the Diocese should have special theological schools (the issue is not how they are named; it is possible to preserve the old name of "seminary") which would accept without distinction children of all social groups who have finished the courses of secondary educational establishments, and who feel the inclination towards the spiritual rank.[51] The subjects taught at these schools would be theological, their mode of life would be strictly religious, and passage from them would be to one thing—service in the Church. The present theological schools may be converted into the secondary educational establishments of the Spiritual Authority,[52] in which the clergy would bring up their children, but the curriculum of these schools must be general. In this way, those who graduate from them could go, if they wish, to higher educational establishments, and those who feel a calling for spiritual service after graduating from them would enter a theological school.

This is the way candidates for priesthood are prepared not only in the non-Orthodox churches, but also in Austria by the Orthodox and the Uniates. The question is, however, who would maintain these schools of the Spiritual Authority? Using Church money? But this money would go for the upkeep of the theological schools. And the Church would hardly give money for the education of those who might not serve it in the future. The government? But it already

---

[51] Meaning that they feel a calling to serve in the ordained ministry.

[52] This phrase is referring to the combined Church-State bureaucracy in Russia.

supports the secondary educational establishments for all without exception, where children of clergy might enter as well. This means that there is no reason to also maintain special schools for them. And the clergy themselves would hardly be able to support such special schools.

On the other hand, no matter how unsatisfactory the theological schools of our day are, nevertheless one might not want to challenge their existence—since some of them have been in existence for over a hundred and fifty years, and they have produced a significant number of outstanding, productive figures in all fields of religious, government, and public service. Therefore, would it not be better and fairer to establish the schools proposed above at the existing seminaries?

In other words, the curriculum of the general secondary school must be introduced at the theological schools and seminaries where the children of the clergy study, while at the same time preserving the character, the religious order, of life that is native to the clergy since childhood. The seminary would have theological courses (lasting three years) taken by those who wish, who have finished the secondary educational program at the seminary or at another civil educational establishment. These courses would provide an educational program and training of a strictly religious character, one which is necessary for future pastors. With this sort of arrangement of things, the question of financing the theological schools is naturally taken off the agenda. The Church and the government and the clergy would take part in it as before.

There is still left for us to say:

5. On the issue of participation of the clergy in public organizations and other matters that might be discussed at the future All-Russia council.

Some are against the participation of the clergy in public institutions because pastors thereby join the stir of worldly events and the bustle of life which is contrary to their direct duties and the eternal principles of pastoral service. To that, however, one might object that since a pastor is the guide of the conscience of a Christian, his spiritual life, as well as spiritual, purely Christian principles, must be reflected and implemented in the area of worldly affairs, especially in a Christian state. And who better than clergy can remind the public institutions about these principles? And is this the time for the clergy to show inactivity and indifference—when the government willingly is inviting elected persons into collaboration?[53] And is this the time to give up the influence of the Church over the government, when circumstances are turning in such a way that the Orthodox Faith is turning from the dominant one in the State to one that is only tolerable—and in some places even intolerable? It is only necessary that the spiritual participants in the public institutions think of themselves specifically as representatives of the Church, advancing Her views there and not their own, even if they might be humane and liberal.

As far as other issues are concerned which might be discussed at the council, there would be quite a few of them. And it would be better for the representatives of the Church authorities to put them on the agenda themselves, and discuss them, rather than to be forced to do so by Mr. Rozanov and other followers of the "new way."[54]

From among these other issues, in light of the decree on tolerance in faith,[55] the issue of the relations of the Orthodox Church with the Old Believers and other confessions is highlighted in the recommendations of the Ober-Prokuror. In accordance with this, a

---

[53] At this time, along with the calling of the Duma, the national legislative assembly, various possibilities for local self-government through elected officials were opening up.

[54] The quotation marks are in the original. This is a reference to the influential journalist Vasilii V. Rozanov (1865–1919), one of the leaders of the Church reform movement in Russia in 1905, who were campaigning for a new era to begin in the structure and life of the Russian Church.

[55] This is a reference to the imperial decree issued on April 17, 1905 (Holy Pascha) that granted religious freedom to all Russian citizens—including granting the legal right for various Old Believer, Uniate, Lutheran, and other non-Orthodox religious bodies to be officially incorporated legally.

question might be raised regarding "unity of faith"[56] (about a bishop who would be in charge of common faith issues, and who would take part in the sessions of the Holy Synod), and about the oaths of the Moscow Council of 1666, which until this day confuse some of those who adhere to the old rites.[57]

For the American mission, it is necessary to receive a resolution of the issue of relations with the Anglicans and their hierarchy—and for all the churches abroad, the resolution of the issue of the calendar.[58] It is necessary also for the representatives of the various Orthodox churches living abroad to coordinate practical matters in liturgical and canonical areas, so that other confessions see that we indeed have "one faith." For the Russian Church, it is necessary to have a new Slavic translation of the liturgical books (the present one is out of date and is incorrect in many places) by which the demands of some to serve in the everyday Russian language might be forestalled. It would not be excessive, it seems, to make certain changes in the liturgical services—for example, to shorten *ektenias*[59] which are repeated often, and to read aloud some "secret" prayers.[60] The fasts also could be discussed, as well as the issue of the relinquishment of one's spiritual rank and the possibility of getting reinstated, etc.

Many of these issues are common to the entire Church. Therefore, when these matters are discussed, it is necessary to hear the voices of representatives of all the eastern and Slavic churches. It is most desirable to invite them to the All-Russia Council (the rectors of the

---

[56] This is a reference to the "One Faith" (*Yedinovertsy*) movement of the late 19th century, whereby the Russian Church sought to reconcile the Old Believers into the "one faith."

[57] This was the council which condemned the old rites, thus in effect creating the Old Believer Schism.

[58] Referring to the issue of the Julian Calendar, which the worldwide Orthodox Church was following at that time, and the Gregorian Calendar, which the Roman Catholic and Protestant Churches were following along with all of the civil societies of the western world.

[59] This word, from Greek, denotes a series, or *litany*, of prayers.

[60] Quotation marks are in the original. This is referring to prayers during the church services done by the celebrant silently.

representation churches in Moscow could serve as the representatives). And it is even more desirable, after the local Church council is held in Moscow, to have a council of all the Orthodox Churches. A great need is felt to have it, and its summoning would bring unquestionable benefit for the [entire] Holy Orthodox Church.

A SERMON[61]

*Preached on the Feast of the Nativity at the New
York Cathedral, on December 25th, 1905*

Thy nativity, O Christ our God, has shown to the world
the light of wisdom.[62]

THESE ARE THE WORDS that the main hymn, the *troparion* of
the present feast, starts with. The Nativity of Christ, according
to the view of the Holy Church, "has shown the world the light of
wisdom"; and people, together with the wise men, learned to worship
the Sun of Truth. They saw, and learned about, the True God.

And is it necessary to say that prior to the Nativity of Christ, people did not have a complete, genuine knowledge of God? Take the
heathen world—everything was divinized there: people, and animals,
and forces of nature—everything aside from the one true God. There
was a deep night of religious ignorance, and its darkness was not
dispersed by a few stars—the thinkers[63] who, although they stood
above the usual lowly understanding of the heathen about God, nevertheless were far from the complete truth about Him.

And then there is the Judaic world. Here the light of the knowledge of God is present, since it is communicated by God Himself
in the Old Testament. But a day does not always happen to be

---

[61] Printed in *Amerikansky Pravoslavny Vestnik*, 1906, #1, pp. 4–7.

[62] These words are from the *troparion* (the main hymn) for the Nativity of Christ.

[63] Most likely St. Tikhon is here referring to the philosophers and sages of the
pre-Christian world.

clear—it often happens that the sun is hidden behind clouds and fog. It is the same way with the Jews, among whom the God-revealed teaching, the Sun of Truth, was clouded over by human inventions, the "traditions of the elders," of which Christ often convicted His contemporaries.

But just as in the visible world, when the sun breaks through the clouds and lights up everything—the mountains, and the valleys, and the most hidden places—in the same way the Sun of Truth shows up in the world. Christ our God enlightens those in darkness and radiates the light of wisdom to the world. "The people which sat in darkness saw a great light" (Matt. 4:16), since "God sent His Son to the people, and He gave light and wisdom, that we may know the true God" (1 John 5:20). Since "the only begotten Son, which is in the bosom of the Father, hath declared Him" (John 1:18), He has shown God to the people. Everything He had heard from the Father, He told them (John 15:15), conveying knowledge about God to such an extent as is possibly attainable by the people. Therefore, there is no new revelation after Christ. In Him there is "the depth of the riches of the wisdom and knowledge of God!" (Rom. 11:33).

And just as two thousand years ago the Nativity of Christ "has shown to the world the light of wisdom," conveying to the people the understanding of God and of themselves, and the meaning of life, in the same way today the celebration of this joyful event brings the "light of wisdom" into our life. It is for us a star that leads us to Christ.

With the coming of the Nativity holidays, each one of us involuntary recalls his faraway, happy childhood. Since these holidays are primarily for the children, they are especially dear for a child's heart. One recalls quiet "family evenings" at "Christmastide," the "Christmas trees" of those days, often quite simple in respect to the decorations and the presents, but joyful and satisfying to have for all. We recall how, having played and run around to our heart's content, we peacefully cuddled up in our child-beds and immediately fell asleep, also holding right there, in our hands, the toys we had just received.

Where are those happy years with innocent joys, when we were "children in malice" (cf. 1 Cor. 14:20), when we wanted everything to be well in the world, when our heart was a stranger to passionate desires, when we were glad to receive some simple toy, when we had not yet become vulgar, had not yet acquired vanity in the whirlwind of the [daily] routine? And who would bring back to us those happy years? "To every thing there is a season under the heaven" (Eccl. 3:1). Childhood passes, and a grown man can no longer live the way he lived as a child.

But at least let us recall our childhood years more often, and refresh our souls with those memories, cleansing them from the vanity and vulgarity of everyday life that have accumulated in them. According to the testimony of wise people, memories of our childhood have for us great significance. They quite often hold a man from improper deeds, especially if those memories are connected with sensations and impressions of a religious nature.

And those indeed are Christmas memories—the brightest, most pure, and most holy. Along with them we always recall the "joyous evening," the procession with a star, caroling. And we recall the marvelous Christmas service with the incessant "Glory be to God in the highest" being sung in it. We vividly imagine the entire captivating story about a quiet night in Palestine, with a manger, in which lies Christ God, Who cannot be contained; the happy Mother who is bending over the Infant with a happy smile; the humble and righteous elder Joseph, who is reverently looking at Him; simple shepherds who are coming to bow down to Him; the angels, singing in the heavens; and the marvelous star, which the wise men from the East used to guide their way.

An old story, and how long it has been known to all! Yet every time when recalling it, a child's feeling comes to life in the soul, which makes a person closer to God, since "for of children is the kingdom of heaven" (Mark 10:14). Again you feel yourself being a child, and again you direct yourself to the Christmas scene in Bethlehem, to an infant lying in the manger.

Let the Christmas holidays shine for us as well with the "light of wisdom," and teach us that the innocence of a child, purity of heart, peacefulness of consciousness, quiet joy, being satisfied with having little, which is inherent to all of us during childhood, comprise what is "most important in the world" for people of any age, constituting a blessing which cannot be exchanged for either honors or wealth or power and influence which are acquired by us with age and the passing of years.

The feast of the Nativity of Christ for us Russians, beloved brethren, also has a special joy and significance: "lying in the manger in Bethlehem like a lamb, You destroyed the strength of our adversaries like a lion and defeated our enemies."[64] Today we remember how, about a hundred years ago, our predecessors did not fear the punishment of God, left the path of the truth of God, and lived according the wills of their hearts. Furthermore, they did not honor the traditions of the fathers, and provoked God to anger with strange gods (cf. Deut. 32:16). For this reason God led foreign people unto them who defeated them in their cities. And as in the old days with the sons of Israel, so it was the same way with our predecessors; for a terrible attack befell them, there was great sorrow, and the capital city was destroyed.

However, the Lord was merciful to the repentance and prayers of His slaves, which had before vanished like smoke. There our enemy, like the ancient King Nebuchadnezzar, proudly exalts himself: "I will ascend into heaven, I will exalt my throne above the stars, I will be similar to the Highest One" (cf. Is. 14:13–14). He vanquishes kings, disturbs the whole world, lays the entire earth barren.

But just as in Bethlehem the gentleness of the Divine Infant put to shame the mindless anger of Herod, who sought the soul of the Child; and the meek, humble simplicity of the One lying in the manger attracted to itself the adoration of the noble wise men;

---

[64] This quotation apparently comes from the Thanksgiving *molieben* (prayer service) on the day of the Nativity of Christ in remembrance of the deliverance of Russia from the invasion of the French under Napoleon in 1812.

in the same way, God showed the world through our predecessors once more that He chooses those who are simple-minded to put to shame those who are wise, and those who are weak to put to shame those who are powerful, and those who are of simple origin to put to shame those of noble descent, in order that no flesh should glory in the presence of God: "him that glorieth, let him glory in the Lord" (1 Cor. 1:27–31). And our predecessors, in that difficult time, "out of weakness were made strong, waxed valiant in fight, turned to flight the armies of the aliens" (Heb. 11:33–34) with their faith, their repentance before God, their ardent prayer for heavenly help, and their readiness to sacrifice everything for the salvation of the motherland—with the humble acknowledgment that all glory belongs to God. So for themselves, their humility was most appropriate.

Grant us, Lord, to have the memory of this glorious visitation of Yours to be firm and constant in us, especially in the present days! Today, just as a hundred years ago, our motherland is going through difficult times.[65] Again there is great sorrow and a terrible calamity, but not from external enemies, but from our own sons, from their inner wavering and confusion. Various ways are sought for ending the disorder and improving the order of the state. But along with the care for external well-being through the granting of various freedoms—freedom of unions, meetings, the press, autonomy, election to the state parliament, to have a constitution, and so on—there are almost no voices heard about the moral perfection of each individual, about humility, about readiness to sacrifice one's pride, one's rights and freedoms.

And how pertinent and salvific it is today to press yourselves close to the Bethlehem manger to learn these virtues from Him, Who "being in the form of God, made Himself of no reputation; and taking upon Himself a form of a servant; and being made in the likeness of men, He humbled Himself, and became obedient unto death, even the death on the cross" (Phil. 2:6–8).

---

[65] In this sentence, St. Tikhon is referring to Napoleon's invasion of Russia in 1812, and to the revolutionary turmoil that erupted in Russia in 1905.

May Thy Nativity, our Christ God, shine with the light of wisdom for us,[66] the Russian people, as well. And may it teach us, by the example of our predecessors, to show "the rules of faith and examples of strength," "which are the truth of everything," and to "acquire" "greatness through humility, treasure through poverty!"[67]

---

[66] Referring to the opening words of the *troparion* (the most major hymn) for the feast of the Nativity of Christ.

[67] These phrases are from the *troparion* of St. Nicholas the Wonderworker.

ADDED NOTES

Concerning the development of Orthodoxy in America

One may hope that with the establishment of the vicariate, the school undertaking in Alaska will grow and will find its inspirer and leader in the Right Reverend Vicar ("Orthodox Gospel Messenger," 1904, #18, p. 58).

One may hope that with the establishment of the vicariate another important and necessary undertaking in Alaska—the opening of a monastery—will soon be implemented ("Orthodox Gospel Messenger," 1904, #17, p. 56).

Regarding the article "Missionary Monastery in Alaska"[68]

I DO NOT CONSIDER this issue exhausted. What kind of a monastery, and where in Alaska, I have already suggested—this was written about not just once in the *Vestnik,* and especially in the article by Fr. T. Pashkovski. "I have no man" (John 5:6–7), but we have to look for one, and of course not among our American monks, since they came here not for establishing a monastery (otherwise I would have established it with them myself), but for parish work; and they bring whatever feasible benefit they can bring, and they do whatever is feasibly possible for them to do.

---

[68] Printed in *Amerikansky Pravoslavny Vestnik,* 1905, #8, p. 158, under the line.

I corresponded with Fr. D. on Athos, and he pointed out Fr. Igumenos Aleksy to me, who resides there, who has previously already established a monastery on Amur[69] and is agreeing to come to America to labor, if the authorities send him. The question regarding him has been cleared up on the eve of the opening of the Alaskan vicariate, and obviously has been left by me to the Right Reverend Vicar to inherit.

Footnote: To the word preached on the day of the holy crowning, 14th of May, 1905[70]

By the way, a reproach was made to our famous preacher, Right Reverend Ambrose of Kharkov, that we clerics praise autocracy now, but with a regime change from the top, we will also praise the constitutional monarch just like an autocratic one ("Faith and Reason," 1901, p. 461). That is not true. We teach and will teach about subordination to any authority (even to the republican, democratic), since all authority is from God [cf. Rom. 13:1]. But without hesitation we state that autocracy is most suitable regarding the idea of the supreme power and the order of the Russian state, which is connected with the spiritual, everyday order of life, and with tribal, geographic, and other conditions.

Regarding the establishment of a monastery community in South Canaan, Pennsylvania[71]

May 31, 1905. God's blessing is called upon the good undertaking of establishing a monastery community in N. America. I order to send for this matter 100 dollars from my salary to the name of Fr. Hieromonk Arseny, whom I appoint the builder of the future

---

[69] A major river in Siberia in the Russian Far East.

[70] Printed in *Amerikansky Pravoslavny Vestnik,* 1905, p. 184.

[71] Printed in *Amerikansky Pravoslavny Vestnik,* 1905, #11, p. 225.

community. The land that is donated should be assigned to the Diocesan authorities.[72]

Regarding Fr. Ingram Nathaniel Irvine joining Orthodoxy from the Episcopalians[73]

On October 22nd, 1905, at the Archpastoral service, the former Episcopalian priest, Doctor of Theology Ingram Nathaniel Irvine, was ordained, after joining Orthodoxy, as a deacon; and on Sunday, October 23—as a presbyter. Newly ordained Fr. Irvine was appointed to the clergy staff of the New York Cathedral, to the position of a missionary for the Americans.[74]

---

[72] In early August of 1905 this new monastery became named for St. Tikhon of Zadonsk. Hieromonk Arseny (Chagovtsov) was pastor of the parish in Mayfield, about ten miles away, but on the other side of a high ridge. He oversaw the building of the first church, which also served as the first monastic residence on the property, and which was dedicated on May 30, 1906.

[73] Printed in *Amerikansky Pravoslavny Vestnik*, 1905, #11, p. 430.

[74] Meaning for only-English-speaking Americans.

YEAR 1906

65. Address given at the consecration of St. Tikhon's Monastery and Church in Pennsylvania, May 17/30, 1906.

66. Sermons preached at the tonsuring at St. Tikhon's Monastery of Monk Anthony on August 13th, and Monk Seraphim on August 14th (1906).

ADDRESS[1]

Given at the consecration of St. Tikhon's Monastery and Church in South Canaan, Pennsylvania, on May 17/30, 1906

THROUGH GOD's speedily acting mercy, the Orthodox Church continues to grow and is strengthened in this land. In various places, Orthodox churches are being established; parishes, brotherhoods, and schools are being organized; a seminary, a seminary preparatory school, and an orphanage are being opened.

Nevertheless, the life of our Church here was not yet full: we did not have an institution which, since ancient times, has been the companion of the Orthodox Church and constitutes her adornment. I mean monasteries, in which the Russian land is so rich. And now, glory and thanksgiving to God! This void is now filled, and we celebrate today the opening of St. Tikhon's Monastery and the consecration of the Monastery's first church.

However, is it not a vain dream and a waste of effort and funds to organize a monastery, with its contemplative, eastern way of life, in a land whose inhabitants are known throughout the world for their practical needs, external efficiency, and a life-style of worldly comforts? Is this fertile soil for the sowing of monasticism? Will its seed not fall among thorns, among those for whom the cares of this world and the seductions of wealth drown out the word, and it bears no fruit? (Matt. 13:7)

[1] Printed in *Amerikansky Pravoslavny Vestnik*, 1906, #11, pp. 208–210.

But are the people here entirely lacking in bursts of idealism, longings for heaven, concerns for "the one thing needful" (Luke 10:42), and a nostalgia for the inner man—all overcome by worldly vanity? Let us not hasten with words of condemnation. For what person knows a man's thoughts except the spirit of the man which is in him (1 Cor. 2:11)? Do not judge by appearances (John 7:24).

And as well there are souls living here and now that thirst for the Lord and long for true, unworldly life. We know that here, among the non-Orthodox, entire monastic communities exist. If people enter them from amongst those who are usually considered to be "practical," then we have reason to hope that our monastery will not remain without inhabitants from among the Russian people who have long been noted for their love and attachment to monasteries, their longing for the heavenly, and their detachment from the worldly things of this life.

Let us hope that our monastery, presently small in the number of its brotherhood, will become like the mustard seed, which is the smallest of all seeds, but when it has grown it is the greatest of all shrubs and becomes a tree, so that the birds of the air come and make nests in its branches (Matt. 13:32). The hopes and desires of my heart go further: I would like our monastery to become, according to the words of the Savior, like a leaven which a woman took and hid in three measures of meal, till it was all leavened (Matt. 13:33).

The future is concealed from man's limited vision, and we do not know at present what will be brought into the life of this land by the constantly increasing wave of Slavic immigration and the gradually growing Orthodox Church. We would like to believe, however, that they will not remain here without a trace, that they will not vanish in a foreign sea, and that they will deposit into the spiritual treasury of the American people the qualities that are peculiar to the Slavic nature and the Russian Orthodox people: a hunger for the spiritual, a passion for the heavenly, a longing for universal brotherhood, concern for others, humility, feelings of repentance, and patience.

The most beautiful nursery for the raising of such feelings, for the preservation and increase of this spiritual leaven, is precisely an Orthodox monastery. "Therefore, look down from Heaven, O God, upon the Monastery now founded, and behold and visit this vine which You have planted with Your right hand, and establish it!"[2]

One more word about our monastery. Not far from it stands an orphanage. Is this appropriate next to a monastery? Is it appropriate for monks who have renounced the world to be preoccupied with cares other than the salvation of their souls? Does not even ministering to their neighbors in the world distract monks from their direct goal?

These questions have preoccupied the minds of both monastics and non-monastics in our fatherland during recent years. Some see ministering to their neighbors in the world as a mere "side-line" for a monk, as something that is not essential to him, as something that can even be dangerous in certain cases. Others, on the contrary, see the very prayers of the monk and his preoccupations with the salvation of his soul as virtually worthless without any ministering to his neighbor. They consider monks to be selfish and idle people.

Who is right? I think that the Synaxarion for Matins of Great Tuesday provides an answer to this question. In it is presented a commentary on the Gospel parable of the Ten Virgins (Matt. 25:1–12). Our Lord Jesus Christ spoke to His disciples about virginity more than once. There is much glory in virginity. Truly, it is a great thing. But in order that one who fulfills this deed [virginity] might not even think of neglecting the other virtues, particularly charity, through which the light of virginity shines, Christ sets forth the Parable of the Ten Virgins. Five of them were wise, for to their virginity they joined the abundant oil of charity. The other five merely preserved their virginity without the oil of charity. They were called foolish, since they accomplished the greater (virginity) while disregarding the lesser (charity).

---

[2] This is the episcopal blessing given by the celebrant at every hierarchical liturgy (i.e., one at which a bishop is serving).

Thus, in the night of this swiftly-passing life, all the virgins fell asleep: that is to say, they died and came before Christ the Bridegroom. The wise entered through the doors of the bridal-chamber, but to the foolish those doors were shut. They had no oil and were forced to go and buy some. But, just as the stores are not open at night, so were the virgins unable to supply themselves with good deeds after death, especially charity. They went away ashamed, for nothing is sadder or more full of shame than virginity defeated by possessions.

Thus monks cannot save themselves by virginity alone. To it they must add good deeds, especially charity. Therefore the orphanage is far from being superfluous to our monastery. In it the monks can serve these little ones with their own labor and with their monastery property, and in this way build their salvation.

I shall end this discourse with the words I spoke to the brotherhood at my first visit to the Monastery. Someone once came to Christ and asked Him, "Good Teacher, what shall I do to inherit eternal life?" "Keep the commandments," answered Christ. "The first and greatest commandment is—You shall love your Lord with all your heart; and the second is like it—You shall love your neighbor as yourself" (Matt. 19:16–17; 22:37–39).

If you, brethren, will live by this rule, you shall inherit the earth, the mercy of God, and eternal salvation. Amen.

SERMONS[3]

Preached at tonsurings at St. Tikhon's Monastery

For Monk Anthony, on August 13th, 1906

I GREET YOU, beloved brother Anthony, with the start on the path of monastic life! I rejoice for you, for today the desire of your heart has come true. It has been several years that you have been consumed with desire to become a monk, and with all your might you have strived to achieve this holy goal.

True, some will condemn you for this and say that you have thrown your life away to no purpose, and especially in these young years. But may your heart not be disturbed by these words. The word of God says something else: Blessed is the man who carries his yoke from his youth. "He who loves his life," says Christ, will lose it, while he who hates his life in this world will keep it for eternal life" (John 12:25). And you in the same way have lost your life as regards this world and its fancies, but instead you have preserved it for life eternal and the Kingdom of Heaven, and in that rejoice!

And our young monastery rejoices, since in you it has acquired its first monk, from among its very own inhabitants. And we can say about you the same as Jacob said when he blessed his first son: "Reuben, you are my firstborn, my might, and the beginning of my children" (cf. Gen. 49:3). And you, brother, are the firstborn of our habitation, and we hope that you will be the beginning of our sons—that

[3] Printed in *Amerikansky Pravoslavny Vestnik,* 1906, #6, pp. 312–314.

others, following your steps and example, will follow after you. We pray and hope that you will be our might and strength and joy—if you follow what you have promised here today. And you should work hard at this last thing most of all.

Today you have been included in the rank of monks, but do not think that with the tonsuring and with being called a monk you have indeed become a monk. No, with that, this endeavor has only started—for today is the beginning of your salvation. In the exhortations read today you have heard what a person must do who wants to become a monk. If you want to be a monk, first of all cleanse yourself from every kind of impurity, acquire the wisdom of humility and obedience, abandon the impudence common to the world, do not complain, be patient in prayer, do not be lazy in watchfulness. And you ought to entreat God through prayer and fasting. You see, brother, what a vast field you have to cross, and today you are only making the first steps on it.

And thus, with God's help, with Christ giving you strength, walk the way you have chosen. "Forgetting those things which are behind, and reaching forward to those things which are ahead, I press toward the goal for the prize of the upward call of God in Christ Jesus (Phil. 3:13–14). And may your new patron, the Venerable Anthony of Pechera [the Kievan Caves][4] be an example for you in this holy undertaking. He, just like you, sought monastic life from youth; and he, like you, received his tonsure in a foreign country, far away from his homeland. With all of my heart and with all of my soul I wish that this resemblance between you and your patron will be not only in name but in deed as well, and not only at the beginning of the struggle but also throughout it, to its glorious end. Let it indeed be!

---

[4] The Kievan Caves Monastery was founded by Saints Anthony and Theodosius in the 11th century near the capital city of Kiev as newly baptized Russia's first monastery. It remains to this day one of the most important monasteries in the Russian/Ukrainian lands.

And as a blessing for this, accept from me the icon of the Mother of God, who came to love monks and who helps them direct their lives to salvation.

For Monk Seraphim on August 14th, 1906

Beloved in the Lord Fr. Seraphim,

Yesterday your young brother Fr. Anthony was made a monk, and today your tonsure has taken place. Those who witnessed yesterday's and today's tonsures might notice a difference—not in the service, since it is the same for everyone—but in the feelings and impressions which accompanied both tonsures. Yesterday, perhaps, some regretted that a young man was becoming a monk, a man at whom the worldly life could smile. At the same time, it was fitting to be concerned about how this young monk would be able to bear the hardship, how he would be able to withstand temptations and seductions.

But different things come to mind about you, beloved brother. You are already a very old man, who has lived in the world for a long time and has experienced its joys and sorrows. Even the self-willed world does not rebel against the tonsuring of a person of your age. We treat your tonsure in a calm way, and we do not worry about your future fate. The world already will not tempt you, since it has lost its luster in your eyes; you will not have to struggle with bodily lusts, since they have long died in you. And nevertheless, my brother, at your tonsure, those who know you well are not less emotional than at yesterday's.

Forgive me if I also briefly mention your life, to show—not to you, since you know it already, but to the others—how profoundly true are the words that stand at the beginning of the service. God desires all people to be saved (1 Tim. 2:4), but in the lives of some it is expressed particularly distinctly. And so it is with you. You used to be a priest once, you had a good position, with good connections, with family joys. Life apparently was smiling at you, but your happiness, just like that of many others, turned out to be short-lived. God sent you a trial. Your young wife died. This was a terrible blow, since a priest who has been widowed cannot be consoled with a second marriage. But you did not understand that trial then. Perhaps the Lord was calling you closer to Himself at that hour, calling you to the monastic path, but you loved the world more than God, and found yourself outside of the priesthood.

Undoubtedly it did not take long after that for you to regret what you had done, since you could no longer minister in God's service and enter into the closest union with Christ. And then, something even bitterer was in store for you: you left your motherland with its temples and holy places, and found yourself in a country and cities without them. How hard it must have been to live through that for someone who had been a servant of the altar himself, who used to nestle in the house of God! I think that more than once you cried bitterly in front of the Lord and offered Him sighs of repentance, that you had broken the high vows of a priest.

And then the merciful God, seeing your repentance, as a father who loves his child, brought you near to Himself again. First, He gave you the consolation of seeing a temple in your town and attending church services in it. Then He healed you from sickness through the intercession of the Venerable Seraphim of Sarov,[5] whose name was given to you today. Not long ago, unexpectedly for you, He called your female companion to the next world and you became free again, yet not for the worldly life, but for a different one.

And just in those very days a monastery was being established here, where you can renounce the world and enter a different path of life. And so today, something happened to you that could have happened 40 or 50 years ago. And once again you belong to a holy order. Once again you live in the courtyard of the Lord. Once again

---

[5] St. Seraphim of Sarov (1754–1833), who was a wonder-working, clairvoyant elder at the Sarov Monastery in Russia, is an especially beloved Russian Saint. His glorification as a Saint at Sarov in 1903 was a national sensation, at which Tsar Nicholas II and his entire family attended.

you participate in reading and singing. Once again you preach the word of God. Once again you see the beauty of the service of God daily! Once again the Lord is close to you and you are close to Him. Here He comes to you in His image, which is presented to you as a blessing from my unworthiness.

Take Your Lord, and from now on do not leave Him; and He will receive you and embrace you and protect you, falling asleep and waking up with you, comforting and bringing joy to your heart, making you worthy of the portion of those saints who forever have shone forth in monasticism. Amen.

YEAR 1907

67. A sermon preached at St. Andrew's Church in Philadelphia on Sunday, January 31, 1907.

68. A sermon preached at the Liturgy at the Mayfield Church on February 18, 1907.

69. Farewell sermon preached on the Sunday of Orthodoxy at the New York Cathedral.

A SERMON[1]

Preached at St. Andrew's Church in Philadelphia
on Sunday, January 31, 1907

YOUR TEMPLE, brethren, is dedicated to one of the Holy Apostles—Andrew the First-Called; and this circumstance gives me reason to be carried in thought to the times of the Apostles, to those Churches that were in existence at the time of the Apostles. One of those Churches carried the same name as yours—the Church of Philadelphia; and it was addressed at one time by God through a seer of mysteries—John: "Behold, I have set before thee an open door and no man can shut it: for thou has a little strength and has kept my word, and has not denied My name. Behold, I will make them of the synagogue, which say they are Jews and are not, but do lie—behold, I will make them to come and worship before thy feet, and know that I have loved thee; hold fast that which thou hast, that no man take thy crown" (Rev. 3:8, 9, 11).

Some of these sayings could be applied to your church as well, brethren, and I would like to wish that the promises spoken by God in regards to the ancient Church of Philadelphia might be fulfilled in you likewise.

"I have set before thee an open door and no man can shut it." About ten years ago in your city the door of the proclamation of the Orthodox Faith was opened—a small handful of people from Austria had come to know the right Faith here. Being persecuted

---

[1] Printed in *Amerikansky Pravoslavny Vestnik*, 1907, #3, pp. 42–43.

by those related to them in the flesh, who remained in the former faith, they organized their own church community and rented a small room for conducting worship services. But there were only a few of them, and they did not have their own spiritual pastor who would look out for them and instruct them in the law of the Lord. It seemed the spark that had just lit up would die out right away, and the enemies were ready to celebrate their victory.

But God did not allow this right and holy undertaking to perish. "You have preserved the word of His patience, and for that He has preserved you in the time of temptation" (Rev. 3:10). People from the great holy Russia came to your city—sailors, whose ships were being built here. Through their sacrifices and through their taking part in the prayers with you, they encouraged you, supported you, and helped you much. Soon you gained a spiritual pastor also, who gathered together your flock, multiplied it, and acquired the present temple. This is how the door for the proclamation of the Orthodox Faith was opened in this great city, and no one can shut it, no matter how hard your enemies would try to do so.

In truth, even now still "you do not have much strength" and are weak compared to your adversaries, but what is important is that in spite of your weakness and shortcomings you still "preserve the word of God, and do not deny" the Orthodox Faith. "Hold fast that which thou hast, that no man take thy crown"—and then, we believe, the promise of God will be fulfilled in you as well regarding the gathering of people who surround you, who are related to you in the flesh and in the former faith, those people who also portray themselves as being Orthodox, yet they are not, and lie; and that those people in time will still come to you and will join you. This will come to be; indeed it will!

But in order for you, brethren, to attract others and bring them to accept your Faith, you must not only profess the right Faith with your lips, but lead the right way of life according to your faith. Unfortunately, quite often "the name of God is blasphemed" (Rom. 2:24) because of our bad way of life; and we, while calling ourselves the ones of the right Faith, sometimes act worse than the unbelievers.

Here your city, for example, bears the name of Philadelphia, which means "brotherly love." This is as if a special behest is given to you, its citizens, concerning brotherly love, to live in peace and concord. And indeed, "How good and how pleasant it is for brethren to dwell together in unity" (Ps. 132:1). But tell me, where do you have this brotherly love? "Slavic discord" and that among the Russians is known the world over, and those who live in this land give one more further confirmation of this discord. Discord between the Orthodox and the Uniates, between the Russians from Russia and the Rusyns from Austria, between the Galicians and the Ugro-Russians, between the "moskal"[2] and the Ukrainians—how often it happens here and how almost daily it is reported about!

And seeing how "you attack one another" (cf. Gal. 5:15), who would come to you? Who would accept your Faith, when it is "dead without good works" (cf. Jas. 2:20, 26)? "If one is wise and smart among you, let him indeed demonstrate it with kind behavior and meekness; but if you have bitter envy in your heart and quarrelsomeness," then "glory not" that you have the right Faith, and "lie not against the truth" (Jas. 3:13–14).

"I write this not to embarrass you, but to admonish you as my beloved children" (1 Cor. 4:14). In the near future you are going to start the construction of a bigger and more splendid temple. Beware, then, not to bring discord into this holy undertaking also; but on the contrary, "laying aside all malice, all guile and hypocrisies, and envies and all evil speaking, and having purified your souls unto unfeigned love of the brethren, love with a pure heart, as lively stones, build up for yourselves a spiritual house and the holy nation that is called to announce to others, who are unaware, the marvelous light of the true Christian Faith" (1 Pet. 1:22; 2:1, 5, 9).

---

[2] The word literally means a "moscovite" (a person from Moscow); it is a derogatory nickname for "Russians" used by Ukrainians and Belorussians.

A SERMON[3]

Preached at the Liturgy at the Mayfield Church on the
opening day of the convention, on February 18, 1907

YOU HAVE HEARD, brethren, the words of the holy Apostle Paul, which were read today at the liturgy, "All things are lawful unto me, but all things are not expedient: all things are lawful for me, but I will not be brought under the power of any" (1 Cor. 6:12). Everything is permissible for a Christian, but not everything is beneficial. Everything is permissible, but he must use what is allowed to him in such a way that it does not prevail over him, does not make him its docile servant. Today's Gospel reading indeed shows in the example of the prodigal son what kind of sad consequences the improper use of what is permissible, and the unskilled use of freedom, can lead to.

"A certain man had two sons, and the younger of them told the father, 'Give me the portion of goods that falleth to me'" (Luke 15:11–12). The younger son felt an overabundance of strength; he wanted to put it to use in action; he wanted to live independently, freely, without guardianship, without restrictions, which might have been at times set unnecessarily by the old father. And this kind of aspiration by the young son alone by itself did not contain anything reproachful. It was acceptable; but as one might expect, it did not turn out to be beneficial. Having nobody to restrain him, held back by no one, far from the loving parental eye, the wealthy young man

---

[3] Printed in *Amerikansky Pravoslavny Vestnik*, 1907, #5, pp. 78–80. This was the opening of the First All-American Sobor of the Russian Missionary Diocese in America, held in Mayfield, Pennsylvania, in February of 1907.

squandered all of his estate by living lasciviously. Friends, wine, and women drove him into miserable poverty. While the money lasted he partied constantly, and then he had to tend to pigs.

Perhaps some of his delights were permissible, but within proper boundaries. The Word of God does not condemn earthly pleasures: "eat thy bread with joy" says the Most Wise, "and drink thy wine with a merry heart, for God now accepteth thy works. Let thy garments be always white and let thy head lack no ointment; live joyfully with the wife whom thou loveth" (Eccl. 9:7–9) and whom He has given to thee. "Rejoice, O young man, in thy youth and let thy heart cheer thee in thy youth while the evil days come not, nor the years draw nigh when thou shalt say, 'I have no pleasure in them.' But know thou, that for all these things God will bring thee into judgment" (Eccl. 11:9, 12:1).

Pure delights and innocent pleasures are quite permissible for a Christian, for they brighten the bitterness of life. But if someone makes them the entire purpose of his life, makes them his goal, and lives only to eat, drink, and party, giving himself to them at all times, then this person is a slave of his passions and a lost man, and the same sorrowful lot awaits him as that of the prodigal son.

And thus the Holy Church, with the sermon of Christ about the prodigal son as well as with the words of the holy Apostle Paul, wishes to warn us and teach us the right use of pleasures and the right exercise of freedom. "All things are lawful unto me, but all things are not expedient: all things are lawful for me, but I will not be brought under the power of any" (1 Cor. 6:12). "For, brethren, we have been called unto liberty"; but may there be no place for frivolousness and the absence of self-restraint among you. Remember that your freedom should not be a reason to satisfy your own wills, but for "serving one another by love" (cf. Gal. 5:13).

I use this present meeting of prayer to also say my farewell word to you. You, of course, know that I am leaving you, and I am seeing many of you for the last time.[4] Under these circumstances, a touching High Priestly prayer of the Savior Christ to the Heavenly Father comes to my mind.

While preparing to say good-bye to His disciples, the Savior prayed to God the Father that He would preserve them in the same way Christ Himself up to that time had preserved them, saved them from enmity, let none of them perish, had them illumined with His Truth, and united them in mutual love (John 17). This prayer is called the High Priestly prayer, since Christ prays it like a Pastor, as the Chief Priest for His flock—for His disciples, and for those who would believe in Him according to their words.

Following the example of our Master of all pastors—Christ—I as well, while preparing to say good-bye to you, departing to another place from you, first of all, offer a prayer to the Heavenly Father for my former flock. There is a union between the Archpastor and the flock, and this union is most of all expressed in mutual prayers. Our life has turned out in such a way that only a few from the flock come in touch with the Hierarch in day to day matters, and the rest see him only in the temple while serving the service and offering prayer for the flock. Usually the flock meets the Hierarch, who has just arrived in the diocese, in the temple. With a prayer he starts his service to the flock, and with a prayer—"the farewell service"—it ends as well. Although, upon the departure of the Hierarch to another place, nothing prevents him from praying for his former flock, since there are no obstacles of space for the spirit, and "charity never faileth" (1 Cor. 13:8).

And thus at my departure from you, the present prayer of mine to the Heavenly Father is that He preserve you in the right Faith and save you from the hostility of enemies. The Savior, when departing from this world, worried about the fate of the handful of His disciples who were being left to face many enemies. "Simon, Simon,

---

[4] By this time St. Tikhon had been told by the Holy Synod of the Church of Russia that he was being transferred to the ancient see of Yaroslavl back in Russia, so he uses this occasion to give his flock a farewell message from him.

behold, Satan has desired to have you, that he may sift you as wheat; but I have prayed for thee that thy faith fail not: and when thou art converted, strengthen thy brethren" (Luke 22:31–32).

How could we not worry for the small flock of ours? How easily can the wind blow out a candle lit in an open room! How easily can the waves of the sea drown the sailor in a fragile vessel! We cannot boast either of our numerousness, or fame, or wealth, or erudition—all that is valuable in the eyes of this world. We are strong here only with the true, right Faith; and even that is "not of yourselves: it is the gift of God" (Eph. 2:8), of which an increase in us we should be asking the Lord.

"Righteous Father! I am no more in the world, but these are in the world" (cf. John 17:11). "I pray not that Thou shouldest take them out of the world, but that Thou shouldest keep them from the evil" (John 17:15). "Holy Father! Sanctify them through Thy truth" (John 17:17), "keep them through Thine own name" (John 17:11). "Neither pray I for these alone" (John 17:20), but for all the faithful. For all those whom Thou has given me at one time, may they know Thee the True God, and may they remain in Thy Holy Church and in the Orthodox Faith.

As for you, brethren, when you will have departed from here and have returned to those who have sent you here, do in turn strengthen your fellow brethren in faith and love for Holy Orthodoxy. Whatsoever you have learned here that is true, honest, and just, whatever you have heard and seen that is of good report, that you should do yourselves and tell others about it (cf. Phil. 4:8, 9).

I will endeavor that you may be able after my decease to have these things in remembrance (cf. 2 Peter 1:15). The Lord be with you all (2 Thess. 3:16).

FAREWELL SERMON[5]

Preached on the Sunday of Orthodoxy in the New York City Cathedral; March, 1907

THIS SUNDAY IS CALLED "The Sunday of Orthodoxy" or "The Triumph of Orthodoxy," since on this day the Holy Church solemnly commemorates her victory over Iconoclasm and other heresies. And this triumph of Orthodoxy took place not just a thousand years ago. No—for due to the mercy of God, the Church up to this day, now here and now there, gains victory and is triumphant over her enemies, of which She has many.

It is not a coincidence that the Church is likened to a ship, sailing amidst a ferocious, stormy sea which is ready to drown it in its waves at any minute. And the further the ship sails, the harder the waves slam against it, the fiercer they attack it! But the harder the waves hit the ship, the further they are thrown away and rejoin the abyss and disappear in it, and the ship continues its triumphant sailing as before. For "the foundation of God standeth sure" (2 Tim. 2:19), since the Church of Christ is built on an immovable rock, and "the gates of hell shall not prevail against it" (Matt. 16:18).

The Church of Christ is the kingdom not of this world, which does not possess any worldly attractions, which is persecuted and slandered, which not only avoids perishing in the world, but grows and defeats the world! This happens everywhere, and here in our

---

[5] Printed in *Amerikansky Pravoslavny Vestnik*, 1907, #6, pp. 96–98. This sermon was St. Tikhon's very last sermon preached in America.

land as well. "We cannot but speak the things which we have seen and heard" (Act 4:20).

It is true that our Church here cannot boast of the quantity of its members, neither of their erudition. Just like the "preaching of Christ crucified" (1 Cor. 1:23), for some it seems lowly and contemptible, and for others it seems simple and foolish; but in reality "God's power and wisdom" (1 Cor. 1:24) are concealed in it. It is strong and rich with the authenticity of the doctrine which has been preserved unaltered, its clarity of rules, a deep sense of liturgical service, and an abundance of grace. And with all of this it is gradually attracting the hearts of people, and it is growing and getting stronger more and more in this country.

You brethren have witnessed and seen for yourselves the growth and strengthening of Orthodoxy here. Just a mere twelve to fifteen years ago, we, aside from faraway Alaska, barely had any churches here. There were no priests, and the Orthodox people numbered only in a few dozens and maybe a few hundreds.[6] And even they lived dispersed, far from one another.

And now? "The Orthodox are seen this day in this country."[7] Our temples appear not only in big cities but in obscure places as well. We have a multitude of clergy, and tens of thousands of faithful—and not only those who have been Orthodox for a while, but those who have converted from among the Uniates. Schools are opened, the brotherhoods are established. Even strangers acknowledge the success of Orthodoxy here. So how can we ourselves not celebrate "The Triumph of Orthodoxy," and not thank the Lord who helps His Church!

---

[6] St. Tikhon is exaggerating a bit here. In 1892 there must have been at least one priest at the Russian Cathedral in San Francisco, the parish in Chicago had had a priest for some years before St. John Kochurov arrived as the new priest there in 1895, and St. Alexis Toth and his Uniate parish of 361 Russin immigrants were received into Holy Orthodoxy in the Spring of 1891 by Bp. Vladimir of the Russian Cathedral in San Francisco.

[7] Quotation marks are in the original; source unknown.

But it is not enough, brethren, to only celebrate "The Triumph of Orthodoxy." It is necessary for us personally to promote and contribute to this triumph. And for this we must reverently preserve the Orthodox Faith, standing firm in it in spite of the fact that we live in a non-Orthodox country, and not pleading as an excuse for our apostasy that "it is not the old land here but America, a free country, and therefore it is impossible to follow everything that the Church requires." As if the word of Christ is only suitable for the old land and not for the entire world! As if the Church of Christ is not "catholic"![8] As if the Orthodox Faith did not "establish the universe"![9]

Furthermore, while faithfully preserving the Orthodox Faith, everyone must also take care to spread it among the non-Orthodox. Christ the Savior said that having lit the candle, men do not put it under a bushel but on a candlestick so that it gives light to all (Matt. 5:15). The light of the Orthodox Faith has not been lit to shine only for a small circle of people. No, the Orthodox Church is *catholic;*[10] She remembers the commandment of Her Founder, "Go ye into all the world and preach the Gospel to every creature and teach all nations" (Mark 16:15; Matt. 28:19).

We must share our spiritual richness, truth, light, and joy with others who do not have these blessings. And this duty does not only lay upon the pastors and the missionaries but on the lay persons as well, since the Church of Christ, according to the wise comparison of the Holy Apostle Paul, is the body, and every member takes part in the life of the body. By means of all sorts of mutually binding bonds which are formed and strengthened through the action of every member according to his capacity, the great Church body receives an increase unto the edifying of itself (Eph. 4:16).

---

[8] Probably quoting from the Nicene Creed: "One holy, catholic, apostolic Church."

[9] Quoting from the service for the Sunday of Orthodoxy.

[10] St. Tikhon is clearly taking the word "catholic" here to mean "universal" or "worldwide."

In the first centuries it was not only the pastors who were tortured, but lay persons as well—men, women, and even children. And it was lay people likewise who enlightened the heathen and fought heresies. And now in the same way, the spreading of the Faith in Christ should be a matter that is personal, heartfelt, and dear to each one of us. Every member of the Church must take an active part in it—some by personal *podvig*[11] spreading the Good News, some by material donations and service to "the needs of the holy persons," and some by profuse prayer to the Lord that He "keep His Church firm and multiply it"—and concerning those unaware of Christ, that He would "proclaim the word of truth to them, open to them the Gospel of Truth, and join them to the Holy Catholic and Apostolic Church."[12] I have told this numerous times to my flock. And today, upon my departing from this land, I once more command all of you to preserve and act upon this, and especially you, brethren, of this holy temple.

You witnessed yourself last Sunday that "The foreknowledge of God drew you closer to the bishop's cathedra, and that the awareness of this closeness elevates your Christian spirit and edifies the nature of your undertakings, inspiring you for everything good."[13] Your temple is a cathedral. It is preeminent in the diocese. And being its parishioners, you, brethren, must give others an example in everything good that concerns the life of the Church, including caring for the Orthodox Faith.

Furthermore, your parish is Russian, almost entirely consisting of people who came from Russia. And to this very day, Russia has been famous throughout the world as a holy Christian land, whose adornment is the Orthodox Faith, the piousness of her people, and her temples of God. So, brethren, uphold here in a foreign land the glory

---

[11] *Podvig* is a rich, distinctive Russian word roughly meaning "ascetic, spiritual struggle."

[12] Quotation marks in the original; from a prayer for the catechumens (those officially learning about the Orthodox Faith in preparation for Baptism and/or Chrismation).

[13] Quotation marks in the original; source unknown.

of your native land. Manifest yourselves before the non-Orthodox as the Russian Orthodox people.

I can say with comfort that in these days, with your zealous attendance at our temple, you've made a good impression on the local residents. And you have especially gladdened my heart and expelled the sadness and grief which were felt, not only by me, in other places at the sight of empty temples during the feastday Church services.

May the Lord strengthen you to excel in the Orthodox Faith more and more—my last prayer is about this. Today I depart from you. And so, farewell, fathers and brethren of this holy temple, who are close to me not only in spirit but in our joint prayers, labors, and residence! Farewell to you, the rest of my flock scattered across the wide horizon of this land! Farewell, all those of you wandering in the deserts, working in the mountains and in the depths of the earth, and those on the islands far out in the sea!

Farewell to you, my cathedral temple! You are dear and close to me. It has been during the time of my service that you were opened, you were adorned during my time as well, and you were made a cathedral during my time. Perhaps for some who have seen the large, magnificent temples in Russia, you might seem small and modest, and you do not shine with gold and silver and precious gemstones like those temples do. But for Russian Orthodox people, who suffered here for a long time without a temple, you represent a precious treasure, and they rejoice that they have you—like the Jews who returned from the Babylonian captivity rejoiced at the time of the construction of the second temple, even though it was not as splendid as that of Solomon.

"O Lord, the God of Israel! May Thine eyes be open toward this house night and day, that Thou mayest hearken unto the prayer of Thy people when they shall pray in this place! ... Moreover, concerning a stranger that is not of Thy people, when he shall come and pray in this house, hear Thou him from Heaven, Thy dwelling place!" (3 Kingdoms 8:26–27, 39–41).[14]

Farewell to you, this country! For some you are the motherland, the place of birth; for others you gave shelter, work, and well-being. Some received the freedom to profess the right Faith in your liberal land. God spoke in ancient times through the prophet, "And seek the peace of the city whither I have caused you to be carried away captives, and pray unto the Lord for it: for in the peace thereof shall you have peace" (Jer. 29:7; Hebrew text).

And so, let us pray to the Lord that He send this country "a plentitude of the earthly fruits, fair weather, timely rain and wind, and preserve it from the cowardly, flood, fire, sword, invasion of foreigners, and civil strife."

Let God's blessing be upon this country, this city, and this temple. And let "the blessing of the Lord, with grace and love for man," rest upon you all, "now and ever and unto the ages of ages. Amen."[15]

---

[14] This is the source in the Septuagint version of the Old Testament, designated as the LXX. In the Hebrew text, the source is 1 Kings 8:28–29, 41–43.

[15] Quotation marks in the original; phrases taken from various liturgical prayers of the Church.

AFTERWORD

By the original editors

THIS PRESENT 4th installment of *"Instructions and Teachings" for American Orthodox Russia by His Holiness Tikhon, Patriarch of Moscow and of All Russia,* during the years of his service while being Vladika of the Aleutians and North America (from 1898 till 1907), ends the publication started on November 21, 1923.

Of course, this series of collections of sermons of His Holiness is far from including everything which is dear to the memory of an Orthodox person in America, and which is connected with the name of the deceased Hierarch-Confessor. The spiritual inheritance of Vladika Tikhon was captured in print by the chroniclers of that time. Step by step they noted the travels of their most gracious Arch-pastor with the evangelism of the Holy Gospel through the most distant corners of America. Many memorable events connected with his name were preserved in their notes, along with sermons and conversations which were almost always literally reproduced from his words. Without a doubt, the compiling together and publishing of these notes on the Evangelical Travels of Vladika Tikhon in America is awaiting its hour.

Likewise it would be useful to collect all the information from official documents related to that period of, so to say, the undivided Orthodox Church in America on one hand, as well as a number of letters of the Deceased relating to the same period on the other hand. The first and the latter are precious, and when published would contribute a great deal to bringing to light the personality and activity of Vladika Tikhon, as well as all of that period in the history of the Russian Church in America, which, according to his name, would enter posterity with the name "Tikhon's."

The publishing committee does not make plans so far in the future. It expresses joy that whatever little it tasked itself with has come into fruition with the help of God today. Glory be to God for everything! Thanks to all those who with their contributions, sympathy, and kind words, as well as labor, have helped to accomplish this task.

First of all, thanks are rendered to His Beatitude Metropolitan Platon, who blessed the start of this undertaking and who looked upon it as the fulfillment of the obligation of the Diocese to the memory of Vladika Tikhon. In spite of the suspicions that are spread by rumors that American Russia is departing from the commands of His Holiness Patriarch, Vladika Metropolitan prompted the publishers to underline the opposite—on the part of the current laborers, a complete reverence for and fidelity to the plans of the life and work of the Orthodox Church in America that were outlined in those days.

Heartfelt thanks are also earned by the all-honorable fathers—Fr. Archpriest Theophan Buketov, who was the first to start personally collecting the sermons and speeches of His Holiness; and Fr. Grigori Shukat, who patiently and diligently wrote down a number of sermons and teachings from issues of the *Amerikansky Pravoslavny Vestnik* from years ago that were difficult to access. And along with them, an honorable participant in this undertaking has been Mr. T. M. Mogilat, who would visit the New York Public Library especially for the purpose of copying the issues that were not readily available.

Mr. A. A. Vonsyatski, who supported the publication with a generous gift, deserves full gratitude, as well as people and parishes who sent their mite for this publication. Also, gratitude is expressed for the kind reviews to the authors of the articles, as well to newspapers which mentioned them.

With sincere respect to all those to whom the memory of the great hierarch of the Russian Orthodox Church, His Holiness Patriarch of All Russia TIKHON, is precious.

The Publishing Committee at the St. Nicolas Cathedral in New York City.

Cathedral Archpriest Leonid Turkevich.[1]
Cathedral sacristan Archpriest Petr Popov.
Archpriest Vasili Lisenkovski.

January 22, 1926.

---

[1] Archpriest Leonid Turkevich would later become Bishop of Chicago in 1933. And from 1950 to 1965 he served as Metropolitan of the Russian Metropolia in America, established in 1924 as the direct successor to the Russian Missionary Diocese. He is buried at St. Tikhon's Monastery in South Canaan, Pennsylvania.